Advances in 21st Century Human Settlements

This Series focuses on the entire spectrum of human settlements—from rural to urban, in different regions of the world, with questions such as: What factors cause and guide the process of change in human settlements from rural to urban in character, from hamlets and villages to towns, cities and megacities? Is this process different across time and space, how and why? Is there a future for rural life? Is it possible or not to have industrial development in rural settlements, and how? Why does 'urban shrinkage' occur? Are the rural areas urbanizing or is that urban areas are undergoing 'ruralisation' (in form of underserviced slums)? What are the challenges faced by 'mega urban regions', and how they can be/are being addressed? What drives economic dynamism in human settlements? Is the urban-based economic growth paradigm the only answer to the quest for sustainable development, or is there an urgent need to balance between economic growth on one hand and ecosystem restoration and conservation on the other—for the future sustainability of human habitats? How and what new technology is helping to achieve sustainable development in human settlements? What sort of changes in the current planning, management and governance of human settlements are needed to face the changing environment including the climate and increasing disaster risks? What is the uniqueness of the new 'socio-cultural spaces' that emerge in human settlements, and how they change over time? As rural settlements become urban, are the new 'urban spaces' resulting in the loss of rural life and 'socio-cultural spaces'? What is leading the preservation of rural 'socio-cultural spaces' within the urbanizing world, and how? What is the emerging nature of the rural-urban interface, and what factors influence it? What are the emerging perspectives that help understand the human-environment-culture complex through the study of human settlements and the related ecosystems, and how do they transform our understanding of cultural landscapes and 'waterscapes' in the 21st Century? What else is and/or likely to be new vis-à-vis human settlements—now and in the future? The Series, therefore, welcomes contributions with fresh cognitive perspectives to understand the new and emerging realities of the 21st Century human settlements. Such perspectives will include a multidisciplinary analysis, constituting of the demographic, spatio-economic, environmental, technological, and planning, management and governance lenses.

More information about this series at http://www.springer.com/series/13196

Li Zi

Online Urbanization

Online Services in China's Rural Transformation

Springer

Simply put, to achieve urbanization, it is a must to integrate urban and rural areas and bridge the gaps.

In the past, what concerns local officials most is how to "urbanize" the land, rather than the people. They acquire land resources, especially those resources of rural lands to finance urbanization. These conducts are likely to cause a deep local financial crisis, or even a national financial crisis. We have learned from past lessons that urbanization, if led by capital and power, would soon evolve into a large-scale land plunder by ripping off farmers. If urbanization tumbles in this pitfall, a profound social crisis may happen.

So, is the technology-empowered Internet enough to create a new model to "urbanize" the people and achieve coordinated regional development?

In this book, the author Li Zi explains how the Internet empowers rural communities and gradually creates a nationwide online business ecosystem in a bottom-up manner, and how and why a series of concurrent events influence the decisions of Chinese policymakers.

China now stands at a critical stage of reform and transformation, where urban and rural development appears to be divergent as more and more rural residents are moving out. As a matter of fact, these problems are exacerbated by the information divide, financial gap, discrepant living standards, and unevenly distributed resources. The author first explains how the capable brains in Suichang County, Zhejiang Province, leverage the power of Internet technology, cooperate with Internet giants like Alibaba, integrate local resources, create jobs locally, and improve commercial and public services. Then, the author analyzes how Alibaba and other Internet businesses acclimatize Internet technology to the traditional rural organization pattern and improve working and living standards of rural residents through innovation and talent cultivation. Against this backdrop, rural e-commerce is rolled out nationwide, but it never loses local characteristics because local innovation is carried out simultaneously. In the end, both policies and resources at local and national level are leaning toward rural e-commerce. Government bodies from the State Council, the ministries and commissions to the local governments are developing policies and raising funds to support rural e-commerce, especially e-commerce-based poverty alleviation programs.

This trend alters China's urbanization approach, because it agrees with the development orientation of regional town clusters. In the vast areas of Yangtze River Delta and the Pearl River Delta, Taobao villages and Taobao towns who benefited from rural e-commerce have multiplied day by day. Thanks to the Internet and information technology, towns and villages are turned into nodes at all sizes, spontaneously creating an urban and rural network and fitting into the regional and even global production chain and living system. The author defines the restructuring of regions, space, and time as "online urbanization." To help the readers understand how the IT-centered flowing factors in urban and rural China will influence urbanization in the short and long run, he further explores best practices in five aspects, including urban and rural human resource flows and cultivation, the urban and rural logistic network and supply chain optimization, urban and rural information flow, effective resource allocation, and ecological and cultural progress.

Based on this concept, the author concentrates his focus on the twin engines of online urbanization—nodes and convection—to establish a conceptual framework of online urbanization.

In retrospect of the vicissitudes in urban and rural China, we may easily realize that be it the booming Caoshi (marketplace) in Song dynasty or the prosperous rural fairs in Ming and Qing dynasty, the rural society had remained autonomous and laid equal stress on agriculture and commerce. This tradition contributes to maintaining a relatively stable urban–rural relationship, differentiating China from Europe where urban and rural areas have been in an antagonistic state. In the era of the Internet, China is likely to find a new approach to balanced regional development by striking a consensus among central and local governments, enterprises, farmers, and other parties involved. This new approach is neither the suburbanization model adopted by the USA, nor the "New Town" model prevalent in European welfare states that was designed to improve living standards and working environment of workers. China is creating a new model to achieve rural development and urbanization in the information era, a model that can be followed by other developing countries, especially those in the Silk Road Economic Belt and the 21st century Maritime Silk Road.

The transforming urban–rural relations enabled by the Internet have eloquently testified the changing relations between the state and society. It serves as a mirror through which we can observe how the Internet reshapes the relations between the state and the society. The Internet has changed the way we live and work, bringing about more frequent interactions between the state and society. These interactions produce diversified results: In some cases, the state and society reinforce each other, while in other cases they are diminishing one another and tend to be more exclusive.

In the current stage, active interaction is the defining characteristic in rural e-commerce development and online urbanization, yet there is little evidence indicating the role of capital and power in urbanization. Generally speaking, farmers still remain a vulnerable group whose interests are always at stake. Therefore, while pushing forward the new-type urbanization, it is imperative for China to try its utmost to safeguard the rights and interests of farmers and promote a fair and reasonable flow of factors between urban and rural areas.

The author Li Zi has been reaching deep into the countryside to acquire firsthand experiences of practicing rural e-commerce. He aims to build an analytical framework by adopting an interpretive approach, which is conducive for readers to better understand the real side of the Chinese society.

This book will help readers comprehend the status quo of rural e-commerce and the future of China's urbanization. Better still, the author tries to conceptualize the phenomenon pertaining to rural e-commerce by combining theories with experiences. Therefore, it is a worth-reading academic work.

Singapore
April 2018

Zheng Yongnian
Director of East Asian Institute (EAI)
National University of Singapore (NUS)

Foreword II

Online urbanization: Online Services in China's Rural Transformation by Li Zi is written at exactly the right time when e-commerce is in vogue. They are groundbreaking urban studies of networked urbanization under the perspective of information sociology. Beginning with the specific case of Suichang County, Lishui City, in southwest Zhejiang Province and the rural strategy of Alibaba, the author then analyzes the development of rural e-commerce and online urbanization. This book is an outstanding academic work, a convincing proof of Li's professional competence as one of the lecturers in Cihu Auditorium (formerly known as Cihu Academy) in Cicheng, Zhejiang.

What we regard as a breakthrough is that Li Zi finds the most in-thing in urban China, things that are most vigorous and unprecedented in human history. The energetic activists in Suichang, Zhejiang, as detailed in the book, reveal the renewed social structure and strong development momentum under the new urban–rural relations. They include farmers, small commodity producers, couriers who deliver packages, and e-commerce practitioners who engage in online trading. They are networkers in the information economy, as well as netizens in the cyber society. Carrying on the traditions upheld by cities and towns in the south of Yangtze River and heritages of countryside markets in Ming and Qing dynasty, Taobao villages and virtual communities came into being. They seized opportunities offered by the new-type urbanization whose focus had been shifted from export to domestic demand. Taobao villages and virtual communities are different from English new towns and American suburbs in the industrial society, who were caught in implacable desires for lands. Instead, those villages and communities borrow power from IT-backed networks and the nodes that flow online. They are gridded into the established city clusters in the Yangtze River Delta. In this way, the urban–rural relation is renewed as networked urbanization proceeds; the space of flows reshapes the correlations between urban and rural areas, as well as local communities.

Li Zi noted in the preface that the potential of e-commerce can be utilized to a greater scale. Central, west, southeast, south Asia, and even Europe and Africa were once important regions in the ancient Silk Road. They still have a big part to play in the Belt and Road Initiative in the current information era. In a time when consumers. Based on these four aspects, the author wishes to reinvigorate the values and social system that are found in the traditional culture in rural China and change the status quo where urban and rural areas impair each other.

The trend of bringing e-commerce to the countryside has just developed buds. As we can see, Internet giants are deploying e-commerce strategies one after another in counties and rural areas; rural business pioneers are leading local communities and organizations to prepare e-commerce platforms and training their fellow villagers so that the fruits can be shared by all; local officials are also considering new development approaches to ease the pressure of transforming traditional export-oriented manufacturing and to realize the hopes of poverty-stricken counties to develop the ecological economy. According to the author, the three parties altogether have struck a delicate balance of commerce and ecology.

E-commerce injects strong impetus into rural China. To be more specific, it highlights the role of men in developing rural areas, reveals the bright prospects of developing the service sector in the Chinese countryside originally dominated by eco-agriculture, and improves the living standards of rural residents. This impetus, further driven by keen capital inflows, passionate startups, and transformed government, has brought real changes to the ecological system in rural China.

However, when developing rural areas, there are many aspects that require more profound experiment and analysis, so that we can draw more experiences. These aspects include: how to build a smart supply chain for eco-agriculture and support it with a traceability system of agricultural products; how to develop and implement quality and safety standards for agricultural products; how to assess the differences between small-scale farming and large-scale agricultural economy, and how to define agricultural modernization based on this assessment; how to interpret the "culture and value system" in the modern countryside; last but not least, how to identify and evaluate corporate social responsibilities of Internet giants, as the e-commerce-based public service system that they build is driven by profits and market share, but is designed to serve the public.

Shanghai, China
March 2018

Wu Chen
Editor-in-chief of The Economist
Global Business Review

Preface

I commit myself to online urbanization research in the first place: to explore how emerging technologies can boost economic development in China and other developing countries; to break down the current urbanization approach driven by capital and power, so that counties and villages can participate in the international production chain and enjoy a global lifestyle; to improve commercial and public services in counties and villages, so that people don't have to abandon their homes to make a living in a strange city. However, in the long run, online urbanization is merely one of the many stages in technological development. It is very likely that we may confront more severe threats later on.

Our future will be brought to extremes by technology revolution. The implications of human activities will be impacted by three major revolutions, and communities will be restructured.

Capitalism Without Men

While Artificial Intelligence (AI), Virtual Reality (VR) and Augmented Reality (AR) are continuing to evolve, capital is poured into virtual world expeditions. As a result, a new production and consumption cycle is about to come into being, or we may say that it has already been formed. Since the establishment of capitalist production relations, humans, once one of the productive forces, has been regarded as a fugitive and disruptive factor (men tend to feel uncertain about their future and have unrealistic expectations) that should be excluded from production means and forces. The newborn capitalism will become a closed cycle without the participation of men, establish new production relations, and generate a steady and constant flow of productive forces.

While the lives of the vast majority are transformed by technology and capital, they also lost the game. More and more people believe that their fate is doomed and out of control. They are somewhat aware of the plight. But how do they think of their role in this plight? Nowadays, more and more elites and grassroots share a pessimistic attitude toward the future. Have they foreseen the embarrassing tomorrow of their children?

Not only producers, but also consumers will soon lose their ground in the game of capital. When technology and capital make the match and create a closed cycle, the virtual world will become the main venue where production and consumption take place. As a result, the industrial world is supposed to reconsider the production means and relations, and make necessary adjustments to consumption relations. In fact, we have already entered this stage. When looking around, one may find that many of their family members, friends, and colleagues are spending much time on video games and online consulting. It is clear that many people are voluntarily living in a virtual world, interacting with their peers, the society, and the nature under the rules dictated by world of algorithm.

When kept stable, the world of algorithm is able to regulate the relation between men (compared with the industrial age where capitalism was in its cradle, economic crisis and social crisis broke out occasionally, and proletariats were working individually). In the new world where reality and virtuality intermingled, we need to redefine the meaning of consumption. Then what are the new implications of consumption? AI consumes data, machines consume energy, and men consume protein. In all these activities, consumption recovers its nature: utilizing and converting energy. Men are no longer the one and only consumer. Instead, robots, cloned men, and machines are new members in the consumer group. The definition of currency will also be changed. Cattle, sheep, shells, gold, silver, banknotes, digital currency, Bitcoin created by blockchain technology, and other consumption mediums used by non-human consumers are new forms of currency. The purpose, approaches, and means of consumption will all be changed.

Humans are emotional. Emotions may affect their expectations on future and further on add sensibilities to capital. But from now on, these sensibilities reflected in production and consumption may be replaced by logic, thanks to technology and algorithm. Therefore, capital as well as the production relations and productive forces of capitalism will become more sensible and stable. Will it break the inherent nature and infinite cycle of economic crisis? Is it possible that economic crisis may escalate social crisis? (The two world wars were outlets for economic crisis.) We may find an answer by looking at the restructured society.

Post-cyberspace in China

Those trends have brought new challenge to the world, meanwhile in China, some new phenomena are emerging.

The unprecedented prospects of China's online services in urban and rural places, especially its soaring popularity in the countryside, have presented something different: that those arguments are applicable not only in cities, the developed countries, Europe and America, but also in the countryside, the developing countries, and the oriental nations. In the meantime, the situation is somewhat different in China.

In this country, the central authorities have been vying with local ones for several thousand years. It boasts a long tradition of political-merchant reciprocity and regional autonomy by local prominent families and gentries. As a result, the information technology is bound to interact and integrate with local communities in unique and diverse forms. However, the uniqueness and diversity share something similar: well-established associations and the interaction between commercial organizations and local governments provide an organizational basis and political guarantee for the flow of various factors in urban and rural areas.

Singapore
December, 2018

Li Zi
University Town, National University of Singapore

Acknowledgements

My profound gratitude, both personal and professional, must go to my supervisor, Prof. Heng Chye Kiang. Without his guidance and suggestions, I could not have completed this study. I also appreciate the great help from Prof. Jurgen Rosemann, A/P Johannes Widodo, and A/P Li Dihua.

Simultaneously, I have been given a lot of advice during the formation of my research topics from Prof. Hsia Chu-Joe (National Taiwan University), Dr. Zhang Ye, Prof. Zheng Yong Nian (East Asian Institute), Tunney Lee (MIT Department of Urban Studies and Planning), A/P Fu Yu Ming, and Prof. Vincent Nadin (TU Delft).

I must say thank you to my friends who have given me hands during the field trip and data collection. To begin with, truly thanks to Mr. Liang Chunxiao, the dean of the Academic Committee of Alibaba, Mr. Gao Hongbing, the director of Ali Research and his colleagues who helped me a lot. Furthermore, I will show my gratitude to the president of Suichang Network Association, Mr. Pan Dongming, and vice-county head of Suichang, Mr. Zhao Wenming.

Meanwhile, I would also like to express my appreciation for the support from my friends: London Cluff, Marine Chuberre, Benjamin Viale, Zhang Le, and Ula Kuczma.

At the same time, I would like to show my sincere appreciation to the publisher Springer Nature, especially project coordinator and book production staffs, Mr. Sanjiev Kumar M., Mr. Prasanna Kumar, Ms. Raghavy Krishnan and Dr. Loyola D'Silva.

Finally, I will express deepest affection to my family, to my Parents and Uncle Li Yu Zhong.

Contents

List of Figures

List of Tables

Chapter 1
Introduction

Through description of phenomenon of ecommerce in rural China, I try to explain the influence on China's urban-rural relationship in a framework. The propose is not to find a solution for existing problem of urbanization in China, but try to reply research questions: 1. What is rural ecommerce? 2. What is the urban-rural spatial relationship under the influence of rural ecommerce in China?

1.1 Background of Research

1.1.1 Critical Issues of Urbanization in China

Unlike highly urbanized European and American cities where social conflicts often stem from cultural, racial and other urban maladies, the economic and social issues of developing countries are often closely associated with urban-rural gap and regional development imbalance. Compared to developed countries that are generally urbanized, in the majority of developing countries in Asia urban population accounts for less than 50%[1] (49.6% of the population is urban in 2018) of the total population. Urbanization drives poverty reduction and the realization of the Millennium Development Goals (MDGs).[2] Nevertheless, if the process of urbanization is poorly managed, it can lead to upsurges in crimes, environmental deterioration as well as social problems. Therefore, countries have been exploring what an efficient, inclusive and sustainable model of urbanization looks like.

[1]http://www.worldometers.info/world-population/asia-population/.
[2]Ki-Moon, B. "The Millennium Development Goals Report 2013." *United Nations Pubns* (2013).

L. Zi, *Online Urbanization*, Advances in 21st Century Human Settlements,
https://doi.org/10.1007/978-981-13-3603-4_1

On April 17th, 2013, the World Bank and the International Monetary Fund (IMF) released "The Global Monitoring Report 2013: Rural-Urban Dynamics and the Millennium Development Goals" (GMR),[3] which sets out to achieve the Millennium Development Goals through sustainable urbanization by creating more jobs, raising rural incomes, improving business and public services, and decreasing poverty around the world, especially in developing countries. From 1990 to 2010, East Asia and Pacific region's poverty had topped the world with nearly 1 billion people (50% of the world total) living on less than 1.25$ a day. However, the region was able to reduce its poverty rate to 12% by 2010 and 6% by 2015.

Like most countries, China's fast economic development has been accompanied by its quick urbanization. People from rural areas are flooding into towns and cities to seek better facilities and more job opportunities. The population in Shanghai has exceeded 20 million, equivalent to that of two and half times the size of New York City. The latest urbanization rate published by the National Bureau of Statistics of China in 2013 was 53.7%. Statistics also show that 289 million Chinese were living away from their registered addresses for at least 6 months, out of whom 245 million people moved to another town or city. Accounting for the documentation of registered addresses, only around 35.7% of citizens have their documentation of registered addresses (*hukou*) of the city where they live and can get their welfare (including right to buy an apartment, public education, public health care and so on) from those local governments. It reveals that the actual urbanization rate in urban areas in China is much lower than the official data (53.7%), and it means 18% of China's population live in their city without welfare provided from that local government.[4]

During this process, the urban-rural chasm has been further deepened, as rural areas are deprived of the chance to be fully included in the regional work division under globalization, lacking power and say in the process. These unbalanced developments cause urban-rural segregation, and additionally cause social problem[5] of the rural and the social fragmentation of the urban.

There are critical issues of urbanization in China:

1. Forced eviction: 16% of rural families have recently encountered forced land renunciation, housing demolition and relocation. (China Data Center, Tsinghua University (CDC), 2013).[6] There have been increasing reports of rural land

[3]Bank, World. "*Global Monitoring Report 2013: Rural-Urban Dynamics and the Millennium Development Goals.*" https://openknowledge.worldbank.org/handle/10986/13330 (accessed May 2, 2013).

[4]http://www.ciudsrc.com/new_zazhi/fengmian/2014diyiqi/2014-02-25/62220.html.

[5]During more than 30 years of urbanization, the rural residences who lives in County including small towns and villages, especial to young people, keep moving to urban areas to lead transformation of rural society. The phenomenon is defined as rural social hollowization.

[6]Zhang Xiaohe 张晓鸽 (2013, Oct. 28th). Zhengdi chaiqian boji 16% jiating 征地拆迁波及 16% 家庭 [*Requisition of land affected 16% Family*]. 2013. China Data Center, Tsinghua University (CDC) (2013), "Large-scale Survey Data of Urbanization in China" (中国城镇化调查大型数据) http://epaper.jinghua.cn/html/201310/28/content_35335.htm.

disputes and fights for resources among farmers, real estate developers and governments.

2. "Cities without citizens": rural workforces migrated to cities are marginalized as they are unable to enjoy the same medical, retirement and educational welfare as the locals, because they are not qualified to update registered addresses to the city registry. There are more than 200 million such rural migrants, and they are not likely to be converted to urban citizens soon.
3. Destruction of environment: the unevenness of development continues to lead to environmental deterioration in both cities and villages, and eco-system crisis.
4. Local government debt, not sustainable: for example, Zhejiang (one of the rich provinces in China), as of June 2013, the province, municipal, county and township governments bore the responsibility to repay the debt of 10.633 billion yuan, 146.71 billion yuan, 328.818 billion yuan and 22.663 billion yuan respectively, with the county government debt accounting for 64.62% of the total.[7] Furthermore, the Chinese government has estimated an average cost of 131,000 RMB to convert one such rural migrant to an urban citizen. For a huge number of rural migrants, the local governments have to suffer this cost.

1.1.2 New Phenomenon: Ecommerce Creates New Opportunities

June 2016, the total number of Chinese Internet users is 709.5 million, and there are 656 million mobile phone users. The number of rural Internet users is 191 million (26.9% of total user). Ecommerce increased from 100 billion (accounting for 1% of total retail sales for the year) in 2008 to 5 trillion in 2016 (accounting for 15%). The percentage in US is nearly 7% (Figs. 1.1, 1.2 and 1.3).

During the Double 11 online shopping festival in 2016, online sales reached 120.7 billion in only 24 h. In a Taobao village of Gengche town, Suqian, for example, an ecommerce business that manufactures furniture, ran out of stock just three seconds past midnight, generating daily sales of over 7 million yuan. Besides, the shopping spree was going on concurrently in 235 countries, where 1.05 billion online payments were finished, resulting in 657 million parcels. Most of the transactions were done with cellphones, accounting for 80% of the total transactions (Figs. 1.4 and 1.5).

As a result of the Internet globalization and blockbuster trade made possible, Internet business has managed to span the world with the convergence of both urban and rural areas. Since the relationship between urban and rural areas stems

[7]Yu Hairong 于海荣, Wang Xinyi 王辛夷. "央地财政关系再调整." [*Central government financial relations and then adjust*]. *Weekly Caixin* 财新周刊 35 (2016): 30–32.

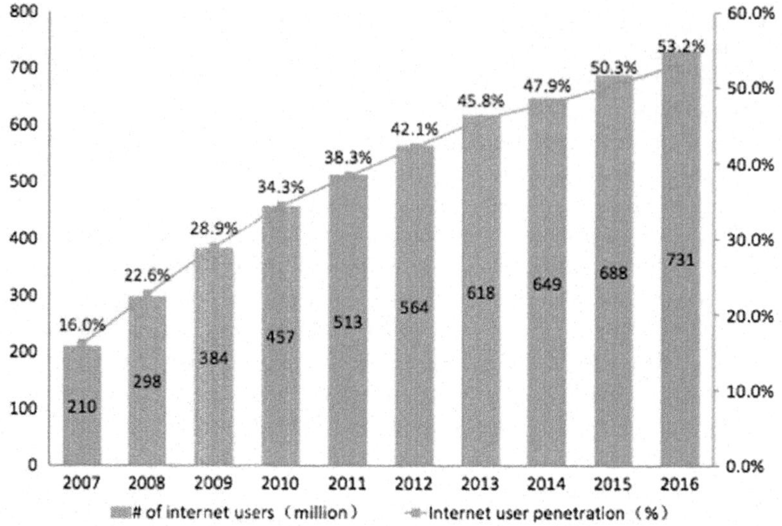

Fig. 1.1 Population and penetration rate of Chinese internet users over 2007–2016. *Source* Aliresearch

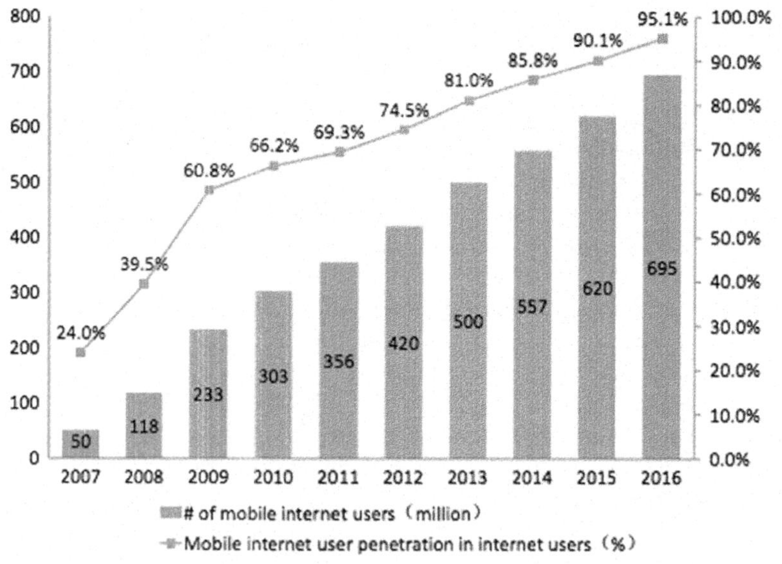

Fig. 1.2 Population and penetration rate of Chinese mobile internet users over 2007–2016. *Source* Aliresearch

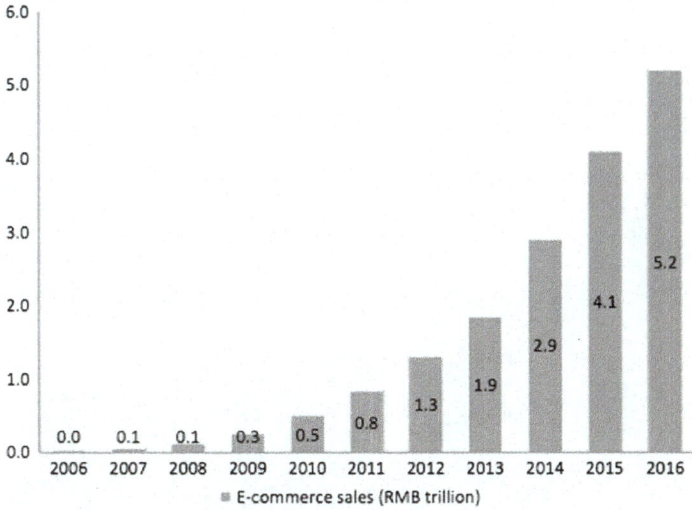

Fig. 1.3 China's ecommerce sales over 2006–2016. *Source* Aliresearch

Fig. 1.4 Service center of rural Taobao in Xingcheng. Photograph taken by the author

Fig. 1.5 Service center at Dayingbuzi village, Caozhuang town, Xingcheng. Photograph taken by the author

largely from geography and distance from economic centers, we can see how the advent of time-space compression[8] is vital, making possible new production chains inclusive of even the most remote rural areas. The undergoing transformation of the urban-rural relationship can be seen in the changes taking place in technology, consumption, production, logistics and transactions, well indicating the prosperous development of the new economy in counties and villages. Thanks to Internet business and consumption, rural areas have a chance to keep up with the cities at a gradual pace.

AliResearch released the development indices of ecommerce in different cities and counties, as well as the distribution data of Taobao villages. Though the original data is unavailable, we can draw a rough comparison of ecommerce development between difference regions based on their rankings. Furthermore, those maps also show the spatial distribution of ecommerce activities. They are also useful references for analysis of urban rural relationship with the impact of ecommerce.

Figures 1.6 and 1.7 demonstrate the spatial distribution patterns of ecommerce in China. They were provided by AliResearch in July, 2015, based on the

[8]Time–space compression (also known as space–time compression and time–space distantiation), articulated in 1989 by geographer David Harvey in *The Condition of Postmodernity*, refers to any phenomenon that alters the qualities of and relationship between space and time. Harvey's idea was rooted in Karl Marx's theory of the "annihilation of time and space".

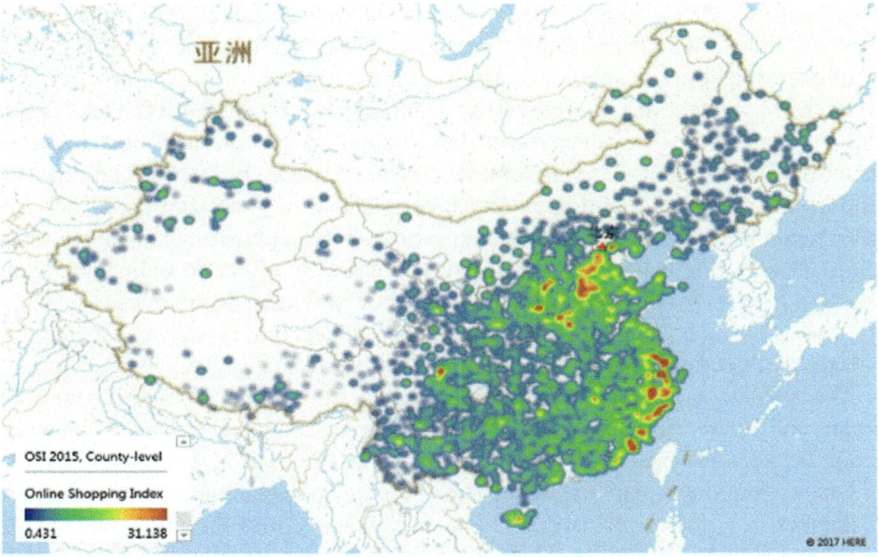

Fig. 1.6 Online shopping index geographical distribution 2015 (county-level). *Source* Aliresearch

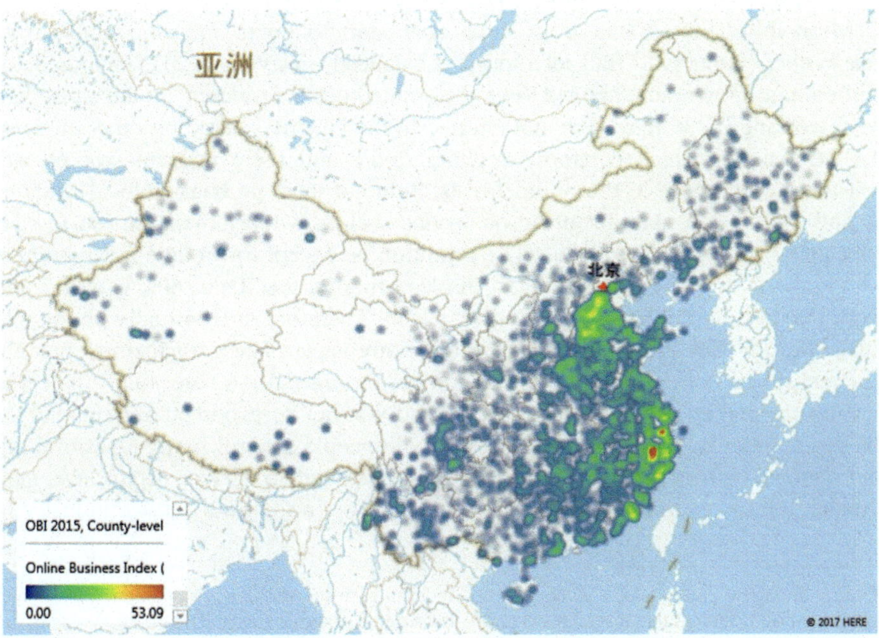

Fig. 1.7 Online business index 2015 (county-level). *Source* Aliresearch

development indices of ecommerce (Online Shopping Index[9] (OSI) and Online Business Index[10] (OBI) in Chinese counties at prefecture-level or above. By virtue of this information, we are able to interpret these indices.

In such a context, the Yangtze River Delta region, the Pearl River Delta region and Beijing-Tianjin-Tangshan region have actually experienced a next round of urban-rural integration through online services. It can be fairly said that the land-based traditional real-estate sectors, commercial business and public services have begun to be replaced by the online service (Internet business) model. Various online factors flow between urban and rural areas from offline to online, including business activities and even some online public services (health care, education, etc.), which creates an alternative urbanization model. In this way, the standard in villages and counties are lifted on the regional level.

The advent of rural ecommerce ecommerce has profoundly transformed the urban-rural relationship in China, thus altering the spatial distribution and interaction between villages and cities.

China's previous path to urbanization, though efficient, has confronted grim challenges in terms of inclusiveness and sustainability. But the informatization of the global network has given China unprecedented opportunities. The opportunity is that China, the country with the largest scale of urbanization, will take the lead in embarking on the road of urban-rural integration against the unique background of informatization, and provide another way to eliminate poverty to revive urban and rural dynamics and achieve the Millennium Development Goals.

Meanwhile, immigrants from rural areas start to go to the cities and towns nearby their families to find jobs to get a balanced lifestyle. In 2015, hundreds of million migrant workers had not yet to be granted urban residency by the cities they were working in, so they were not entitled to the benefits shared by other citizens. As the export-oriented economy declines, more and more migrant workers are considering returning to their hometowns. Some of them go back to local counties to find jobs in the manufacturing or service sectors, while others choose to start their own businesses in villages. The condition is, except for middle-aged workers who know farm work well, younger people born after the 70s or 80s, who live and work in cities, hardly know how to till the land. Therefore, it is virtually impossible for them to follow the plough, nor are there any vacant lands for them to plough. The real situation is, only those left-behind farmers aged 50–60 are still proficient at farm work, so they are the major work forces for agriculture, both at present, and for the years to come. Just like in Japan, many old people are still living a pastoral life and content with it, while young people are engaged in service sector. We may wonder is there a similarly deep yet unfulfilled gap in the rural service industry in

[9]Online Shopping Index (OSI): A constructed index measuring the density of online buyers and the percent of online buyers with annual online consumption above RMB 10,000. The value of the index ranges from 0 to 100. The higher the value, the more developed the online purchase.

[10]Online Business Index (OBI): A constructed index measuring the density of online stores and the percent of online stores with annual online sale above RMB 240,000. The value of the index ranges from 0 to 100. The higher the value, the more developed the online sales.

China? County and rural service industry is able to provide rural dwellers with public and commercial services as enjoyed by urban residents.

Moreover, there is another benefit to it: it serves as an excellent opportunity for service and other industry chains to reach out from cities and villages. This is reflected in urban networks. Those urban networks, centering on commercial towns and business centers, have long been serving the teeming crowds living in the vast land of urban and rural areas. Therefore, those towns and business centers become different nodes connecting urban and rural China.

Therefore, with the opportunities of ecommerce development, and the situation of movement of rural immigrants back to their hometown (normally, they settle down at township and county downtown), ecommerce in rural China (township and county level) is emerging and develops fast. Furthermore, urban rural spatial relationship is impacted by rural ecommerce. To those new phenomena, I addressed my research questions.

1.2 Research Question

1. What is rural ecommerce in China?
2. What is the urban-rural spatial relationship under the influence of rural ecommerce in China?

1.3 Literature

In this chapter, I briefly introduce literature of this research.

Rural Ecommerce was firstly defined as online retail whose registered address was in a rural area.[11] This concept was addressed by Liang Chunxiao and Wang Xiangdong.[12] In Dec, 2011, AliResearch reported the volume of rural ecommerce as 1.31 million.[13] Wang Xiangdong defined rural ecommerce in two models: top down model in the 90s (government-led movement); 2. bottom up (market-oriented

[11]Rural Ecommerce was firstly mentioned in Seminar of Rural Ecommerce and Shaji model ("农村电子商务暨'沙集模式'高层研讨会") by Chinese Academy of Social Science, Ali Research Center and Suining County Committee at 18th–19th, Dec., 2010. http://iqte.cass.cn/dtbd/xsdt/201012/t20101230_1790829.shtml.

[12]China Academy of Social Sciences and Ali research released the research report on Shaji model Taobao village. http://www.aliresearch.com/Blog/Article/detail/id/12860.html.

[13]The survey of "rural ecommerce report" used random sampling call interview, and separated survey targets as rural online shop owner and farmers without ecommerce experience. http://www.aliresearch.com/Blog/Article/detail/id/16871.html.

platform driven by online retailers and organizations).[14] The former is based on external power, such as government; the latter is based on commercial sector's motivation including ecommerce platform, farmers and so on.

2012, Zhou Haiqin defined rural ecommerce as the transaction process transferring products to the market by simple, fast, low-cost electro-communication, and during the process buyers and sellers do not need to meet.[15]

However, rural ecommerce developed very fast in the last 5 years, and there are 3 main phenomena:

1. Suichang Model
2. Alibaba Rural Strategy (Taobao Villages and Rural Taobao).

To answer the first question, I define the rural commerce at the end of his book. To reply the second question, about the relationship between ecommerce and space, I generally introduce theories from outstanding scholars here and more reference is address in Chap. 2.

In which aspects I can analysis phenomena of ecommerce in rural China? Saskia Sassen analyzed global cities including: 1. major stock exchanges and indexes on flows of labors and capital[16]; 2. international political affairs and cultural institutions on cultural identity; 3. media hub on flow of information; 4. transit networks and airport and impact on transport and logistics; 5 skyline on spatial image.

Manual Castells analyzed space of flow as having at least three layers of material supports by: 1. a circuit of electronic exchanges (virtual space); 2. its nodes and hubs (place); 3. the spatial organization of the dominant, managerial elites that exercise the directional functions around (elites).[17]

Learning from those theories and methodology, I observed and analyzed urban rural flows through rural ecommerce as having 5 aspects: 1. human resources; 2. flow of capital (e.g. investment); 3. logistics; 4. informational tech; and 5. cultural interaction. Thus, I proposed 5 aspects to define the concept of online services and online urbanization firstly, and will explain it in chapters later.

Online services are accurate, economical and convenient services provided through Internet business (including ecommerce, long distance education, long distance health care, logistics, financial technologies and so on). The measure of "online

[14]Rural Ecommerce: change moment after development for 20 years (农村电商:20年、 新变局), Dec 31st, 2015. http://blog.sina.com.cn/s/blog_593adc6c0102w4xy.html.

[15]Zhou Haiqin and Zhang Chaiming, "Analysis of key elements of rural ecommerce development in China" *Information China* 1(2012): 17–19. (周海琴, 张才明. "我国农村电子商务发展关键要素分析." 中国信息界 1 (2012): 17–19).

[16]Sassen, Saskia. *The mobility of labor and capital: A study in international investment and labor flow*. Cambridge University Press, 1990: 12–14.

[17]Castells, Manuel. *The space of flows*. Wiley-Blackwell, 1996.

services" includes the urban and rural flows which are manifested in five aspects: fostering and flow of urban and rural human resources; the urban and rural logistics supply chain; information flow; effective resource allocation; and ecological and cultural progress. This can be summarized as the flow of people, goods, information, capital, ecology and culture.

Furthermore, I introduce Online urbanization which base on online service system. It can be interpreted as a large number of residents in towns and townships beginning to use the Internet (including ecommerce, mobile commerce and other business and public services opportunities provided by the Internet) to enter the market and join the urban and rural production chain and local lives, build socializing networks, promote products online, and organize offline production, acquisition, transportation and community building, achieve local development, create jobs and improve business and public services; it is manifested in five aspects including fostering and flowing of urban and rural human resources, the improvement of urban and rural logistics supply chain, the narrowing of urban and rural information gap, the effective resource allocation and urban-rural ecological and cultural progress. The urban and rural areas are unified as one network; different nodes of flowing factors and their touch points are integrated into the regional and even global production chain and living system.

I started a research about rural and urban relationship since 2005, when I was engaged in a project of metropolitan park around Beijing city, China. The main conflicts is Green policy from municipality for long term view against local development for local farmers in short term view. Without benefits from their lands, local people have chosen to abandon land or abuse use of natural recourses. To this project, I started to think about how to empower locals to manage their own resource. From 2004 to 2013, I have worked with developers local communities, and local government on a new economical model with rebalance their interests. But with the land financial system in China, it's difficult to let the local communities to play their role without equal right compared with other group's. With my practice as urban planner and urban designer, I critique the urbanization in China. Therefore, instead, I discovered internet business as a new economy with new service industries. The new media as ecommerce provides the direct access to market provide new research questions to me.

From 2013, especially during a field trip for Suichang ecommerce association in Zhejiang Province, I found the rural ecommerce as a tool to empower local communities with management of local resources including human resources, land, service, social relationship, financial supports, products and so on. New phenomena have emerged in Suichang counties. Then Alibaba Group adapted rural ecommerce model to national scale.

As a young scholar, I stayed at Suichang to participate on rural ecommerce there and try to analysis the phenomena with writing and recording. With the observation of Internet society and advanced in field trip, the concept and case studies of online urbanization has become more and more clear. With research and participation of

Suichang Rural Ecommerce Model and then Alibaba rural strategy, I developed my concept of "letting local community manage their resources with new medias". It's a way of de-centralization of business and community development system, and benefit local community, compared with urbanization with real estate in last 30 years in China.

I published "Analyze the Sixth Big Revolution from the Changes of Urban-Rural Relations"[18] in Ali Business Review in July 22, 2014. I try to conclude the new mode of urbanization led by the development of online service, especially Ecommerce service. In the forum on Urbanization in Beijing on Nov. 8 of the same year, I made a speech of Development of Global Ecommerce and Urbanization in Rural China[19] and further elaborated the concept of online service and urbanization. "Analyze the Sixth Big Revolution from the Changes of Urban-Rural Relations"[20] in Ali Business Review and concluded the new mode of urbanization led by the development of ecommerce. In this paper I reviewed the history of urbanization on vertical aspect ask a question: what's the relationship between new urbanization with impact of ecommerce with the grassrooting markets and grassrooting town during more than a thousand years in China? Furthermore, November of the same year, in sub forum of Urbanization, Beijing Forum, I made a speech of Development of Global Ecommerce and Urbanization in Rural China[21] to further elaborate the concept of online service and urbanization. This opportunity help me to make a summery of survey and participate of rural ecommerce in Suichang, and start to follow the Alibaba Rural Strategy (including Taobao, Ali Healthy, Cainiao Logistics, Ali entertainment, Ants Finance and other departments) and Taobao Villages Phenomenon. I started to do research on framework of online service and online urbanization.

[18]"阿里商业评论 | 从城乡关系变迁，看中国第六次"大变革"-资讯-阿里研究" [Ali Business Review | Analyze the Sixth Big Revolution from the Changes of Urban-Rural Relations]. 2014. Aliresearch.Com. http://www.aliresearch.com/blog/article/detail/id/19452.html.

[19]"李玫:全球电子商务发展与中国农村新型城镇化_名人谈_景观中国". [Li Zi: the Development of Ecommerce and the New Mode of Urbanization in Rural China] 2018. Landscape. Cn. 2014. http://www.landscape.cn/news/comment/celebrity/2014/1113/171849.html.

[20]"阿里商业评论 | 从城乡关系变迁，看中国第六次"大变革"-资讯-阿里研究" [Ali Business Review | Analyze the Sixth Big Revolution from the Changes of Urban-Rural Relations]. 2014. Aliresearch.Com. http://www.aliresearch.com/blog/article/detail/id/19452.html.

[21]"李玫:全球电子商务发展与中国农村新型城镇化_名人谈_景观中国". [Li Zi: the Development of Ecommerce and the New Mode of Urbanization in Rural China] 2018. Landscape. Cn. 2014. http://www.landscape.cn/news/comment/celebrity/2014/1113/171849.html.

From 2015 to 2016, I posted a series of articles on Ali Business Review[22] and academic journals.[23] In these articles, I tried to analyze different aspects of urban rural relationship impact by flows created by ecommerce to make a framework of online services and online urbanization (2018.5.20).

In "the Spring up of Ecommerce and the position of Online Urbanization",[24] "Waiting for the Chance—Development of Rural Community and Ecommmerce" and "Sustainable Rural Community Development Mode—Local Identity With the Internet", I tried to explain why the ecommerce in rural China is an opportunity to rethink of the last decades of urbanization in China to create a new path of

---

[22]"新加坡国立大学李孜:乡村在线城镇化, 不能让乡村旅游变成"迪士尼"现象-资讯-阿里研究院". Rural Online Urbanization, Rural Tourism Should not be Disney] 2017. Aliresearch.Com. http://www.aliresearch.com/blog/article/detail/id/21255.html.

"李孜:从双十一到淘宝村, 每个人的在线城镇化-资讯-阿里研究院". [From Double 11 to Taobao Village, Online Urbanization for everyone]. 2016. http://www.aliresearch.com/blog/article/detail/id/21185.html.

"李孜:在线城镇化, 有别于欧美城镇化的独特途径? | 活水专栏-资讯-阿里研究院". [Online Urbanization, Unique Way Different from European?]. 2016. http://www.aliresearch.com/blog/article/detail/id/20981.html.

"活水专栏 | 李孜:关于在线城镇化的5个观点-资讯-阿里研究院" [Li Zi: Five Points about Online Urbanization]. 2016. Aliresearch.Com. http://www.aliresearch.com/blog/article/detail/id/20971.html.

"中国区域协调发展独特途径:在线城镇化-资讯-阿里研究院" [Online Urbanization: Unique Way to Coordinate Area Development in China]. 2015. Aliresearch.Com. http://www.aliresearch.com/blog/article/detail/id/20705.html.

"阿里商业评论|时空重构之农村电商涌现与在线城镇化-资讯-阿里研究院" [Time and Space Reconstruction: the Spring up of Rural Ecommerce and Online Urbanization]. 2015. Aliresearch.Com. http://www.aliresearch.com/blog/article/detail/id/20533.html.

"阿里商业评论|农村电商涌现与在线城镇化途径的历史坐标-资讯-阿里研究院" [The Spring up of Ecommerce and the position of Online Urbanization]. 2015. Aliresearch.Com. http://www.aliresearch.com/blog/article/detail/id/20475.html.

"阿里商业评论|农村电子商务涌现与在线城镇化途径-资讯-阿里研究院" [the Spring up of Ecommerce and the Approach of Online Urbanization]. 2015. Aliresearch.Com. http://www.aliresearch.com/blog/article/detail/id/20451.html.

[23]Li Zi 李孜. Dai kechengzhiji, Zuo qiadaohaochu——Xiaoji xiangcun shequ yingjian yu nongcun dianzi shangwu fazhan 待可乘之机, 做恰到好处——小记乡村社区营建与农村电子商务发展 [Waiting for the Chance—Development of Rural Community and Ecommmerce]. World Architecture 世界建筑, 2, 010.

Li Zi 李孜. Nongcun dianzishangwu chuangxin yu zaixian chengzhenhua qiji 农村电子商务创新与在线城镇化契机 [Innovation of Ecommerce in Rural China and a Way to Urbanization Online-Mobile]. Eco-city and Green Building 动感(生态城市与绿色建筑), 1, 2016.

Li Zi 李孜. Kechixu xiangun shequ yingjian moshi tantao—hulianwang xiade diyu rentong 可持续乡村社区营建模式探讨——互联网下的地域认同 [Sustainable Rural Community Development Mode—Local Identity With the Internet]. Journal of Human Settlements in West China 西部人居环境学刊 2015, 30(03): 18–22

Li Zi 李孜. Lianjie xiangcun 链接乡村 [Sustainable Rural Community Development Mode—Local Identity With the Internet]. Garden 园林, 2015, 11: 30–33.

[24]"阿里商业评论|人, 农村电商涌现与在线城镇化的核心-资讯-阿里研究院" [People, the Spring up of Rural Ecommerce and the Core of Online Urbanization]. 2015. Aliresearch.Com. http://www.aliresearch.com/blog/article/detail/id/20514.html.

community development nowadays. Then, I was invited to write Taobao village report 2016, 2017, and share my reports in some important conferences, such as 2016 New Economy Think Tank Summit.[25]

With the interview by Wu Chen, the editor in chief with Economist Global Business Review, my concept of online urbanization has become a hot topic in the fields of Internet, real estate and urban planning in China. Furthermore, the publishing of "Rise of Ecommerce in Rural China: From Ecommerce Service in County to the Online Urbanization" in Chinese helped me make an academic structure of literature of theories, description of phenomena and a framework of online urbanization.

The value of this online urbanization research might give a new approach for developing areas when meeting the opportunities and challenges of urbanization and informatization.

China's urbanization, led by the Internet and the mobile Internet, may break through the several models of urbanization after World War II: the British "new town" model under the welfare state system that aims at improving the living conditions of the working class; the US's suburban development model driven by consumerism and real estate; and the new industrial district model that is in progress in most developing countries. China is forming a new type of online service model focusing on developing an information society in urban and rural areas with Chinese characteristics. By bringing industrial products offline and agro-products online and the great potential for improving public and business services, such an online service pattern is able to link the rural areas to the around-the-clock global production chain, consolidate the production, circulation and distribution of different regions and make the global market and technologies accessible to rural areas. This urbanization pattern will serve as another paradigm for the development-oriented urbanization in developing countries.

After reaching the Information Era, the Network Society emerges.[26] Space of flows and grassrooting space of flows[27] have turned into a phenomenon within the globalized urban development. The definition of space of flows can be simplified to be the global network and urban spaces formed by the Information Network and Financial Capital. However, space of flows and the grassrooting of space of flows in Euro-America and other more developed regions and cities contrast with the ones in China, as they are more aggressive and less harmonious considering the rivalries

[25]"新年特辑|从心链接乡村 - 规划头条" [Link Rural from Heart]. 2017. Upnews.Cn. http://www.upnews.cn/archives/27179.

[26]Castells, Manuel. *The rise of the network society: The information age: Economy, society, and culture*. Vol. 1. John Wiley & Sons, 2011.

[27]The empowerment furnished by the Internet in the process of globalization, stimulated by elites in this information era, and also the production of anti-globalization regional grass-root activities. The space of flows can be described as the physical and virtual space in which all higher-level transactions (monetary, communicative, informational, etc.) take place, while "grassrooting" refers to the integration these transactions into local communities.

within the urban-rural binary structure.[28] There are limits in current literature[29] in that it does not address the urban-rural dynamic. Now, the Internet has brought opportunities to readjust the urban-rural relationship and unite virtual and rural offline communities, providing an alternative to the predominant urban-rural relationship. Analysis of the new phenomenon of online service in rural China could expand the literature of space of flows and grassrooting space of flows to fill the gap in explaining the new urban-rural relationship from developing countries in Information Era. The intended contribution of this book is to address and incorporate these new developments. In order to get a clear image of the rural ecommerce and the spatial regeneration of the villages, it is helpful to briefly detail a few examples on the way that rural ecommerce transforms the everyday life of people, changing the way they interact with space.

1.4 Methodology

There was very limited references in 2013 when I started this research. Therefore, to understand and redefine the rural ecommerce in China, I started qualitative research with case studies on: 1. Suichang Model, 2. Rural Taobao, 3. Taobao Villages and Towns.

Mainly, I use Ethnographic method to collect Empirical data by observation, in-depth interviews and participation for years. I also collected data from rural ecommerce reports, company files and various public and private databases (Table 1.1).

The methods explanation is based on four aspects: observation, analysis, reflection and theorization. In last 4 years, I visit more than 25 counties, specially at Suichang (more than 10 times in 2 and half year).

Rural Taobao as Alibaba's rural Ecommerce strategy and Taobao village are the national scale objects. As guest researcher of Ali research, I observed, participated and interviewed different players through 5 aspects to analysis the urban rural flows in national scale. I gave request (For example, spatial distribution of rural taobao in China) to my colleagues in Alibaba and got the results. Those data is helpful to illustrate the distribution and average situation. But to spatial transformation of nodes, I take field trip with Observation, Participation, Interviews and so on.

Suichang is the first organized and uninterrupted rural Ecommerce county. my role in Suichang rural ecommerce model is participants and observers. Besides reports about Suichang as recourse, I got diverse sources of data with close

[28]The rapid urbanization is the progressive widening of urban-rural gap and accelerating prominence of an urban-rural binary structure.

[29]The current theory on space of flows and grassrooting space of flows focuses primarily on urban areas and does not adequately account for urban-rural relationships that have developed in the last ten years in some areas. As a compelling case study, China's urban-rural conflict presents interesting elements.

Table 1.1 Analysis of methodology

Case studies	Suichang Ecommerce Association	Rural Taobao; Taobao village
Ethnographic methods Observation, Participation, Interviews	Data gathering from 5 aspects: Human resource, logistic, flow of capital(etc. investment), culture and informational tech; open data, Report; internal statics; primary data from interviews	Data gathering: 5 aspects: Human resource, logistic, flow of capital (etc. investment), culture and informational tech back end statics; network in Taobao village; primary data from interviews
Analysis	Data analysis in 5 variables Human resource: population; age and gender etc.; logistic system with distribution; analysis of flow of capital (etc. investment) cultural interaction between urban and rural in cases informational tech	
Reflection	Urban-rural spatial relationship influenced by Suichang model, Taobao village and Rural Taobao	
Theorization	Spatial changes brought by Ecommerce might be a new paradigm for urbanization in China	

Source Author

relationship with team of Suichang ecommerce association, local government officers, and local communities. Those data reflected on spatial transformation of county scale, to village scale by land use and infrastructure.

The meaning of case study of Suichang is its innovation of ecommerce service system by local ecommerce association and platform in county level. Firstly, Suichang is small or middle scale county (260 thousand residents) out of around 2800 counties in China. It's not about the quantity of ecommerce of Suichang, but its representation of normal condition as other counties in southeast China. Secondly, the ecommerce service in country level was developed earlier there and became a remarkable case in China. This is why I still choose Suichang as case study, even if it is not on the top counties list about ecommerce index (AliResearch) base on the quantity of ecommerce.

To region scale, the unbalanced development of different regions in China is also addressed by development of ecommerce. There are some ecommerce index of cities and counties, especially, one from AliResearch. Those report were addressed to explain the general situation of national scale in China with comparison of different regions' ecommerce condition. It's just one aspect to understanding the impact on the urban-rural relationship from ecommerce with some scholars' analysis.

I focus on rural ecommerce with urban-rural flows of elements (capital flow, flow of goods, flow of human resource, flow of information and technology and flow of culture). This research way based on literature of research ways.

To ecommerce in urban China, Alibaba and other platforms started urban ecommerce at the end of the 90s, much early then the development of rural ecommerce (the concept of the Taobao village was firstly defined in 2006, and the first phenomenon of ecommerce association in county level emerged at around 2010). The urban ecommerce, especially in first to third class cities, is developed better than one in counties and villages. Furthermore, But, based on low levels of ecommerce service, rural ecommerce develops faster than the urban ecommerce by the data in national scale nowadays. Therefore, it's interesting to analysis rural ecommerce with their fast development and how it impact the urban rural relationship nowadays.

There is limitation of this research. Firstly, as a cross sectional research, data was collected in only from 2014 to 2017. Secondly, in China, there are diversification case, and this research mainly based on 3 case studies (Suichang Rural Ecommerce Model, Rural Taobao and Taobao villages) in China. To next step, more case studies in different regions should be studied to understand the unequal development in west-east, south-north regional contexts. Thirdly, sample size of interviews becomes a constraint.

To the problem or negative parts (i.e. business relation, social relationship and spatial relationship) of rural ecommerce development, I will add discussion in case study of Suichang Model and Alibaba Rural Strategy, and finally make summary about it in the chapter of conclusion.

1.5 Introduction of Each Chapter

This chapter serves as an introduction to the book. It emphasizes the problems caused by uneven urbanization in China and presents online services, especially ecommerce, as a potential solution. It is the hope of this book that the research may find possible extensions in other countries. Research questions, mythology and research design are addressed to directly emphasize contributions to fill the limitations in current literature.

Chapter 2, theories on "space of flows" and "grassrooting space of flows" from Manual Castells explain accurately the empowerment furnished by the Internet in the process of globalization, stimulated by elites in this information era to inspiring the review of China's urbanization model in last decades years.

In Chapter 3, the flow of information, cultures, goods, capital, and human resources echo off each other inside the urban-rural network, while offering urban-rural integration based on market economy in traditional Chinese societies. The author will further address how the rural-urban relationship in traditional Chinese society may be considered as an interesting background to highlight contemporary issues regarding the rural-urban relationship.

Chapter 4 emphasizes on the Suichang ecommerce model, in which people were empowered by Internet technology which contributed to integrate local resources, increase employment in their localities, and improve business and public services. This case is helpful to explain the online service phenomenon in China' s rural area on county level.

Chapter 5 Alibaba Rural Strategy is presented as one of the primary providers of rural online service on the national scale. Rural strategy is investigated to explain rural ecommerce under global and national influence. The study is the premise to an understanding of new urban rural relationship impacted by online services.

By focusing on different aspects of the County and rural areas, Chap. 6 questions how the ecommerce shapes the local and regional scale of study in China.

Chapter 7 answers the research questions and introduces a new framework for online service and online urbanization, and an attempt to respond to the theory introduced in this chapter and Chap. 2 is made.

References

1. Ki-Moon B (2013) The millennium development goals report 2013. United Nations Pubns
2. World Bank (2013) Global monitoring report 2013: rural-urban dynamics and the millennium development goals. https://openknowledge.worldbank.org/handle/10986/13330. Accessed 2 May 2013
3. Zhao G 赵冈 (2006) The history of urban development in China 中国城市发展史论集. New Star Press 新星出版社
4. Zhou H, Zhang C (2012) Analysis of key elements of rural ecommerce development in China. Inf China 1:17–19 (周海琴, 张才明. 我国农村电子商务发展关键要素分析. 中国信息界)
5. Sassen S (1990) The mobility of labour and capital: a study in international investment and labour flow. Cambridge University Press, Cambridge, pp 12–14
6. Castells M (1996) The space of flows. Wiley-Blackwell, USA
7. http://www.ciudsrc.com/new_zazhi/fengmian/2014diyiqi/2014-02-25/62220.html
8. Zhang X 张晓鸽 (2013) Zhengdi chaiqian boji 16% jiating 征地拆迁波及16%家庭 [Requisition of land affected 16% family]. China Data Center, Tsinghua University (CDC) (2013) Large-scale survey data of urbanization in China (中国城镇化调查大型数据) http://epaper.jinghua.cn/html/201310/28/content_35335.htm
9. Yu H 于海荣, Wang X 王辛夷 (2016) 央地财政关系再调整 [Central government financial relations and then adjust]. Weekly Caixin 财新周刊 35:30–32
10. http://iqte.cass.cn/dtbd/xsdt/201012/t20101230_1790829.shtml
11. http://www.aliresearch.com/Blog/Article/detail/id/12860.html
12. Rural ecommerce report 2011. http://www.aliresearch.com/Blog/Article/detail/id/16871.html
13. Rural ecommerce: change moment after development for 20 years (农村电商: 20年、新变局), Dec 31, 2015. http://blog.sina.com.cn/s/blog_593adc6c0102w4xy.html
14. 阿里商业评论｜从城乡关系变迁, 看中国第六次“大变革”-资讯-阿里研究 [Ali Business Review | Analyze the sixth big revolution from the changes of urban-rural relations] (2014) Aliresearch.Com. http://www.aliresearch.com/blog/article/detail/id/19452.html
15. 李孜: 全球电子商务发展与中国农村新型城镇化_名人谈_景观中国 [Li Zi: The development of ecommerce and the new mode of urbanization in rural China] (2018) Landscape.Cn. 2014. http://www.landscape.cn/news/comment/celebrity/2014/1113/171849.html
16. 新加坡国立大学李孜: 乡村在线城镇化, 不能让乡村旅游变成“迪士尼”现象-资讯-阿里研究院 [Rural online urbanization, rural tourism should not be Disney] (2017) Aliresearch.Com. http://www.aliresearch.com/blog/article/detail/id/21255.html
17. 李孜: 从双十一到淘宝村, 每个人的在线城镇化-资讯-阿里研究院 [From double 11 to Taobao village, online urbanization for everyone] (2016) http://www.aliresearch.com/blog/article/detail/id/21185.html

18. 李孜: 在线城镇化, 有别于欧美城镇化的独特途径? | 活水专栏-资讯-阿里研究院 [Online urbanization, unique way different from European?] (2016) http://www.aliresearch.com/blog/article/detail/id/20981.html
19. 活水专栏 | 李孜: 关于在线城镇化的5个观点-资讯-阿里研究院 [Li Zi: Five points about online urbanization] (2016) Aliresearch.Com. http://www.aliresearch.com/blog/article/detail/id/20971.html
20. 中国区域协调发展独特途径: 在线城镇化-资讯-阿里研究院 [Online urbanization: unique way to coordinate area development in China] (2015) Aliresearch.Com. http://www.aliresearch.com/blog/article/detail/id/20705.html
21. 阿里商业评论|时空重构之农村电商涌现与在线城镇化-资讯-阿里研究院 [Time and space reconstruction: the spring up of rural ecommerce and online urbanization] (2015) Aliresearch.Com. http://www.aliresearch.com/blog/article/detail/id/20533.html
22. 阿里商业评论|人, 农村电商涌现与在线城镇化的核心-资讯-阿里研究院 [People, the spring up of rural ecommerce and the core of online urbanization] (2015) Aliresearch.Com. http://www.aliresearch.com/blog/article/detail/id/20514.html
23. 阿里商业评论|农村电商涌现与在线城镇化途径的历史坐标-资讯-阿里研究院 [The spring up of ecommerce and the position of online urbanization] (2015) Aliresearch.Com. http://www.aliresearch.com/blog/article/detail/id/20475.html
24. 阿里商业评论|农村电子商务涌现与在线城镇化途径-资讯-阿里研究院 [The spring up of ecommerce and the approach of online urbanization] (2015) Aliresearch.Com. http://www.aliresearch.com/blog/article/detail/id/20451.html
25. Li Zi 李孜 Dai kechengzhiji, Zuo qiadaohaochu——Xiaoji xiangcun shequ yingjian yu nongcun dianzi shangwu fazhan 待可乘之机, 做恰到好处——小记乡村社区营建与农村电子商务发展 [Waiting for the chance—development of rural community and e-commmerce].World Architect 世界建筑 2:010
26. Li Zi 李孜 (2016) Nongcun dianzishangwu chuangxin yu zaixian chengzhenhua qiji 农村电子商务创新与在线城镇化契机 [Innovation of ecommerce in rural china and a way to urbanization online-mobile]. Eco-city Green Build 动感(生态城市与绿色建筑) 1
27. Li Zi 李孜 (2015) Kechixu xiangun shequ yingjian moshi tantao—hulianwang xiade diyu rentong 可持续乡村社区营建模式探讨——互联网下的地域认同 [Sustainable rural community development mode—local identity with the internet]. J Hum Settlements West China 西部人居环境学刊 30(03):18–22
28. Li Zi 李孜 (2015) Lianjie xiangcun 链接乡村 [Sustainable rural community development mode—local identity with the internet]. Garden 园林 11:30–33
29. 新年特辑|从心链接乡村 - 规划头条 [Link rural from heart] (2017) Upnews.Cn. http://www.upnews.cn/archives/27179

Chapter 2
From Globalization to China's Urbanization

The theories on "space of flows" and "grassrooting space of flows" from Manual Castells explain accurately the empowerment furnished by the Internet in the process of globalization, stimulated by elites in this information era, and also the production of anti-globalization regional grass-root activities. The notion of space of flows can be described as the physical and virtual space in which all higher-level transactions (monetary, communicative, informational, etc.) take place, while "grassrooting" refers to the integration of these transactions into local communities. These are the two sides of the same coin. However, there are limitations in the current literature. The current theory on space of flows and grassrooting space of flows focuses primarily on urban areas and does not adequately account for urban-rural relationships that have developed in the last ten years in some areas. As a compelling case study, China's urban-rural conflict presents interesting elements. In China, the integration of space of flows are clearly reflected in the urban-rural unity and social practices, epitomized in the emergence of county-level rural e-commerce. This is the new phenomenon of China's Urban-Rural Relationship. One of the main contributions of this book is to attempt to use China as a reference to gauge the accuracy of these theories. During its development with globalization in the last couple of decades, and with emerging ecommerce in the past 20 years, China has unquestionably gone through significant changes.

L. Zi, *Online Urbanization*, Advances in 21st Century Human Settlements,
https://doi.org/10.1007/978-981-13-3603-4_2

PRC has experienced free market economy[1] in a short period of time, witnessing the whole process of government intervention from its conception to its experimental implementation. It has also attempted two diametrically opposite economic systems (from Communes to the Reformation). In the vast land of China, regional developments and urbanization are indeed extremely uneven and accompanied with drastically different culture and history. Globalization has guided urbanization and urban-rural relationships in different areas, with some regions displaying signs of co-existence and congruence of both urban and rural dynamics. Undoubtedly, there are quite a number of regions in China which are still far away from realizing modernization, in particular villages. However, there are some villages (some with over thousands of residents) which have been influenced profoundly by Information Technology and have already become a part of the network society. China followed another path than the one taken by Europe and America to the extent that it entered the information era without reaching an urbanization rate as high as Europe and America.

However, it is now crucial to highlight that the shift towards informatization is characterized by its progressive evolution.

---

[1]Prof. Zhao Gang pointed out that the traditional stages of China's historic social system development were not accurate. (Zhao Gan, 赵冈, Chen Zhongyi 陈钟毅. *Zhongguo tudi zhidu shi* 中国土地制度史 [*History of Chinese Land System*]. New Star Press 新星出版社, 2006) The mainland scholars, in particular, divide the historic social system based on Marxism's division of European history, including stages of Primitive Communism, Feudalism, Capitalism, and ultimately socialism. According to Prof. Zhao Gang, this division fits the European context, but not the Chinese context. Chinese scholars had been using this Europe-centric framework to analyse the Chinese history, thus adding a stage of feudal landlord economic system (vs. the European feudal lord system) and a stage of feudal lord system in end of Western-Zhou dynasty. Prof. Zhao Gang argues that China's land system after the western Zhou (西周) dynasty was totally different from Feudal lord system of European land system. In another words, should we argue that there was Feudalism from the warring states (东周战国) until Qing dynasty, because the land ownership and development right was really traded in the market. The landlord did not get land from the Emperor or King, as what was the case in Europe's Feudal lord system, but instead bought the land from the market. Prof. Fu Yiling (傅依凌, 1988) replaced the term "feudal society" by "traditional society" in his last paper '中国传统社会:多元的结构' ("China's traditional society: a diverse/multi-variate structure"), admitting that China has had a dynamic social structure since the end of primitive society. He pointed out that the Chinese society has had a long and complicated evolvement history, with social systems constantly transforming from old to new and combining features of the two. Many different production systems co-existed for a long period in history. He also pointed out that the property system in China had long ago led to a market economy which was dynamic and flexible. Prof. Zhao Gang approached the analysis of the Chinese market economy under private ownership system by illustrating the school of thought of economic systems that property ownership was equivalent to decision making power. In his illustration, the Chinese private ownership system was established early in history, supported by the legal evidence of rural land private ownerships started by the Reforms of Shang Yang (秦国商鞅变法) in the warring states (东周战国). Private ownership system stimulated the formation of markets. Markets are places for transfer and exchange of property ownership (Zhao Gang 赵冈. "论中国传统社会的性质" ("The Characters of Chinese Traditional Society"), 中国社会经济史研究 *2* (*The Journal of Chinese Social and Economic History*) (1998):1–6).

2.1 Globalization

The American transition from an agricultural to an industrial economy began in 1914 when Henry Ford shocked the world by introducing 8-h working days and $5 per day wages. This system increased the efficiency of machinery production. Henry Ford maybe aware that mass production would bring mass consumption, and that the new work system would influence people psychologically. This new relationship with production came with a new lifestyle, a new way of thinking, and a new life experience.

In the early 1960s, a major crisis hit Ford. Due to the saturation of the domestic market, the company had to start exportation. The economic downturn and shortage of oil in 1973 further exacerbated Ford's crisis. Meanwhile, Toyota, another automobile company, was one of the first to use the "just-in-time"[2] operation system which relied on flexibility in work processes, the labor market, product and consumption. The labor market changed totally in the face of a volatile global market, vigorous competition and a reduction in profits. Employers began to employ excess labor to gain more flexible contracts and systems. Employment formats went from regular full-time employment to also include part-time jobs and subcontracting. Meanwhile, new technology served as the catalyst of the "just-in-time" system, as well as furthering its promotion. Restructured financial systems strengthened the trend of time-space compression.[3] Flexible capital flows encouraged individualism and new market re-configuration,[4] and this trend swept the globe with globalization.

Everywhere and every minute of time has since been absorbed by the time-space compression and consumption system in its dynamic promoting of economic liberalism. From an extensive production-oriented economy to a demand-oriented

---

[2]Companies who use what is sometimes called "just-in-time" production rely on the flexibility of small batches and numerous small contracts and subcontracts.

[3]Time–space compression (also known as space–time compression and time–space distanciation), articulated in 1989 by geographer David Harvey in *The Condition of Postmodernity*, refers to any phenomenon that alters the qualities of and relationship between space and time. Harvey's idea was rooted in Karl Marx's theory of the "annihilation of time and space".

[4]Firstly, products, production and monetary devaluation occurred, as shown by the economic crisis that occurred in the 1930s, leading to tremendous devaluation of capital and money. The Second World War was significantly detrimental to European productivity. Secondly, because of the capitalist tendency of over-accumulation, a balance had to be maintained after the Second World War between Fordist production and Keynesian macro-control. However, the balance remained fragile. Thirdly, the control and eventually the absorption of over-accumulation may be achieved by shifting the time and space features. One of the key elements during this process may be the virtual capital formation as well as the diversification of financing channels on a global scale. Therefore, the Just-In-Time production as a system covering the whole global economy by following a logic of capitalist consumerism may be an important step to achieve this new approach towards space and time. Therefore, the shift from the Fordist production to the Just-in-time production is correlated to the transition from a large-scale production-oriented extensive economy to a market demand-oriented intensive form of economy. Harvey, David. *From space to place and back again: Reflections on the condition of postmodernity* (1993), and Harvey, David. *The condition of postmodernity: An enquiry into the conditions of cultural change* (1990).

intensive market, the shopping-space has become more powerful and has had a huge impact on the urban development. Therefore, the consumerist culture and rapid urbanization in developing countries have become integrated by global production and the consumer market.

> The work of running a global economic system, the practices of global control, and the infrastructure of low wage jobs is necessary to service the global economy, the emergence of new spatial order in global cities, all these terms have now become part of the optic or the conceptual landscape through which I attempt to understand the condition of cities that are deeply articulated with global economy.[5]

Cities, as places of consumer activities, naturally extend to and engulf the rural areas. With the convergence of labor and resources, the urban areas expanded to new boundaries. Meanwhile, businesses along the urban-rural borders become more active, giving opportunities to form huge markets.

If there is a seasonal economic crisis such as overproduction in the capitalist world as Marx predicted, the production processes should focus on consumers to integrate resources and labor in order to keep a benign cycle of the global economic system. In his book *The Protestant Ethic and the Spirit of Capitalism,*[6] Weber explained the relationship between the major western ideologies and the spirit of capitalism that evolved in Europe before being brought to America. He combined economic and religious sociology to elaborate on the interaction between economy and society. Durkheim also analyzed capitalism and moral order from a positivist approach. Their contributions created the foundation for economic sociology.[7] Talcott Parsons and Neil J. Smelser later built largely on Weber's work to identify the basic concepts and scope of this new field of study. They tried to improve the economic integration theory and social theory to construct a comprehensive analysis of a unified theoretical framework of economy and social relationships.

Karl Polanyi in his *The Great Transformation: The Political and Economic Origins of Our Time* gave a vivid and detailed description about the influence on rural society brought by the Industrial Revolution. As the instigator of the revolution, England had become the indisputable World Factory, leading the extensive globalization and colonization. However, Karl Polanyi was able to put the technical reformation/innovation and economic globalization into the corresponding social transformation/reformation of various countries, and proposed a relationship of 'Embeddedness' between Economy and Society. Polanyi used embeddedness to explain 'family', 'reciprocity' and 'redistribution' as the principle economic system in history to satisfy social structure. Compared with this economic system in history, the free economic current market system has negative impacts on social structure.[8]

---

[5]Sassen, Saskia. *The global city: New York, London, Tokyo*. Princeton University Press, 2001.

[6]Weber, Max. "The Protestant ethic and the spirit of capitalism, trans." *T. Parsons. Charles Scribner's Sons.* [*SA*] (1958).

[7]Durkheim, Emile. *The division of labor in society*. Simon and Schuster, 2014.

[8]Polanyi, Karl. "The great transformation: Economic and political origins of our time." *Rinehart, New York* (1944).

Later, Mark Granovetter wrote an article—"Economic Action and Social Structure: The Problem of Embeddedness" in 1985. He proposed the idea that economic action is impacted by a social structure. In this paper, he also remarked on the concepts of 'Over-socialized' and 'Under-socialized'. Over-socialized is generally explained as the condition of "people being overwhelmingly sensitive to the opinions of others and hence obedient to the dictators without being perceived as a burden." Under-socialized, on the other hand, is generally explained as "arguments that disallow any impact of social structure and social relations on production, distribution, or consumption".[9]

All these discussions are about the problems of social-reconfiguration faced mostly in urban-rural societies as the result of free economy globalization and urbanization.

Like Henri Lefebvre mentioned in his *The Production of Space*:

> If it is true that (social) space is a (social) product, how is this fact concealed? The answer is: by a double illusion, each side of which refers back to the other, reinforces the other, and hides behind the other. The two aspects are the illusion of transparency on the one hand and illusion of opacity, or 'realistic' illusion, on the other.[10]

Therefore, space is not only the goods for use or consumption, but also a mode of production. It generates concrete social behaviors. Furthermore, Henri Lefebvre points out that land, labor and capital as the important elements in expression. The globalization in terms of the production process is reflected in the re-allocation of land, labor and capital. But globalization also creates regional discontinuity while generating a hierarchical order, which are embodied in the urban space. Urbanization characterizes capitalist industrialization, which has remodeled urban space constantly through the period of industrial society as well as urban society.

Nowadays, the competition for urban space and power has extended to the information age, turning into the battle between space of flows and grassrooting space of flows.

2.2 Space of Flows and Grassrooting Space of Flows

"Technology is society, and society cannot be understood or represented without its technological tool".[11] The influence that Internet technologies are exerting on nations and societies, simultaneously deep and vast, might be just the beginning of

---

[9]Granovetter, Mark. "Economic action and social structure: The problem of embeddedness." *American journal of sociology* 91, no. 3 (1985): 481–510.

[10]Lefebvre, Henri. *The production of space*. Vol. 142. Blackwell: Oxford, 1991.

[11]Bijker, Wiebe E., Hughes, Thomas P. and Pinch, Trevor (eds) (1987). The Social Construction of Technological Systems: New Directions in the Sociology and History of Technology, Cambridge, MA: MIT Press.

its infiltration into all aspects of social life. This statement is strengthened by Manuel Castells, when he points out:

> Although technology and technical relationships of production are organized in paradigms originating in the dominant spheres of society (for example, the production process, the military–industrial complex) they diffuse throughout the whole set of social relationships and social structures, so penetrating and modifying power and experience. Thus, modes of development shape the entire realm of social behavior, of course including symbolic communication. Because informationalism is based on the technology of knowledge and information, there is an especially close linkage between culture and productive forces, between spirit and matter, in the informational mode of development. It follows that we should expect the emergence of historically new forms of social interaction, social control, and social change.
>
> Technological innovation and organizational change, focusing on flexibility and adaptability, were absolutely critical in ensuring the speed and efficiency of restructuring. It can be argued that without new information technology global capitalism would have been a much limited reality, flexible management would have been reduced to labor trimming, and the new round of spending in both capital goods and new consumer products would not have been sufficient to compensate for the reduction in public spending. Thus, informationalism is linked to the expansion and rejuvenation of capitalism, as industrialism was linked to its constitution as a mode of production.[12]

The underlying drive behind this force is the pursuit of an optimal allocation of resources—a new economic system called 'informational capitalism'.[13]

In the following tables (Tables 2.1 and 2.2), Dr. Zhou Zhiheng highlights the main evolutions in the structure of the economy, underlying the tendency towards informationalism in the context of globalization. These shifts in the economy therefore helped facilitate the transformation of transactions, from cashier counters to an online platform economy.

The new economy builds new urban-social relationships. The competition for urban space and power between elites of urban capitalist and local communities is exacerbated. Lefebvre forewarned the contestation of the average masses against the elite urban capitalists for the right of urban space as 'space is power'[14] as well as for the control over the different levels of information technology. Resistance followed control, which was exactly what happened in the 1968s student movement in Paris. In Henri Lefebvre's in-depth analysis of globalization, *The Urban Revolution* he asserted that with the expansion of the financial, commercial, and industrial networks, the traditional social structures and the morphology of the city would suffer from disintegration.[15] Diffusion of debris, including suburban, residential groups, industrial complexes, tourist resorts and the distant edge of the city and so on have already appeared and reveals this phenomenon.

---

[12]Castells, Manuel. *The rise of the network society: The information age: Economy, society, and culture*. Vol. 1. John Wiley & Sons, 2011, 18 & 19.

[13]Castells, Manuel. *The rise of the network society: The information age: Economy, society, and culture*. Vol. 1. John Wiley & Sons, 2011, 18.

[14]Hickman, John. *Space Is Power: The Seven Rules of Territory*. London: Lexington Books, 2016.

[15]Lefebvre, Henri. *The urban revolution*. U of Minnesota Press, 2003.

Table 2.1 Comparison of the evolution from old economy to new economy

Old economy	New economy
Partially covered (large number of intermediate steps, long chain, agency relationships)	Fully covered (full-crew transaction subject/main body)
Production centered	Transaction centered
Business-oriented	Individual-oriented
Report-driven	Data-driven
Counter economy	Platform economy
Production big bang/outburst	Transaction big bang/outburst
Physical environment—cost, distance, law	Mathematical and scientific environment—data, algorithm and program

Source Zhou Ziheng is from China Academy of Social Sciences furthered the comparison between the characteristics of Old and New Economy, bringing forward the differences between Platform Economy and Counter Economy

Table 2.2 Comparison of the evolution from counter to platform economy

<table>
<tr><th colspan="2">Counter economy</th><th colspan="2">Platform economy</th></tr>
<tr><td colspan="2">Reach and complete a transaction at the same time; goods and money settled immediately</td><td colspan="2">Focus only on the transaction-reaching process; the completion of transaction is on-line</td></tr>
<tr><td colspan="2">“Heavy” economy</td><td colspan="2">“Light” economy</td></tr>
<tr><td colspan="2">Partially covered: crew, goods and services</td><td colspan="2">Fully covered: crew, goods and services</td></tr>
<tr><td colspan="2">Round-the-clock non-stop transactions</td><td colspan="2">On and off transaction</td></tr>
<tr><td colspan="2">Scattered transaction</td><td colspan="2">Concentrated transactions</td></tr>
<tr><td colspan="2">Concentrated goods and customers</td><td colspan="2">Scattered goods and customers</td></tr>
<tr><td colspan="2">Property, energy, manpower, financial law</td><td colspan="2">Data, algorithm, program, system</td></tr>
<tr><td rowspan="2">Financial term and possibilities:</td><td>1. Inventory carry rate and Turnover Rate of Inventory</td><td rowspan="2">Financial term and possibilities:</td><td>1. Zero/null inventory or negative inventory</td></tr>
<tr><td>2. Current period inventory/ Proportion of Products Sold is definitely smaller than 1 in long term</td><td>2. Current period inventory/ Proportion of Products Sold can be larger than 1 in long term</td></tr>
</table>

Source Zhou Ziheng is from China Academy of Social Sciences furthered the comparison between the characteristics of Old and New Economy, bringing forward the differences between Platform Economy and Counter Economy

Manuel Castells explained the network society through the concept of “space of flows[16] and “grassrooting the space of flows” and defined the concept of “space of

[16]Manuel Castells explained the space of flaws: The “space of flows”, as the material form of support of dominant processes and functions in the informational society, can be described (rather than defined) by the combination of at least three layers of material supports that, together, constitute the space of flows. The first layer, the first material support of the space of flows, is

flows" in his book *The Information Age: Economy, Society, and Culture*[17] He simplified the network of advanced city services to the flow of information and knowledge production, which includes banking, insurance, real estate, consulting, legal services, advertising, design, marketing, public relations, security, information gathering, and management information systems, and also incorporates research and development as well as science and innovation. (All these sectors are the cores of the economic process, whether they belong to the manufacturing, agriculture or service industry.)

These flows established a spatial pattern, which on the one hand influence employment and investment growth rate in the world, and on the other hand are concentrated in the flow line of the city's interior nodes. This system and process is defined by Castells as 'the space of flows' in opposition to the system of 'the space of places'. 'The space of places' can be described as independent from the global system of production network and lifestyle. It's a non-international space led by the process of localization and relying on local cultural resources. From the early 1980s to the 1990s, the international elites of the space of flows first mastered the Internet and thus became the controllers of the flow of information, strengthening their global leadership. For instance, this process is exemplified by the model of the CBD in international metropolises (most notably Wall Street) as well as the new technological parks (such as Silicon Valley). These two models have indeed no

actually constituted by a circuit of electronic exchanges (micro-electronics-based devices, telecommunications, computer processing, broadcasting systems, and high-speed transportation—also based on information technologies) that, together, form the material basis for the processes we have observed as being strategically crucial in the network of society. This is indeed a material support of simultaneous practices. Thus, it is a spatial form, just as it could be "the city" or "the region" in the organization of the merchant society or of the industrial society. *The second layer of the space of flows is constituted by its nodes and hubs.* The space of flows is not placeless, although its structural logic is. It is based on an electronic network, but this network links up specific places, with well-defined social, cultural, physical, and functional characteristics. Some places are exchangers, communication hubs playing a role of coordination for the smooth interaction of all the elements integrated into the network. Other places are the nodes of the network; that is, the location of strategically important functions that build a series of locality-based activities and organizations around a key function in the network. Location in the node links up the locality with the whole network. Both nodes and hubs are hierarchically organized according to their relative weight in the network. But this hierarchy may change depending upon the evolution of activities processed through the network. Indeed, in some instances, some places may be switched off the network, their disconnection resulting in instant decline, and thus in economic, social and physical deterioration. The characteristics of nodes are dependent upon the type of functions performed by a given network. *The third important layer of the space of flows refers to the spatial organization of the dominant, managerial elites* (rather than classes) that exercise the directional functions around which such space is articulated. The theory of the space of flows starts from the implicit assumption that societies are asymmetrically organized around the dominant interests specific to each social structure. The space of flows is not the only spatial logic of our societies.

[17]Castells, Manuel. *The rise of the network society: The information age: Economy, society, and culture*. Vol. 1. John Wiley & Sons, 2011.

connection to local communities (representing the space of places), and do not follow the local and traditional way of life and production.[18]

Stephen Graham also recognized this point and explained it from an urban planning point of view:

> A final set of problems surround the limits that inevitably exist on the power of even progressive and creative urban policy maker to alter the deep-seated structural dynamics, which are broadly shaping the development of contemporary cities. The nature, geographies, politics, and social relations of cities and urban regions are currently being transformed so rapidly under the influence of neoliberal capitalism and the ICT technologies that are intrinsic to it. This limits the "maneuvering space" at the local level, to shift to different path of city-ICT relations.[19]

Space of flows and local spaces are two distinct worlds. As the majority of the population is concentrated in cities, both spaces are presented as urban spaces in Europe and the US. The space of flows is led by globalized elites, unquestionably guiding people and resources in local and regional spaces. Social functions, wealth and power are organized in the space of flows whereas regional and local spaces are led by traditional and regionalist dynamics. Globalized elitism aims to dominate and the logic they adopted thoroughly changes the meanings and dynamics of the local and regional spaces. Ultimately, then, people are the object for the reformation. This is the power of space of flows.

Meanwhile, the wave of the world anti-globalization has never ceded. The opposition against the reformation by the Global Elite Class on the lifestyles of the masses has become a norm. The space of flows is undergoing changes of alienation.

To explain this phenomenon, Castells published "Grassrooting the space of flows"[20] in the electronic information and city conference in Atlantic on 21st March, 1998. The article supplemented his theories about "space of flows", and he further postulated that "the space of flows is not confined to electronic spaces; real

[18]Manuel Carstells has a detailed illustration under the chapter "The Space of Flows" in the book.

[19]Stephen Graham, (ed), The Network Society: A New Context for Planning (Routledge 2005), 105.

[20]Castells specified five points regarding to the dimensions of the space of flows:

"First, I will refer to a series of dimensions of autonomous expression of social meaning in the space of flows, with emphasis in electronic spaces, but in interaction with the space of place."

"A second dimension for autonomous expression is represented by purposive, horizontal communication, not just personal feeling of casual communication."

"Third, there is a fast growth of networks of solidarity and cooperation in the internet, with people bringing together their resources, to live and to survive."

"The fourth dimension is social movement. The net is used increasingly by social movements, of all kinds, as their organizing ground and as their privileged means to break their isolation."

"Fifth, linkages are a development that we have to pay close attentions to, increasing linkage between people and institutions in an interactive process."

"The attempt by capital, media, and power to escape into the abstraction of the space of flows, bypassing democracy and experience by confining them in the space of place, is being challenged from many sources by the grassrooting of the space of flows."

regional spaces have combined with information technology at varying levels, the Internet is used by the Mass".[21]

2.3 Impact of Internet on Urban Civil Society and Space

The Internet has changed people's lives, family relationships, and urban society. In the American cities, working at home through the Internet has become a trend, and people's leisure life is gradually occupied by the Internet.[22] The consumption forms that do not need to be met by e-commerce are also slowly accepted by the public, etc. Of course, the urban society has been greatly affected. These have quantitative statistics in the *Internet and Society* report, and the Internet has changed the behavior patterns of citizens.

Meanwhile, Augmented Reality add digital information to users' everyday interaction with the real world.[23] For example, if you are lost, you can use the special eyeglasses to instantly let you stand in the heights to see the surrounding environment and determine your position. Of course, Augmented Reality's game is also a way to understand how people behave in a way that interacts with the community. Poketto Monsuta's research[24] on Pokémon also gave a reference of how in Augmented Reality impact players' community in urban area nowadays.

Artificial Intelligence is another digital development with transformation of urban life. In Artificial Intelligence and Life in 2030,[25] *the* outlines the implications of several key dimensions of AI, including:

- Large-scale learning or algorithms that crunch ever-larger datasets
- Deep learning procedures that recognize images, video, audio, speech, and language
- Reinforcement learning that shifts from pattern recognition to experience-driven decision-making
- Robotic devices that can physically interact with environments and people
- Computer vision that allows computers to see and perform tasks better than people

---

[21]Castells, Manuel. "Grassrooting the space of flows." *Urban Geography* 20, no. 4 (1999): 294–302.

[22]Nie, Norman H., and Lutz Erbring. "Internet and society." *Stanford Institute for the quantitative study of society* 3 (2000).

[23]Feiner, Steven, Blair MacIntyre, Tobias Höllerer, and Anthony Webster. "A touring machine: Prototyping 3D mobile augmented reality systems for exploring the urban environment." *Personal Technologies* 1, no. 4 (1997): 208–217.

[24]Nikou, Shahrokh, Julian Tarvoll, and Anssi Öörni. "Impact of Playing Pokémon Go on Wellness." In *Proceedings of the 51st Hawaii International Conference on System Sciences*. 2018.

[25]Stone, Peter, Rodney Brooks, Erik Brynjolfsson, Ryan Calo, Oren Etzioni, Greg Hager, Julia Hirschberg et al. "Artificial intelligence and life in 2030." *One Hundred Year Study on Artificial Intelligence: Report of the 2015–2016 Study Panel* (2016).

- Natural language processing that does more than react to requests—it communicates through speech
- Collaborative systems, crowdsourcing, and human computation
- Algorithms and computational tools that can apply economic and social data to realign incentives for people and businesses
- The "Internet of Things" that networks appliances, vehicles, buildings, and cameras
- Neuromorphic computing that mimics biological neural networks to improve the efficiency and robustness of computer systems.[26]

Internet, AR, AI and other digital technologies are developing fast, and also have affected the lives and work of citizens. Some scholars believe that due to the popularity of the digitalization in cities, the influence of citizens on identity and its roots has become the source of social conflicts. From Europe and America to Asia, scholars have a lot of arguments: on the one hand, the professionalism of information technology is allowing a few people to monopolize data and become a newcomer in new economy; on the other hand, the empowerment of information technology on urban grassroots people has promoted civil society in urban area. For example, The discussion of space of flows and grassrooting space flow shows that the impact of informatization on the development of urban society is universal and profound.

Skeptical scholars question the digital divide that will create new inequalities. Firstly, there are still many people in underdeveloped areas who cannot connect to the Internet because of economic and infrastructure reasons. Meanwhile, for some countries, there are certain restrictions on the Internet. Secondly, the spread of the Internet is also dominated by some governments or companies due to false news and other unfair issues, and the risks are increasing. For example, the impact of social media on political activities, large Internet companies through social media restrictions on innovative SMEs. Third, the monopoly of data has caused the privacy of citizens to be violated.

Stephen Hawking,[27] believe that while the lives of the vast majority are transformed by technology and capital, lots of people who will be no involve in those industry also lost the game. More and more people believe that their fate is doomed and out of control. They are somewhat aware of the plight. But how do they think of their role in this plight? To create their community to find the belonging is new phenomena.

Meanwhile, optimistic scholars believe that new information technologies such as the Internet give citizens the opportunity to pay more attention to culture and identity, to join the community on the Internet and to build their own communities

[26]When Artificial Intelligence Rules the City, Richard Florida, May 16, 2017 https://www.citylab.com/life/2017/05/when-artificial-intelligence-rules-the-city/509999/.

[27]Cellan-Jones, Rory. "Stephen Hawking warns artificial intelligence could end mankind." *BBC News* 2 (2014): 2014.

in terms of their own value orientation.[28] This new community has become part of the citizen's social movement. Alberto Melucci attempts to create a framework to analyze the relationship between action and identity, as well as a re-discussion about the relationship between personal and collective characteristics, and challenges of urban collective action in the information age, including the terms such as 'collective violence', 'collective behaviour', 'protest', 'social movements', or 'revolution'.[29]

As Jodi Dean points out:

> The dependence of networked interconnections on global capitalism does not mean that such interconnections cannot serve as a vehicle for critical conversations about and struggles against market inequities. Indeed, precisely because new political threats appear with the movement of transnational capital throughout the globe, a model of civil society that emphasizes from the outset nonstate forms of political assemblage is crucial for theorizing the various meanings and effects of this movement.[30]

Berry Wellman said that each person has his/her own "personal community",[31] than fitting into the groups around them. Furthermore, he addressed:

> Computer networks are social networks. Social affordances of computer-supported social networks – broader bandwidth, wireless portability, globalized connectivity, personalization – are fostering the movement from door-to-door and place-to-place communities to person-to-person and role-to-role communities.[32]

The world will soon be reshaped. With more and more communities on new media built on similar identities, the state power pattern will make due adjustments. The new governance system and power pattern need to be efficient, inclusive and inspiring enough to soothe the complexities among communities, both in the virtual and real world. The new governance system will be built on rules that are commonly accepted by communities on new media. It will respond swiftly, make real-time decisions and execute the decisions. Better enough, people will be entitled to design trouble-shooting mechanisms by themselves. Therefore, it is reasonable to predict that autonomy and decentralization will be the new trends. What is equally important in the future is data collection and processing. Applied properly, data can improve communities in a comprehensive, precise and proper manner. In real life, a governance system for online payment, e-commerce and social media platforms has taken shape. In other words, Internet and technology tycoons like Google, Facebook and Twitter are competent enough to bring order to communities on new

---

[28]Castells, Manuel. *End of millennium*. Vol. 3. John Wiley & Sons, 2010.

[29]Melucci, Alberto. *Challenging codes: Collective action in the information age*. Cambridge University Press, 1996.

[30]Dean, Jodi. "Cybersalons and civil society: Rethinking the public sphere in transnational technoculture." *Public culture* 13, no. 2 (2001): 265.

[31]Wellman, Barry, and Barry Leighton. "Networks, neighborhoods, and communities: Approaches to the study of the community question." *Urban affairs quarterly* 14, no. 3 (1979): 363–390.

[32]Wellman, Barry. "Physical place and cyberplace: The rise of personalized networking." *International journal of urban and regional research* 25, no. 2 (2001): 227.

media. In addition, they can rally the most vigorous communities, no matter their sizes and locations.

As a result, these platforms become a global platform for participation, allowing diversity of public opinions to be presented to the public, allowing citizens to participate in a wide range of public issues and public spheres. At the same time, this method has broken the monopoly of traditional media to a certain extent, especially the government official media monopoly of some countries, thus promoting the development of civil society. Such an opportunity also played a role in the government's further opening of data, such as the Helsinki Region Infoshare (HRI), the public sector, private sector and community data sharing system. Helsinki metropolitan government has established a database that can be shared for innovation on the basis of participation and innovation.

> Open data increases citizens' knowledge and understanding of their living area, its history and future development. This increases the overall activity, participation and interaction of citizens. Open data can be seen as a facilitator for creating new services and business opportunities, as well as supporting research and development. The value of public data increases the more it is used.[33]

As Frank Webster pointed out:

> It continued to review features of the argument which claims that 'new politics' is part of the tumultuous change that envelops us. From this point of view, New Social movements, novel forms of campaigning, high-tech, media-sensitive and Lifestyle politics appear to be taking over the political ground.[34]

About Asia, David Lyon points out: "whatever freedom and fun may be generated in cyberspace, the reality is that the Internet does not create a 'space apart,' a realm of technologically enabled liberty. Rather, as the Internet is increasingly integrated with everyday life in Asia as elsewhere, so it provides some new ways of engaging old practices."[35] This situation also applies to the process of Internet government policy in Asia, especially in China. Governments play an important role in digitalization, especially in China.

The unprecedented prospects of China's internet business in urban and rural places, especially its soaring popularity in the countryside have presented something different: that those arguments are applicable not only in cities, the developed countries in Europe and America, but also in the countryside, the developing countries and the oriental nations. In the meantime, the situation is somewhat different in China.

But how has China's urbanization followed digitalization to shape interesting routes? Might the grassrooting movement in China be empowered in other ways by Internet business compared to the social media cases in Europe and the US?

---

[33]https://hri.fi/en_gb/hri-service/what-is-hri/.

[34]Webster, Frank, ed. *Culture and politics in the information age: a new politics?*. Routledge, 2002: 13.

[35]Ho, Kong-Chong, Randy Kluver, and C. C. Yang, eds. *Asia. com: Asia encounters the Internet*. Routledge, 2003: 68.

The pervasiveness of space by Internet connectivity breaks down, one might say, over-runs Castells's space of flows paradigm. It's not that there is a separate, emerging space of Internet connectivity that over-rides customary political and social relations. That is a paradigm defined from a pre-cyber perspective. In the post cyber perspective taken in this book, where the Internet of everything is coming upon us, space of flows is so pervasive, that there is practically no non space of flows. Every interaction between consumers, producers and buyers and government has a cyber dimension. The author's work is pushing on this edge by showing the rapid growth of Internet use and the tremendous implications this has for economic development and social change. This in my opinion is as far as one can go with the data and evidence developed so far.

Furthermore, in this country, it boasts a long tradition of political-merchant reciprocity and regional autonomy by local prominent families and gentries (detailed in Chap. 3). As a result, the information technology is bound to interact and integrate with local communities in unique and diverse forms. However, the uniqueness and diversity shares something similar: well-established associations (Suichang Model) and the interaction between commercial organizations and local governments provide an organizational basis and political guarantee for the flow of various factors in urban and rural areas. To understand it, let's first review China's Urbanization.

2.4 China's Urbanization and Globalization

The situation in China is drastically different from the one in highly-urbanized regions like Europe and the US. On the one hand, multitudes of Central Business District (CBD) and new industrial districts are appearing constantly in Beijing, Shanghai, Guangzhou and in other first, second and third tier cities; the urban expansion widens the urban-rural gap, and there is the co-existence of depopulated villages and blood and sweat factories in city outskirts. On the other hand, from south-eastern coastal areas to the west, some counties and villages have shown signs of new development under the influence of the Internet, mobile internet, and in particular e-commerce.

Now, let's take a brief walk through the different aspects of rural areas in China from the British enclosure movement to the prosperity of American Silicon Valley. Time has been compressed by the space to consolidate and intermix within this country, where the development of rural and urban areas is so unbalanced. The example of China, of course, is also an epitome of Asia.

Globalization contributed to the reconfiguration of urban-rural societies by shaping the process of urbanization. By 1978, discussions on setting up special economic zones were started, and a few such zones were set up by 1983 along the east coast, such as the Shenzhen city economic zone (set up in May 1980). The year 1989 was also a turning point, because the central government took back the fiscal controls, focusing more on developing state-owned enterprises. In 1990, a financial

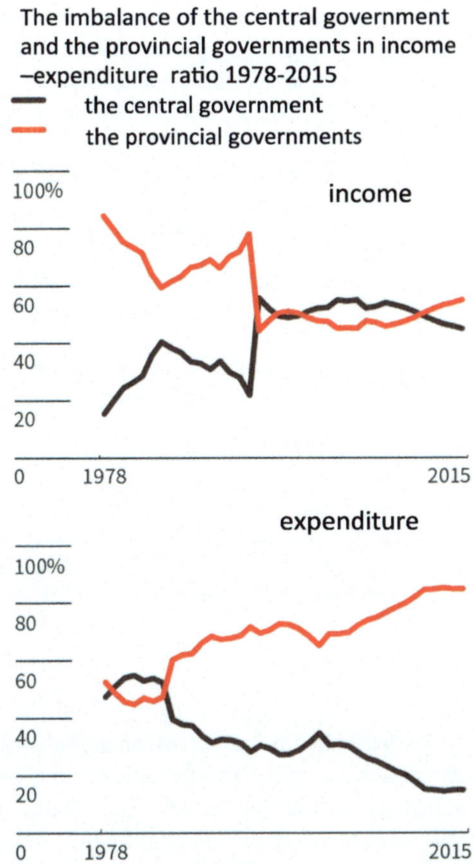

Fig. 2.1 The imbalance of central government (black line) and provincial governments (red) in income (above)-expenditure (below) ratio. *Source* Yu Hairong 于海荣, Wang Xinyi 王辛夷 (Yu Hairong 于海荣, Wang Xinyi 王辛夷. "央地财政关系再调整." [*Central government financial relations and then adjust*]. *Weekly Caixin* 财新周刊 35 (2016): 30–32)

center was set up in Shanghai Pudong with the support of the central government. Deng Xiaoping's Southern Trip to Shenzhen in 1992 started an export-oriented city economy development model. In 1994, Premier Zhu Rongji changed the fiscal allocation between the central and local government, after which the central fiscal revenue grew from 22% in 1993 to 55.7% in 1994 and was finally maintained at 45%.[36] Urbanization thus became a priority of local development. It became a stable source of income for local governments, guaranteeing two sources of earnings: land transfer fees in the short run and business taxes in the long run. In 2001, China became a member of WTO and a plethora of international capital began to flow into China and affect the process of China's urbanization. The urbanization rate increased quickly from 35% in 2001 to 53.7% in 2013 (Fig. 2.1; Table 2.3).

[36]Yu Hairong 于海荣, Wang Xinyi 王辛夷. "央地财政关系再调整." [*Central government financial relations and then adjust*]. *Weekly Caixin* 财新周刊 35 (2016): 30–32.

Table 2.3 Mark events of urbanization after China's opening up 1978–2013

1978	Discussions on setting up special economic zones were started, and a few such zones were set up by 1983 along the east coast
1990	Shanghai Pudong financial center with the support of the central government (China's urbanization rate: 25% (Niu Wenyuan 牛文元. *Zhongguo Chengshi Fazhan baogao* 中国城市发展报告 [*the report of cities' development in China*]. Beijing: 电子工业出版社, 2005)
1994	Change of the fiscal allocation between the central and local government, after which the central fiscal revenue grew from 22% in 1993 to 55.7% in 1994, and was finally maintained at 45%; Urbanization starting become a stable source of income for local governments, guaranteeing two sources of earnings: land transfer fees in the short run and business taxes in the long run
1999	China's western development program
2001	Joining WTO, and urbanization attracting more foreign capitals (2001–2013 China's urbanization rate rising from 35 to 53.7%)
2013	Urbanization leading local government debt: for example, Zhejiang Province, as of June 2013, the municipal, county and township governments bore the responsibility to repay the debt of 10.633 billion yuan, 146.71 billion yuan, 328.818 billion yuan and 22.663 billion yuan respectively, with the county government debt accounting for 64.62% of the total (Yu Hairong 于海荣, Wang Xinyi 王辛夷. "央地财政关系再调整." [*Central government financial relations and then adjust*]. *Weekly Caixin* 财新周刊 35 (2016): 30–32)

Source Author

Underneath this rapid urbanization is the progressive widening of urban-rural gap and accelerating prominence of an urban-rural binary structure. The rural areas are linked to the production chain of the globalized time and space only through cities. Local governments employ the "buy low, sell high" (land finance) strategy to push rural, but mostly suburban lands, into the market to attract global investment, drive farmers into cities to become cheap laborers, and attain rapid urbanization and urban development (Fig. 2.2; Table 2.4).

The problems it has brought are reflected first of all in land finances, the increased premium of rural land during urbanization was not connected with local sustainable development but resulted in conflicts between the local residents and the government. There have been increasing reports of rural land disputes and fights over resources among farmers, real estate developers and government. 16% of rural families have recently encountered forced land renunciation, housing demolition and relocation (Fig. 2.3).[37]

Rural workforces migrating to cities are marginalized in terms of their residential status and residential welfare. Hundreds of millions of people are indeed experiencing unequal treatments compared to the urban population. The conditions for their children and offspring are still deteriorating. They are bearing the cost of

[37]Zhang Xiaohe 张晓鸽 (2013, Oct. 28th). Zhengdi chaiqian boji 16% jiating 征地拆迁波及*16%*家庭 [*Requisition of land affected 16% Family*]. 2013. http://epaper.jinghua.cn/html/2013-10/28/content_35335.htm (accessed Oct., 28, 2013).

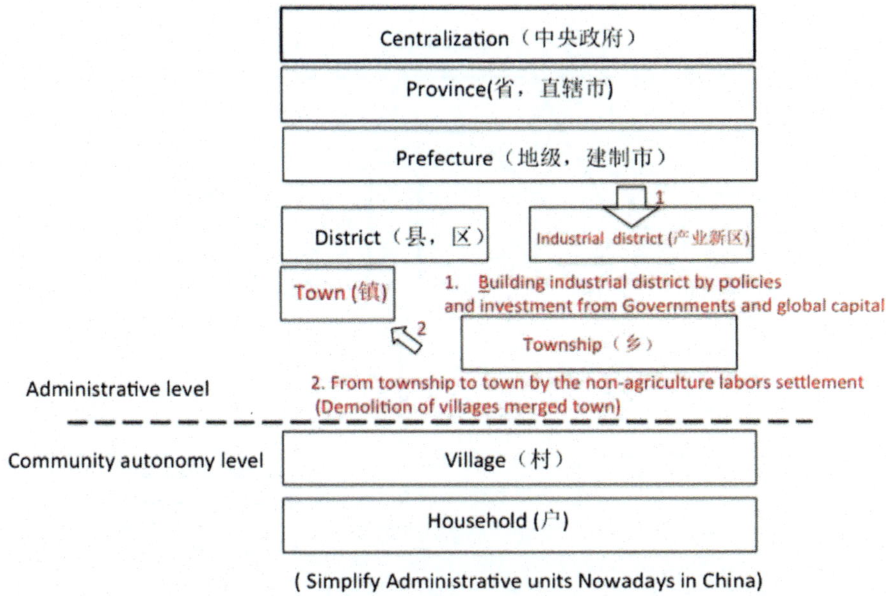

Fig. 2.2 China's current administrative system and urbanization mechanism. *Source* Author

Table 2.4 The changes in numbers and sizes of cities

	Year 1978	Year 2010
Cities	193	658
Over 10 million population	0	6
5–10 million population	2	10
3–5 million population	2	21
1–3 million population	25	103
0.5–1 million population	35	138
Below 0.5 million population	129	380
Towns	2,173	19,410

*Year 2010 data was consolidated based on the Sixth Nation Population Census database

Source National Plan on new urbanization (2014–2020) (The State Council of the People's Republic of China, 2014)

urbanization as they are unable to enjoy the same rights entitled to the city residents. The Chinese government has estimated an average cost of 131,000 yuan (20,000 USD) to convert one such rural migrant to an urban citizen. As a result, some people have chosen to return to their hometowns and villages, despite being landless, to obtain lower living costs and live closer to family members.

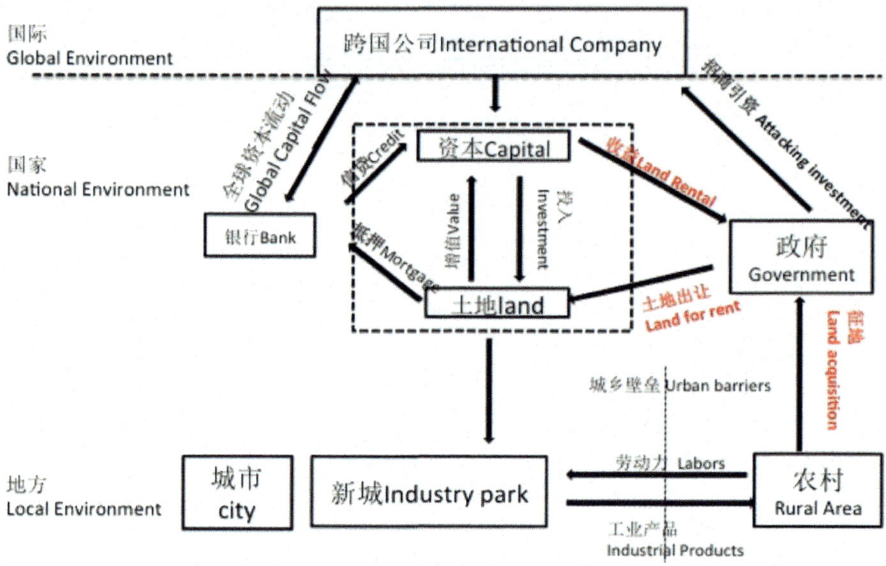

Fig. 2.3 The theoretical framework for the establishment of new towns. *Source* Wu Tinghai 武廷海, Yang Baojun 杨保军, Zhang Chengguo 张城国. Zhongguo xincheng: 1979–2009 《中国新城: 1979–2009》 [*Chinese New Town: 1979–2009*]. *Journal of Urban and Regional Planning* 城市与区域规划研究, (2011 年 02), 19–43, P29

Assaulted by the shrinking international market in 2008, the appreciation of RMB, and the transfer of outsourcing manufacturers from Mainland China to Southeast Asia, rural enterprises faced harsh competition and diminishing profits. The industrial structure of county economies needed an urgent transformation. E-commerce is the solution to advance the upgrade and reformation of traditional economy.

China connected to the World Wide Web for the first time in 1993, however, by 2013 online-shopping already comprised 7.9% of total consumption. China had realized 618 million netizens (network citizens) and there were 302 million Chinese citizens shopping online.

The growth of online Taobao shops in rural China began to take momentum around year 2010. In 2015, there were more than 780 Taobao villages. The widespread development of Taobao villages reflects that in China, empowerment of the grass-root is not only happening in cities but is also extended to villages and counties, which is a phenomenon that has never appeared in Euro-America or any other developed country or region.

We can say that China overall is still being urbanized under industrial globalization. Some regions have already entered the new wave of globalization led by information technology. The unification between space of flows and the local scale are reflected from the social practices and China's urban-rural system. This exactly represents the emergence of county level rural e-commerce services and Taobao villages. Through the Internet, the rural grassroots residents are connected to the system of space of flows, breaking the monopoly of the elites. This is also a process of resource re-distribution of city-town clusters and transformation of rural industries. This analysis of the current literature, especially on space of flows and grassrooting space of flows will be explored over the next several chapters ultimately.

2.5 E-commerce and the Urban-Rural Relationship

In fact, rural e-commerce empowers individuals and families, and underpins Internet-based platforms providing commercial and public services.[38] As it bridges those gaps, more jobs, new civil organizations and lifestyles come forth with it. As this process continues, counties and villages are likely to become an indispensable link in the living and production system, even at a global level. With more human resources flowing in, those counties and villages are able to improve their logistics, narrow the information gap, allocate resources more effectively, improve their ecological system and promote their indigenous culture. The Chinese rural communities, depending on either agriculture or commerce throughout thousands of years, are now about to traverse the misty industrial age, and usher in a new era of information technology.

Lefebvre strongly advocates for the theory of urban revolution,[39] while Castells champions a more grassrooted space of flows.[40] Very naturally, these two trends will begin to develop in rural China. As we have noticed, some international enterprises built on Internet platforms that are already founded, thanks to the information technology and its financial bulwark. These enterprises are borrowing strength from globalization and setting foot in towns and villages. Intermingling with local enterprises organized in a conventional way, their joined forces are reshaping the economic landscape in the Yangtze River Delta and Pearl River Delta.

A number of villages and small towns are merged into the regional market network, a prelude to urban-rural revolution. If we take a closer look, we may find some factors contributing to this urban-rural convergence: global economy, informationalism, enriched local work forces, networked networks[41] and urban-rural

[38]Landscape China. (2014.11.13) Li Zi: Global E-Commerce Development and the New Pattern of Urbanization in Rural China. (Sorted based on Mr. Li's speech delivered at the sub-forum themed "Urbanization" for the "2014 Beijing Forum" in Peking University on 8th, Nov. 2014) Landscape China: http://www.landscape.cn/news/comment/celebrity/2014/1113/171849.html.

[39]Lefebvre, Henri. The urban revolution. U of Minnesota Press, 2003.

[40]Castells Manuel. GRASSROOTING THE SPACE OF FLOWS [J]. Urban Geography. 1999 20 (4), 294–302.

[41]Networked network is formed due to decentralized conglomerates, semi-autonomous business units, increasing number of SMEs, networks established by SMEs, or merely by small or large enterprises working together.

supply chain. Clearly, globalization is the biggest driver of capital flow and Internet-based information flow, while it is the online service sector that contributes to frequent flows of human resources, logistics and cultural exchanges. These factors give eloquent proof of the ongoing new urbanization pattern.

According to the analytical methods of this research mentioned at Chap. 1, I will briefly analyze the urban and rural flows brought by e-commerce in urban and rural areas.

(1) Globalization propels capital and information flow between urban and rural China

Whether it is the early-stage development of Suichang E-commerce Association or Alibaba's rural strategy, they all are dependent on the Internet platforms of Alibaba, especially Taobao. In retrospect, it is because China began to deploy global capital flows and information technology.

In 1994, China's accession to the Internet indeed raised government concerns. However, it should be noted that transnational capital has long been playing the role of promoting global informatization. In the case of Alibaba, Goldman Sachs, Soft Bank and Yahoo deserve part of the credit for improving its online service sector. Alibaba conceives its rural strategy based on the online service sector, or the dynamic system of global capital and information technology. At the same time, this global system sustains China's urban-rural capital flow, as is proved by Ant Financial, an integral part of Alibaba's rural strategy. To be more specific, Ant Financial raised 30–50 billion yuan to support Alibaba's rural strategy.

It shall be noted that for a very long time, the Suichang model has been developed based on Taobao's platform. Therefore, we have reasons to believe that Alibaba, the international financing system for Internet-based industries, facilitates the capital flows between urban and rural areas. At different stages in its early development, Suichang depended on Alibaba for its globalized Internet platform at different levels. We can find numerous evidences to support this point. Suichang E-commerce Association grooms local talents for e-commerce businesses, lobbies government departments, and encourages local talents to enroll in Taobao University, the e-commerce training system under Alibaba. Besides, as the most representative e-commerce facilitator, Suichang wins support from Alibaba's publicity division, government PR department, and its model is widely discussed in news media. Suichang is also endorsed by Taobao as the first county-level Taobao pavilion to showcase its specialties. Furthermore, through its farm pig program, Suichang establishes close ties with Suichang E-commerce Co., the county government and Juhuansuan.com, the group-purchasing website of Taobao. By bringing manufactured goods to the countryside, Ganjie.com reformed the business model of Taodiandian.com, a mobile platform of Taobao providing catering services. Moreover, village-based purchasing agencies are born out of its efforts. The cases above are eloquent proofs of Suichang's cooperation with Alibaba. As a local-level Internet platform, Suichang, together with related organizations, continues to attempt repeatedly to utilize information technology and improve its business model. The driving forces that made it happen are Alibaba's technological advantages as a nationwide Internet platform, and its globally distributed financing channels.

Clearly, the global economy has pushed forward the information economy. That means to boost productivity; we need to attach greater significance to the utilization of knowledge and information in our management, production and distribution.[42] As of June 2016, Chinese Internet users totaled 709.5 million, and mobile phone users reached 656 million. 448 million Chinese people purchased online, of which 401 million[43] made their purchases with mobile phones (see Footnote 8). What's more, dozens of millions of people subscribed to online services including instant messaging, as well as banking, social, and other mobile apps. Netizens and mobile phone users also constitute another foundation for Suichang model and online services of Alibaba's rural e-commerce platform. Technology and organization pattern is shifting from developed areas to less-developed ones and from cities to the countryside. The penetration of Internet technology results in extensive information flows between urban and rural areas. Of China's Internet users, rural users accounted for 26.9% or 191 million, and the number is increasing rapidly.

Besides, Alibaba is actively building information infrastructures. One way is to integrate telecommunication resources so that villagers have access to affordable, efficient and quality phone and data services and contracts. The Graphical County Governance program of Alibaba also consolidates large volumes of data to aid in government decision-making and policy-making. These data come from the government, Rural Taobao, Alipay, MYbank and Cainiao Logistics. WeChat is another socializing tool for rural communities. Take Lishui, Zhejiang as an example, village officials discuss different public affairs in different WeChat groups. Suichang E-commerce Association and Ganjie.com are negotiating with telecom giants like China Mobile for better terms concerning network installation fees, Internet and mobile Internet data charges. These efforts are delivering concrete results.

In conclusion, capital and information flows in urban and rural areas are major contributors to the growth of rural e-commerce. These flows are playing an important role in reshaping the urban and rural spatial pattern.

(2) Flows of local human resources and culture

The information economy is creating a flexible production model in the form of network companies. It has been proven in the relations between Suichang E-Commerce Association and Taobao of Alibaba. Platformed and decentralized conglomerates provide cooperation networks for SMEs, and networked networks

[42]Foray, D., and C. Freeman. "Technologie et Richesse des Nations Economica." (1992).

[43]According to the 38th *Statistical Report on Internet Development in China* released by CNNIC in July 2016, up to June 2016, the number of netizens in China reached 710 million, with 21.32 million more users in the first half of 2016, an increase of 3.1%. http://www.cnnic.cn/gywm/xwzx/rdxw/2016/201608/W020160803204144417902.pdf?sukey=3997c0719f1515206532f1c7a66bb8b11d4628bded1c5c4a9ca8e52d71b4fba3ed5d094eacf871ac6772576fb511ae09.

are born out of this trend.[44] There are several parties in this network. The first is Internet giants like Alibaba. They are improving business infrastructure for rural businesses through Taobao and other platforms. The second one is local e-commerce platforms like Suichang E-commerce Association. They go deep into villages and rural households. They organize local suppliers (family-run farms, cooperatives), service providers (local logistics) and small and micro e-commerce businesses to provide comprehensive services to local communities. The third one is specialized local family farms and rural cooperatives. They are keen on improving production techniques and making innovations. The last one is government officials. They offer policy support to local e-commerce businesses, coordinate interests of various parties and perform their original duties to subsidize and supervise agriculture production.

Each party finds its own niche. In this way, it is possible to maintain a delicate balance between the organization pattern and business ecological system. SMEs conducting rural e-commerce are also major members of this community. It extends to cover the whole country and is becoming an efficient, transparent platform to share insights. Active participants in this platform include both elites and ordinary people from all sectors including e-commerce, real estate, art, NGO and so on. People in different walks of like can exchange their experiences so that human resources are revitalized.

To ease the way for Rural Taobao strategy, Alibaba is designing a selection regime to recruit partners from groups of youngsters who return home to start businesses, college graduates and locals. Besides, it devises a peer-learning and training system. It will combine with Taobao University's training ecosystem to provide multi-level trainings. Rural Taobao offers targeted training courses for the government, enterprises and villagers, the three parties of rural service sector. Rural Taobao establishes a nationwide training system by delegating powers to local entities to run its training regime. In doing so, the training is no longer confined to the narrow scope of transforming villagers' ideas towards consumption and disseminating knowledge and expertise to empower rural online service providers. Rather, it now also focuses on educating government officials by opening courses to mayors and county magistrates. Apart from this, Ali Health partners with local medical institutions and pharmaceutical groups to probe the telemedicine sector. As an example, Ali Health works with the Central Hospital of Wuhan and Jointown Pharmaceutical Group to explore the electronic prescribing[45] and tiered medical treatment system, in an attempt to channel more medical resources to areas with insufficient medical staff.

These efforts have led to a convection of human resources between urban and rural areas.

---

[44]Imai, Ken'ichi. "Joho netto waku shakai no tenbo [The Information Network Society]." Tokyo: Chikuma Shobo (1990).

[45]"九州通试点电子处方 与阿里健康、武汉市中心医院构建完整远程医疗体系" [Jointown Pharmaceutical Group trials electronic prescribing to build a complete telemedicine system with AliHealth and the Central Hospital of Wuhan]. 2016. Vcbeat.Net. http://vcbeat.net/28303.

We should beware of the fact that while capital goes global, most of the labor forces remain confined in their localities.[46] A major cause of this situation is local relations (with family members, folks and between government and businesses) and indigenous culture. Suichang E-commerce Association and Suichang E-commerce Co. raise funds and recruit talents through local networks (through connections with family members, government, local businesses and folks). As a subsidiary to Suichang E-commerce Association, Ganjie.com (merged by Suichang E-commerce Co. and Ganjie.com) recruits most of its employees locally. They find partners from their fellow villagers to ease the process of procurement, warehousing, logistics, quality control and package designing. In addition, this approach proves to be a great success in ensuring smooth communication. As we can see, the e-commerce system in Suichang is a strong network woven tightly by family bonds and kinships. Of course, such a business model should be built upon the needs of villagers. That is why their organization pattern and business model have close links with local culture and customs. For example, each village has a grand auditorium, where people celebrate cultural activities, especially those associated with the 24 solar terms, to promote their offerings and services.

The relationship between government and local business is another important factor that I have to mention here. Mo Wenjian, an expert on county e-commerce once said, "e-commerce harmonizes the relation between government and local business in an unprecedented way". Compared with the central government, local governments are more acquainted with local conditions and more adaptable to local customs. This advantage indeed makes local governments themselves more flexible and resilient in the informationalism process.

Local government are able to protect interests of local businesses, establish close ties with communities, respond to their needs and seize development opportunities. Therefore, the local government takes on the role to coordinate the interests of various parties to adapt to the changing organization pattern in the information society. The role of local government is indeed reinforced in the information era. Or as Manuel Castells says, the Internet has reached out to localities and local states will take the place of nation-state, which is incompetent in maintaining efficiency and performance at the core of its bureaucratic system. It seems to be an interesting topic in China, which has existed as a nation-state for merely 100 years. On the contrary, when local government needs to motivate its folks, it should involve community organizations and the public. In this sense, local government will become an important link in the dynamic development of our society and economy (Fig. 2.4).

In his book *The Power of Identity*, Manuel Castells points out that involving grassroots may give rise to a mindset that is overly defensive and protective. Rural people may find it hard to communicate with others because of the strong identity caused by their distinctive culture. In the long run, they tend to isolate themselves from all social relations. As time passes, local communities have the potential to

[46]Campbell, Duncan. "Foreign investment, labour immobility and the quality of employment." Int'l Lab. Rev. 133 (1994): 185.

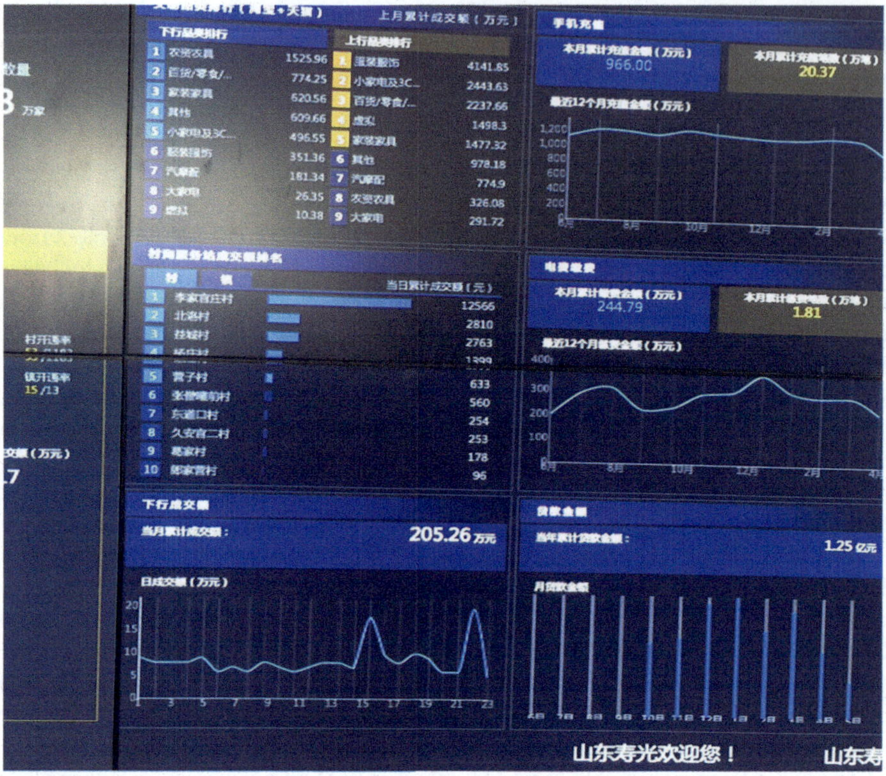

Fig. 2.4 Information displayer of Alibaba's "Graphical County Governance". *Source* Author

become alienated places where people cut off connections with the outside world and where violence runs rampant. We need to find solutions to overcome such a destructive process.[47] In some countries, fundamentalist communities are indeed alienated in the Internet era. However, in rural China, the online service sector and rural e-commerce are able to develop in a peaceful and inclusive manner. Self-identity and local customs are merged into a new functional system by commercial activities. There is something worth our attention in the flows of ecological culture and the establishment of local identity.

As we can see, the Internet empowers grassroots through a global platform and thus encourages cultural exchanges between urban and rural areas.

(3) Integration of urban-rural supply chain

All of the flows we have discussed take logistics as the fundamental factor to make them happen. The unfinished last miles of roads connecting a county and a

[47]CASTELLS, M. "The information city: information technology, economic restructuring, and the urban-regional process. Padstow (Great Britain)." (1989).

village have always been a bottleneck for rural e-commerce development. Whether it is about improving city logistics or building an urban-rural supply chain, Suichang and Cainiao Logistics attach great significance to information integration. In doing so, they strive to gain competitive edges in terms of delivery number, speed and efficiency, and use these edges as the key to connecting upstream and downstream markets for more value-added. What's more, EMS, supply and marketing cooperatives,[48] JD.com,[49] SF Express[50] and YouCan Group[51] are completing their already-diverse offerings with an urban-rural logistic system. Besides, shopping platforms such as Taoshihui,[52] Lecuntao[53] and Cuncunle[54] are actively exploring business models and logistic services appropriate to local conditions.

By now, we have analyzed the flow of capital, information, local human resources, ecological culture and logistics. We can infer from these analysis that Suichang and Alibaba are leveraging the Internet and mobile Internet technologies to encourage convections of factors involved in urban-rural life and production, boost local development, create jobs and improve commercial and public services. Therefore, the author proposes a research structure to analyze the cases of rural e-commerce in 5 aspects: 1.fostering and flowing of urban and rural human resources; 2. the improvement of urban and rural logistics supply chain; 3. the narrowing of urban and rural information gap; 4. the effective capital allocation; 5. urban-rural ecological and cultural progress. The urban and rural areas are unified as one network; different nodes of flowing factors and their touch points are integrated into the regional and even global production chain and living system. Before the analysis of rural ecommerce, I introduce the history of urban and rural relationship as the context of this research.

[48]According to *Decision on Comprehensively Deepening Reform of Supply and Marketing Cooperatives* published by the State Council, "it is imperative to adapt to the profound changes in business model and consumption. We will encourage supply and marketing cooperatives to develop e-commerce. We aim to integrate operations that covers online transaction, warehousing, logistics and delivery, so that online and offline businesses can grow in a coordinated way."

[49]JD.com have their own logistic.

[50]SF is exploring a new delivery model for raw and fresh foods.

[51]YouCan Group intensifies its efforts to improve its supply chain for agricultural products and focuses on innovating cold chain for raw and fresh foods in Hangzhou.

[52]On the one hand, Taoshihui connects rural shops via the Internet to create a new model: build an online platform while running chain stores offline; it expands offerings of rural shops by introducing e-shelves; it focuses on counties while deliver goods with those of rural shops, so that it creates a commodity and service marketing network in rural areas. on the other hand, to sell its agricultural products to other places of the country, Taoshihui establish a cross-supplying and purchasing platform that links various counties so that local specialties can be sold elsewhere.

[53]Lecuntao is an 020 e-commerce platform in rural China. It upgrades the existing grocery stores in villages into offline experience centers, so that villagers can shop online occasionally, deliver packages in batches, and manufacturers and businesses can sell to villagers directly via the Internet in wholesale price.

[54]Cuncunle is a web portal through which villagers can have access to news, local information, commercial trends and social services. By now it has 10 million registered users.

References

1. Castells M (2011) The rise of the network society: the information age: economy, society, and culture, vol 1. Wiley, USA, pp 18 & 19
2. Harvey D (1989) The condition of postmodernity: an enquiry into the origins of social change. Blackwell, Malden, MA
3. Sassen S (2001) The global city. Princeton University Press, New York
4. Marx K (2011) Capital, Volume I: a critique of political economy (Vol. 1). Courier Corporation.
5. Weber M (1958) The protestant ethic and the spirit of capitalism. Charles Scribner's Sons, New York
6. Durkheim, E (2014) The division of labor in society. Simon and Schuster, New York
7. Parsons T, Shils EA, Smelser NJ (eds) (1965) Toward a general theory of action: theoretical foundations for the social sciences. Transaction Publishers, USA
8. Polyani K (2007) The great transformation: the political and economic origins of our time. Beacon Press, Boston
9. Granovetter M (1985) Economic action and social structure: the problem of embeddedness. Am J Sociol 91(3):481–510
10. Lefebvre H (1991) The production of space, vol 142. Blackwell, Oxford
11. Bijker WE, Hughes TP, Pinch T, Douglas DG (2012) The social construction of technological systems: new directions in the sociology and history of technology. MIT Press, Cambridge
12. Hickman J (2016) Space is power: the seven rules of territory. Lexington Books, London
13. Lefebvre H (2003) The urban revolution. University of Minnesota Press, USA
14. Albrechts L, Mandelbaum S (eds) (2007) The network society: a new context for planning. Routledge, London, p 105
15. Castells M (1999) Grassrooting the space of flows. Urban Geogr 20(4):294–302
16. Nie NH, Erbring L (2000) Internet and society. Stanford Institute for the Quantitative Study of Society, p 3
17. Feiner S, MacIntyre B, Höllerer T, Webster A (1997) A touring machine: prototyping 3D mobile augmented reality systems for exploring the urban environment. Pers Technol 1 (4):208–217
18. Nikou S, Tarvoll J, Öörni A (2018) Impact of playing Pokémon go on wellness. In: Proceedings of the 51st Hawaii international conference on system sciences
19. Stone P, Brooks R, Brynjolfsson E, Calo R, Etzioni O, Hager G, Hirschberg J et al (2016) Artificial intelligence and life in 2030. One hundred year study on artificial intelligence: report of the 2015–2016 study panel
20. When artificial intelligence rules the city, Richard Florida, May 16, 2017. https://www.citylab.com/life/2017/05/when-artificial-intelligence-rules-the-city/509999/
21. Cellan-Jones R (2014) Stephen Hawking warns artificial intelligence could end mankind. BBC News, p 2
22. Castells M (2010) End of millennium, vol 3. Wiley, USA
23. Melucci A (1996) Challenging codes: collective action in the information age. Cambridge University Press, Cambridge
24. Dean J (2001) Cybersalons and civil society: rethinking the public sphere in transnational technoculture. Public Cult 13(2):265
25. Wellman B, Leighton B (1979) Networks, neighborhoods, and communities: approaches to the study of the community question. Urban Aff Q 14(3):363–390
26. Wellman B (2001) Physical place and cyberplace: the rise of personalized networking. Int J Urban Reg Res 25(2):227
27. What is hri. https://hri.fi/en_gb/hri-service/what-is-hri/
28. Webster F (ed) Culture and politics in the information age: a new politics? Routledge, London, p 13

29. Ho KC, Kluver R, Yang CC (eds) (2003) Asia.com: Asia encounters the internet. Routledge, London, p 68
30. Mengin F (2004) Cyber China: reshaping national identities in the age of information. Springer, Berlin, p 8
31. Foray D, Freeman C (1992) Technologie et Richesse des Nations Economica
32. Campbell D (1994) Foreign investment, labour immobility and the quality of employment. Int Lab Rev 133:185
33. Yu H 于海荣, Wang X 王辛夷 (2016) Yangdi caizheng guanxi zaitiaozheng 央地财政关系再调整 [Central government financial relations and then adjust]. Weekly Caixin 财新周刊 35:30–32
34. Niu W 牛文元 (2005) Zhongguo Chengshi Fazhan baogao 中国城市发展报告 [The report of cities' development in China]. Beijing 电子工业出版社
35. Guo WY 国务院 (2014) Guojia xinxing chengzhenhua guihua 国家新型城镇化规划 (2014–2020 年). The state council national new urbanization plan (2014–2020). Beijing 北京. http://www.gov.cn/zhengce/2014-03/16/content_2640075.htm. Accessed 16 Mar 2014
36. Zhang X 张晓鸽 (2013) Zhengdi chaiqian boji 16% jiating 征地拆迁波及16%家庭 [Requisition of land affected 16% Family]. http://epaper.jinghua.cn/html/2013-10/28/content_35335.htm. Accessed 28 Oct 2013
37. Wu T 武廷海, Yang B 杨保军, Zhang C 张城国 (2011) Zhongguo xincheng: 1979–2009 《中国新城: 1979–2009》 [Chinese new town: 1979–2009]. J Urban Reg Planning 城市与区域规划研究 19 (2011 年 02)
38. Landscape China (2014.11.13) Li Zi: Global E-commerce development and the new pattern of urbanization in rural China (Sorted based on Mr. Li's speech delivered at the sub-forum themed "Urbanization" for the "2014 Beijing Forum" in Peking University on 8th, Nov 2014). Landscape China. http://www.landscape.cn/news/comment/celebrity/2014/1113/171849.html
39. The 38th statistical report on internet development in China http://www.cnnic.cn/gywm/xwzx/rdxw/2016/201608/W020160803204144417902.pdf?sukey=3997c0719f1515206532f1c7a66bb8b11d4628bded1c5c4a9ca8e52d71b4fba3ed5d094eacf871ac6772576fb511ae09
40. 九州通试点电子处方 与阿里健康、 武汉市中心医院构建完整远程医疗体系 [Jointown pharmaceutical group trials electronic prescribing to build a complete telemedicine system with AliHealth and the Central Hospital of Wuhan] (2016) Vcbeat.Net. http://vcbeat.net/28303

Chapter 3
A Unique Path: The Evolution of China's Urban-Rural Relationship

The flow of information, cultures, goods, capital, and human resources echo off each other inside the network, while offering urban-rural integration based on market economy in traditional Chinese societies. Grassroot market towns and village markets were actually very well developed in traditional Chinese societies. In the extensive connections among urban and rural lives, business transactions brought about by the flow of every single production and life element determined the model for China's traditional society[1]—market economy. [2]Prof. Hsia, Chu-joe mentioned: "carrying on the traditions upheld by cities and towns in the south of Yangtze River and heritages of countryside markets in Song, Ming and Qing dynasty, Taobao villages and virtual communities came into being. They seized opportunities offered by the new-type urbanization whose focus had been shifted from export to domestic demand.[3]"

In this chapter, whether or not rural-urban transformation in traditional Chinese society contributed as a foundation to today's rural-urban relationship brought by the Internet will be further discussed.

---

[1]Prof. Fu Yiling (傅依凌, 1988) replaced the term "feudal society" by "traditional society" in his last paper '中国传统社会:多元的结构'("China's traditional society: a diverse/multi-variate structure"), admitting that China has had a dynamic social structure since the end of primitive society.

[2]Prof. Zhao Gang approached the analysis of the Chinese market economy under private ownership system through the school of thought of economic systems that believed property ownership was equivalent to decision-making power. In his illustration, the Chinese private ownership system was established early in history, supported by the legal evidence of rural land private ownerships started by the Reforms of Shang Yang (秦国商鞅变法) in the warring states period (东周战国). Private ownership system stimulated the formation of markets. Markets are places for transfer and exchange of property ownership (Zhao Gang赵冈. Lun zhongguo chuantong shehui de xingzhi 论中国传统社会的性质 *[the Characters of Chinese Traditional Society]. The Journal of Chinese Social and Economic History,* 中国社会经济史研究 *2(*1998*):1–6*).

[3]Li Zi 李孜. *Nongchun Dianshan Jueqi* 农村电商崛起 *[Rise of Ecommerce in Rural China].* Beijing: Publishing House of Electronics Industry, 2016: VI.

L. Zi, *Online Urbanization*, Advances in 21st Century Human Settlements,
https://doi.org/10.1007/978-981-13-3603-4_3

3.1 Historical Transformations of Urban-Rural Relationship in China

3.1.1 Urban-Rural Division and the Implementation of Hukou System in 1950s

In Chinese history, there were three channels through which rural food surplus flowed into cities: (1) small farmers selling surplus in exchange for cash; (2) government taxation; (3) purchases by landlords.[4] These three channels had existed for nearly 2000 years before the changes took place in 1952.

When the new PRC was founded, grain/food imports decreased drastically. Consumption in cities had to again rely on supplies from rural areas. The government pushed through land reformation against the landlords and wealthy farmers. As a result, farmers started to stock the food surplus instead of selling it to cities. In autumn 1953, there was a food shortage in the cities. Instead of farmers reserving for the their own needs and then selling surplus, the government would purchase entire harvests to be sent to cities. The national storage system would then ration food back to the farmers. Over the course of this policy, millions of people in rural areas died from starvation as urban areas were prioritized. Considering the need to "rob the farmers" to ease the plight, the government finally started to monopolize the purchase and marketing of food.[5]

The monopolization of the purchase and marketing of commodity food to be distributed to cities at designated amounts was not adjustable by people's free will. The urban-rural population movement was confined, when the Hukou system was implemented. In such a monopoly system, people's commune became the best organization to manage food and farmers.[6] The rural markets slowly faded out. From 1957 to 1959 (Table 2.4), the increase in the commodity rate of agricultural products was mainly a result of government monitoring in the commodity food market. At the same time, from 1955 to 1956 (Table 2.5) the government started to increase state's shares in the previously private-owned industries, ultimately controlling the market with state-owned enterprises and building a state-planned economy. Market forces ceased to function, lowering motivation to produce. Absence of market regulation led to product shortage and economic depression till 1978 (Table 3.1).

---

[4]Zhao Gang 赵冈. *Zhongguo chengshi fazhan shilunji* 中国城市发展史论集 *[History of Chinese Urban Development]. New Star Press* 新星出版社, 2006.

[5]Chen Yun 陈云. *Chen yun wenxua:1949–1956* 陈云文选: 一九四九–一九五六年 *[Anthology of Chen Yun: From 1949 to1956]*. People's Publishing House人民出版社, 1984.

[6]Jin Guantao 金观涛, Liu Qingfeng 刘青峰. *Kaifangzhong de bianqian* "开放中的变迁." *[the variations during the open]. Hong Kong: Chinese University Hong Kong* (1993).

Table 3.1 Private industrial output as a percentage of total industrial output value (1949–1955)

Year	1949	1952	1954	1955
Percentage (%)	63	39	25	16

Source Jin Guantao 金观涛, Liu Qingfeng 刘青峰. *Kaifangzhong de bianqian "开放中的变迁." [the variations during the open]. Hong Kong: Chinese University Hong Kong* (1993)

3.1.2 Urban-Rural Relationship During Development of Township Enterprises in 1980s

China's central government started economic reform in 1978. Economic development and approval powers were delegated to local governments, stimulating local economic development. Township enterprises boomed.

In early years of economic reform in 1980s, township enterprises were able to expand with accumulated wealth from agricultural industries, when villages started to recover economies. The development reached a peak in 1991 with total production exceeding 1.1 trillion RMB, contributing to 1/3 of total domestic production, almost the same as state-owned enterprises. 100 millions farmers, "voluntarily and enthusiastically working very hard at zero cost to the nation" were transformed into workers in the township enterprises.[7] It was an experiment to industrialize rural areas, successfully transforming local economies and starting urbanization. It created an opportunity for China to follow this experience and achieve its own unique integrated urban-rural development model.[8] The economic boom in the 1980s was exactly because of central government learning from successful development models from local government and then customizing, legislating and pushing it to the rest of the countries (Household Contract Responsibility System, and Township enterprises model etc.).

During this period, economic progress was remarkable in villages as a result of both closed domestic market and village reforms. Some farmers were even earning higher income than residents in the cities. The integrated urban-rural relationship was an important trend in that period.

---

[7]Fei, Hsiao-Tung. *Peasant life in China*. Read Books Ltd, 2013.

[8]Several models of development were recognized by scholars (周爾鎏,张雨林, 1994): Su Nan Model (South of Jiangsu province), Zhu Jiang Model (in Fujian and Guangdong provinces), Wen Zhou Model (in North of Jiangsu province), Bao Ji Model (Shaanxi Province), Chang De Model (in Hunan province), Min Quan Model (in Henan province). During this period, economic progress was remarkable in villages because of both closed domestic market and village reforms. Income gaps narrowed between cities and villages. Some farmers were even earning higher income than residence in the cities. Integrated urban-rural relationship is a trend in that period.

3.1.3 Rapid urbanization by globalization

From 1990 to 2013, China's urban population had risen from 25% to 53.7% due to the impact of globalization (discussed in chapter 2) (Table 3.2).

3.2 The Inherited Urban-Rural Relations

"All true history is contemporary history."—Benedetto Croce

From "City and the rural as one", in Zhou Dynasty, to the grassroots market towns in Song Dynasty, and municipal markets in Ming and Qing Dynasties, the mechanism behind the evolution of China's urban-rural relationship brought forward opportunities for this old country with the longest history of civilization to embrace the potentials of the Internet Era.

In traditional China's society, the Land Policy (which allowed the annexation of land), tax policy (land rent and labor servitude) and organizational changes (the neighborhood administrative system[9] and Baojia system[10]) (Table 3.3), promoted the spontaneous emergence of small towns and development of commercial networks with markets as centers.[11]

A highly developed flow of urban-rural factors and configuration of resources are important in order to establish unified urban-rural markets and an integrated commercial industry. They also played indispensable roles in the rapid development of grassroots market towns and prosperity of rural markets. Of course, underlying reasons also include the rapid increases in population during Ming and Qing Dynasties, as well as the consequential decline in arable land per capita, which made it difficult to support a large number of urban residents who had completely disengaged themselves from agriculture. Without enough land to subsist only through farming, rural people took up handicrafts and commerce to supplement

[9]The neighborhood administrative system and labor servitude system were the fundamental policies in rural self-governance. The central government was not willing to extend its administration below levels of District; the administrative work was outsourced to local representatives. The principles of neighborhood administrative system and labor servitude system were to have neighborhood monitoring each other to maintain social order, ensure tax collections and oversee/control/enforce labor servitude. The local wealthy clans took turns to take on these responsibilities. They had to set themselves as good examples in community by submitting taxes timely and conforming to labor servitude system, and also perform free administrative and military defense services.

[10]Zhao Gan,.赵冈, Chen Zhongyi 陈钟毅. *Zhongguo tudi zhidu shi* 中国土地制度史 *[History of Chinese Land System]*. New Star Press 新星出版社, 2006.

[11]Yo Shinobu Shiba 斯波义信. *Songdai jiangnan jignjishi yanjiu* 宋代江南经济史研究*[the Ecnomic History of Jiangnan in Song Dynasty]*. NanJing: Jiang Su People Pubishing 南京: 江苏人民出版社, 2012.

Table 3.2 Rural-urban development in Chinese history

	Urban-rural relationship
Traditional Chinese society before five-port commerce in 1843	The urbanization model in China's traditional society evolved from development of large cities in Tang and Song Dynasties to development of market towns and rural market settlements. The development in large cities was restricted at the end of Qing Dynasty before Five-port commerce in 1843. Capital was accumulated locally through agricultural activities on the land, used to develop other productions, and stimulated commerce
Period from five-port commerce till the founding of the Republic of China in 1949	Harbor cities, especially large scale ones, developed rapidly. The urban-rural market landscape started to change, with imports flowing into cities and exports (silk, tea, etc.) shipping out to foreign markets. Imports included industrial products and even agricultural products to be consumed in cities. The off-ground landlords who lived in towns and cities to develop their industry used rural land rent. Capital accumulation in villages was slow
Unified sales and purchasing policies and rural cooperatives in 1950s	Hukou System (Chinese registered permanent residence system) was created in the 1950s leading to urban-rural division by unified sales and purchasing policies. The new Chinese government enjoyed the entire rural resources through rural cooperatives and the aforementioned policies, in order to maintain city consumption and industrial development. [Chen Yun 陈云. *Chen yun wenxua:1949-1956* 陈云文选: 一九四九–一九五六年 *[Anthology of Chen Yun: From 1949 to1956]*. People's Publishing House 人民出版社, 1984.] It was one of the main causes of widespread food shortage in the villages
Household Contract Responsibility System promotion and rapid development of township enterprises in 1980s and 1990s	The growth of township enterprises stimulated a balanced development of urban and rural areas in the 1980s and 1990s after the Household Contract Responsibility System. The system returned partial land rent back to the farmers, not only allowing them to be self-sustained, but also accumulate capital for the upcoming boom of township enterprises. Land was well utilized for the villages, further promoting urban-rural unity. [Zhou Erliu 周尔鎏, Zhang Yulin 张雨林, Wu Dasheng 吴大声. Zhonggguo chengxiang xietiao fazhan yanjiu 中国城乡协调发展研究 *[Research on Coordinated Development between Urban and Rural in China]*. Oxford University Press 牛津大学出版社, 1994.]

(continued)

Table 3.2 (continued)

	Urban-rural relationship
Fast growth in Special Economic Zone and newly developed cities after 1994	The urban population increased and economies boomed in cities but slowed down in villages after 1994, particularly after China joined WTO. Urbanization was mainly driven by local government's profit seeking through land purchasing at low prices and selling high to the market. Consequently, farmers migrated into cities and became cheap labor forces, rural land rent converted into urban-rural rent, bringing considerable capitals for city development [Yang Tenhai 武廷海,Yang Baojun 杨保军, Zhang Chengguo 张城国. *Zhongguo xincheng:1979 ~ 2009 中国新城: 1979 ~ 2009[Chinese New Town:1979-2009]. Journal of Urban and Regional Planning* 城市与区域规划研究, (2011 年 02), 1.] The land transformations and cheap labor from rural China has powered urbanization in China for the past few decades, widened urban-rural gaps, and is an unsustainable model in view of the recent real estate market downturn in China. This urbanization model has become highly controversial in recent years

Source Author

their income. Rural areas and small towns through the half-farming and half-business model fed the larger population.

In the Song Dynasty, there were three administrative levels: centralized government (中央集权政府), prefecture (州, 府); and county (县). While these levels were part of a top-down system, smaller groups such as townships (乡), villages (村), and household (户) were more autonomous and organized by local authority (for example: clan). Professor Yoshinobu Shiba, in his book *The Economic History of Jiangnan in Song Dynasty*, thoroughly described the urban and rural-administrative relationship from the Song Dynasty onwards and analyzed the formation of the Song Dynasty settlement model. The table below illustrates in detail this classification. While there are cross-sections between the hierarchy of administrative centers and of economic centers, at the same time, each had their own independent systems. This allowed a more vibrant market within the administration by centralized government and by provincial (local) self-governance. From the flow among cities to the flow among towns and villages, markets of different levels functioned at varying degrees, forming a market network between the urban and the rural. This type of network further disrupts the self-sustained (self-sufficient) farming lifestyle in the villages. As one of the richest periods in China's history, the Song Dynasty villagers were able to pursue more than just

Table 3.3 Land polices in Chinese history

Xia (2100–1600 BC), Shang (1600–1050 BC) and Zhou (Western Zhou (1046–771 BC) Dynasty	Well-field system (井田制) [The well-field system was a Chinese land distribution method existing between the ninth century BCE (late Western Zhou Dynasty) to around the end of the Warring States period. Its name comes from Chinese character 井 (*jǐng*), which means 'well' and looks like the# symbol.]as public land ownership system
The Warring States Period (475–221 BC), Qin Dynasty (221–206 BC) and Han Dynasty (206 BC–220)	Chinese private ownership system was established, supported by the legal evidence of rural land private ownerships, started by the Reforms of Shang Yang (秦国商鞅变法) [Shang Yang (390–338 BC) was an important statesman of the State of Qin during the Warring States period of Chinese history. Born Wei Yang in the State of Wey, with the support of Duke Xiao of Qin Yang enacted numerous reforms in Qin.] which officially legalized land privatization and the Collateral Punishment Law (连坐法). [It is a rule which imposes same punishment as the perpetrator to those merely aware of the crime.]
The Three Kingdoms period (三国) (220–265) and Jin (晋) (265-420)	Wealthy households and their servants were able to get special exemptions, as a result farmers were attracted to join as servants with their land as assets. The Limiting Farmland System (限田制)[A Law to limit people's ownership to land and limited the trade of land from Western Jin Dynasty] and the Equal-Field system (均田制) [The Equal-field system or Land-equalization system was a historical system of land ownership and distribution in China used from the Six Dynasties to Mid-Tang Dynasty.] were adopted to limit trade of land
Sui (581–618) and Tang (618–906) Dynasties	Continuance of the Equal-Field system (均田制); ZuYongDiao System (租庸(调) [Zu-Yong-Diao System was the succession and development of Zu-Diao System in Wei-Jin resulted to the transition from capitation to property]tax.as tax system. However, in 780, the Equal-Field system (均田制) was disrupted because of land disaggregation and increase in number of mulberry field
Song Dynasty (960–1279)	The cumulative effect of all of the previous periods was the creation of a relatively stable centralization process. Opening the trade of land with the Neighborhood Administrative system (Tax system); high agricultural productivity led to bustling merchant exchanges in markets; excess rural labor moved to towns to find jobs; big towns proliferated; so did grass-root rural markets town system as urbanization

(continued)

Table 3.3 (continued)

Yuan Dynasty (1279–1368) and Ming (1368-1644)	Tuntian (military) system (屯田制) [Tuntian (屯田) system is a system of storing fields for defensive or government's agriculture fields cultivated by farmers as core.]
Qing Dynasty (1644–1912)	Allocation of Land to Bannerman System (旗地制度) in Qing Dynasty to protect interests of Bannerman
Early periods of PRC 1949–1980	In 1960, the communist movement abolished the private ownership system and pushed forward Peasants' Cooperative Policy (农村合作社制度) [The people's commune was the highest of three administrative levels in rural areas of the People's Republic of China during the period of 1958 to 1982–85 until they were replaced by townships. Communes, the largest collective units, were divided in turn into production brigades and production teams. The communes had governmental, political, and economic functions. (Wiki)] and Great Leap Forward ('大跃进') [The Great Leap Forward of the People's Republic of China (PRC) was an economic and social campaign by the Communist Party of China (CPC) from 1958 to 1961.], the progress of which caused disruption for the next few years; it incurred tremendous costs to society, resulting in millions of the population starving to death during the so called "3-year Natural Disaster". [Xie Tao 谢韬. *Minzhushehui zhuyi moshi yu zhongguo qiantu" 民主社会主义模式与中国前途." [the Model of Democratic Socialism and the Future of China]. Yan Huang Chun Qiu 炎黃春秋* 2007, no. 2 (2007): 1–8.]
From 1980	Household Responsibility System;[The collective remained the owner of the collective land and if so desired by collective members, the collective land and other means of production could be leased to any household in the collective. (In 1978,Xiao Gang village created this way, first and all of the farmers there were on the risk of imprisonment. The movement is bottom-up process.) The lessee did not need to pay any rent to the collective, but had to pay taxes to the government. The object so leased could be released among collective members.] the upcoming boom of township enterprises; rapid urbanization

Resource Author

survival, but also strove to create a better life for themselves. The productive and human elements flowed into the network.

An important and interesting factor promoting the development of gross-root markets was the neighborhood administrative system and labor servitude system. The combination of the two forced the wealthy families in villages to move closer to form markets.[12] The principles of the neighborhood administrative system (Fig. 3.1) and labor servitude system essentially encouraged neighbors to monitor one another to maintain order in society, ensuring tax collections and monitoring labor servitude. The local wealthy clans took turns taking on these responsibilities. They had to set examples in community in submitting taxes and conforming to labor servitude, as well as perform free administrative and military defense services. Depending on the year, the government might demand more or longer public service. In order to extend their influence, the majority of clans chose to move away from poorer rural villages to wealthier grass-root market towns. The gathering of clans created a lot of job opportunities, causing a boom in the commercial, handicraft and livestock industries, which accelerated the growth of grass-root markets. Later when the government started to set tax authorities, grass-root markets had transformed into grass-root market towns, which further accumulated manpower and wealth.

Song urbanized quickly (the city of Lin'an had a population of 200 million), and the city began to develop grassroot market towns from rich township and poor township[13].

To use Southern Song Dynasty as an example, its sea, water and land transportation connected a flowing network from national level to the regional and local levels. (Fig 3.2). The hierarchical network linked the capital Lin'an (Hangzhou), regional capitals, regional cities, major cities, local cities, central markets,[14] middle

---

[12]Fu zongwen 傅宗文. *Songdai caoshizhen yanjiu* 宋代草市镇研究 *[Study of town in Song Dynasty*] 福州: 福州人民出版社, 1991.

[13]Poor township (窄乡or 狭乡) means population without enough fields to do agriculture. (Xing Tang Shu."Shi Huo Zhi Yi"新唐书. "食货志一.")

[14]Based on the study of Chinese market system and combined with central place theory raised by the German scholar Walter Christaller (Walter Christaller), Skinner proposed a center-edge theory. He divided China's geographical center into two levels: the central region and the regional system, and the central region is proposed to function as an economic center. According to different economic functions of the varying centers derived a division of different classes, based on which corresponding regional systems were formed. In regional systems Skinner proposed a core - periphery structure theory, in various parts of the local government system, the responsibilities born by core government in social management was lighter than that of peripheral regions, (*Note*: Skinner: " Cities and Local System level" Yeguang Ting such as translation, Skinner editor of " late Imperial China city"). Skinner believes bureaucracy focused on the central areas, while the regional system is concentrated with informal politics and subcultures (*Note*: Skinner: " Cities and Local System level " translated by Ye Guangting, Skinner editor of " Chinese late Imperial city "). In calculating the primary market coverage and ratio between the primary markets and mid-markets, Skinner introduced a hexagonal pattern. This model is based on the assumption of complete homogeneity, that is to say, Skinner must first assume that all of the background and market conditions were equal, they were at the same latitude, all were located in the plains, without

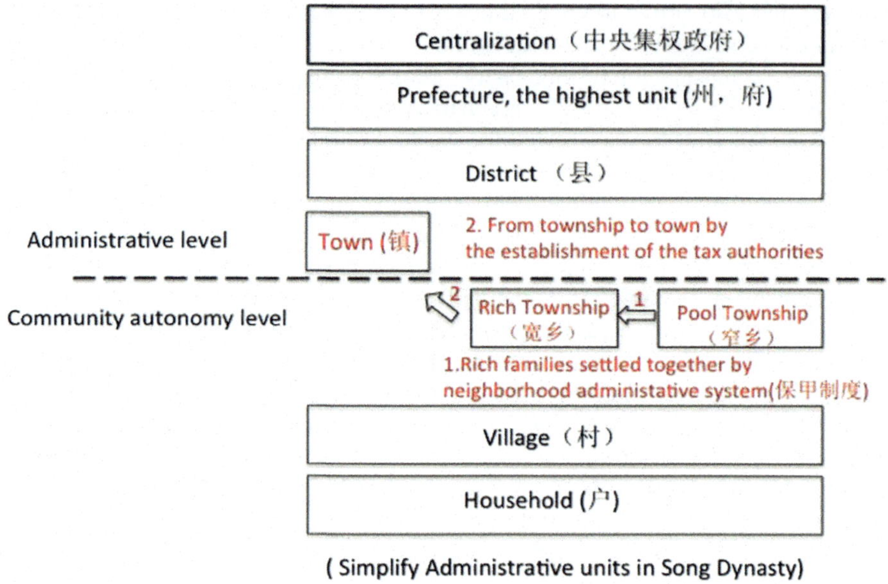

Fig. 3.1 Administrative system and mechanism of urbanization in song dynasty

markets, niche markets and villages in a network of goods, capital and people. It extended from Sichuan province to Jiang Zhe and to Min and Yue areas.

Thus, Yoshinobu Shiba summarized in one sentence: beginning from Song, it was rather an "urbanized civilization" than a "pure agricultural civilization", as the social system exhibited more inherent characteristics of the former. Before the Song Dynasty, clans possessed their own armies and acted without any accountability or

obstacles like rivers, and resources were evenly distributed, all the villages scattered uniformly in this area. therefore, geometrically speaking, to achieve a seamless connection between market areas, the coverage area of each of the primary market has only three options: a deltoid, a square or a hexagonal The principle of equidistance left the shape of any market and neighboring markets to have only one option: regular hexagon. Put it another way: each standard area of the market are circular, however, when a large number of circular were present, they squeezed each other to become an overall honeycomb. Based on the same principle of uniform division, each hexagon must contain the number of same village, so, from the geometric segmentation point of view, only 6, 18 and 36 and other limited number segmentation could arise. Skinner calculated the ratio of number of villages to the number of markets in the whole Guangdong Province in the 1890s found it to be 19.6, thus proving the "Eighteen villages in a market" model in China's rural social to be valid. Skinner used this model to analyze Sichuan, Zhejiang and other rural society, and found out most of the market covered 17–21 natural villages, theory and reality matched surprisingly well. Skinner used this hexagonal model to further infer:, the primary markets in more favorable location may have upgraded to the middle market, middle market covered not only the original site of the primary market, but also part of the adjacent six grassroots markets, which might be located at the six corners of the hexagon (model a), or at the midpoint of the six sides (model B), regardless of which model, mid-market and must be set on collection of all the staggered primary market around.

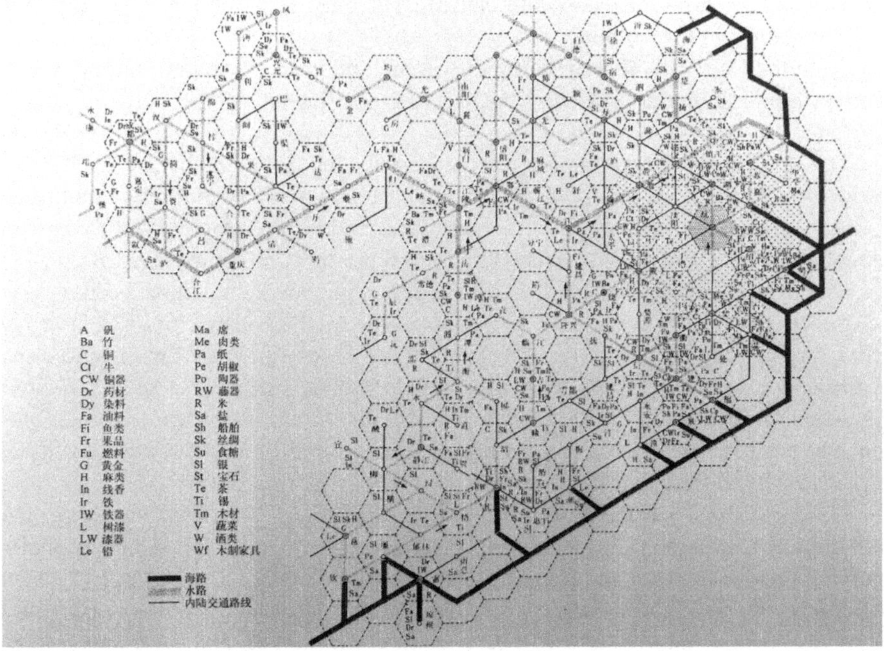

Fig. 3.2 The commercial hinterland for Hangzhou in southern song dynasty. *Source* Yoshinobu Shiba 斯波义信. *Song dai Jiang nan jing ji shi yan jiu* "宋代江南经济史研究". Nanjing: Jiangsu people's publishing house

ties to a central government. The centralization in Song, therefore, caused a relative decline in the power of clans. Additionally, bureaucratic society featured an imperial examination system, simultaneously yielding results in transportation, agriculture, commerce and urban reformations.[15]

The analysis made by Professor Skinner on the urban networks in Yangtze River Basin during the Qing Dynasty is also an important document. He carefully thought through some of the subtle and complex phenomena of urban-rural continuums. In this network, the flow of commerce and economic activities was highly developed. As he mentioned, in the 1890s, within the boundaries of 18 provinces of China,

[15]In his "Study of Jiangnan's economic history in Song Dynasty", Shiba Yoshinobu mentioned while explaining the characteristics of the period of time, that the Song elevated itself from the prolonged continuation of the " aristocracy " society, and established a " monarch centralization." He also regarded Song as the watershed in the Chinese imperial millennium. is within the scope of this Bureaucratic empire to examine this watershed, which started from agriculture, commerce until the political, social and cultural aspects, until a new combination was produced. Chinese bureaucratic system in a series of economic growth manipulation adapt itself to this kind of upheaval, and lasted for a thousand years longer.

there were 39 thousand economic centers, yet only 1546 of them became local administration in the empire.

From the level of commercial regions in big and local cities and central, middle, and primordial market systems, we can see the layout of the network market system.

The flow of information, cultures, and goods echo one another inside the network, while offering urban-rural integration based on market economy in traditional Chinese societies. The grass-root market towns and village markets were very well developed. State and society existed and continue to exist in a process of constant competition and cooperation and has crafted a unique model of China's urban-rural.

In summary, after the end of the Opium War in 1843, port cities began to rise after the opening of five ports in the late Qing Dynasty. The Chinese traditional Confucian system of ruling gradually collapsed under the impact of the Western capitalist industrial civilization. The concept of "urban and rural area as one" disintegrated, while the connection between urban and rural areas was substituted by international trade.

In the history of the PRC, township enterprises promoted an integrated urban-rural relationship in the 1980s. After the government stopped monopolizing purchase and marketing and introduced Household Contract Responsibility System (家庭联产责任承包制), farmers became more motivated towards agricultural activities. The economy started to recover in town markets and rural areas. Rural industry started and expanded rapidly. However, as I introduced before, since the mid-1990s the fast urbanization with global investment has made a huge gap between urban rural areas again.

After a brief inspection of the theoretical logic behind the urban-rural flow of crucial elements in the profile of Chinese urban-rural integration, more discoveries will be explored as we look at online-urbanization in the Internet Era.

Rural e-commerce rises and online-urbanization emerges. May it be considered as the return to old time of village self-government and business traditions? The current phenomenon seems to be both the continuation and reformation of traditional Chinese rural society. Today, when there is a rapid development in rural e-commerce, we have to pay attention to what forces are behind the urban-rural convection of information, manpower, goods and capital: the global integration of production and living elements

Through the historical changes and the new urban-rural integration brought by rural e-commerce, we can see that rural-urban migration in the Internet Era is more efficient. The urban-rural reformation is a continuation of the promotion of balanced development in urban and rural areas. Promoted by online services, especially e-commerce, rural China has already greatly increased the flow of urban-rural information, goods, means of production and human resources, which will enhance the development of urban-rural markets. Industrialization of rural, bottom-up development has not stopped, the upgrade from agriculture and rural manufactures to services industries is already in progress.

I take Suichang county case and Alibaba Rural Strategy to analyze this new phenomenon.

References

1. Fu Y 傅衣凌 (1988) Zhongguo chuantong shehui: Duoyuan de jiegou "中国传统社会: 多元的结构." [Chinese traditional society: a multi-variate structure]. J Chin Soc Econ Hist, 中国社会经济史研究 3:1–7
2. Zhao G赵冈 (Lun zhongguo chuantong shehui de xingzhi "论中国传统社会的性质." [the Characters of Chinese Traditional Society]. J Chin Soc Econ Hist, 中国社会经济史研究 2 (1998):1–6
3. Li Zi 李孜 (2016) Nongchun Dianshan Jueqi 农村电商崛起 [Rise of ecommerce in rural China]. Publishing House of Electronics Industry, Beijing VI
4. Timeline Of Chinese History And Dynasties| Asia For Educators| Columbia University. 2009. Afe.Easia.Columbia.Edu. http://afe.easia.columbia.edu/timelines/china_timeline.htm. Accessed 5 May 2015
5. Zhao G 赵冈 (2006) Zhongguo chengshi fazhan shilunji 中国城市发展史论集 [History of chinese urban development]. New Star Press 新星出版社
6. Rozman G (1973) Urban networks in Ch'ing China and Tokugawa Japan. Princeton University Press
7. Wu H 吴慧 (1985) Zhongguo lidai liangshi muchan yanjiu 中国历代粮食亩产研究 [Study on grain yield of ancient China]. China Agriculture Press 农业出版社
8. Chen Y 陈云 (1984) Chen yun wenxua:1949–1956 陈云文选: 一九四九–一九五六年 [Anthology of Chen Yun: From 1949 to1956]. People's Publishing House 人民出版社
9. Fei H-T (2013) Peasant life in China. Read Books Ltd
10. Jin G 金观涛, Liu Q 刘青峰 (1993) Kaifangzhong de bianqian "开放中的变迁."[The variations during the open]. Chinese University Hong Kong, Hong Kong
11. Guangzong 穆光宗 M (1989) Woguo nongye shengyu laodongli zhuanyi de lishi kaocha "我国农业剩余劳动力转移的历史考察."[A historical investigation on the transfer of agricultural surplus labor in China]. Chin Rural Ecnomoy 中国农村经济 3:40–51
12. Erliu Z 周尔鎏, Zhang Y 张雨林, Wu D 吴大声 (1994) Zhonggguo chengxiang xietiao fazhan yanjiu 中国城乡协调发展研究 [Research on coordinated development between urban and rural in China]. Oxford University Press 牛津大学出版社
13. Yang Tenhai 武廷海, Yang B 杨保军, Zhang C 张城国, Xincheng Z 1979 ~ 2009 中国新城: 1979 ~ 2009[Chinese New Town:1979–2009]. J Urban Reg Plann 城市与区域规划研究, (2011 年 02), 1
14. Zhao G 赵冈, Chen Z 陈钟毅 (2006) Zhongguo tudi zhidu shi 中国土地制度史[History of chinese land system]. New Star Press 新星出版社
15. Xie T (2007) 谢韬. Minzhushehui zhuyi moshi yu zhongguo qiantu "民主社会主义模式与中国前途." [The model of democratic socialism and the future of China]. Yan Huang Chun Qiu 炎黃春秋 2007, (2): 1–8
16. Shiba Y 斯波义信 (2012) Songdai jiangnan jignjishi yanjiu 宋代江南经济史研究[The ecnomic history of Jiangnan in song dynasty]. Jiang Su People Pubishing, NanJing 南京: 江苏人民出版社
17. Fu Z 傅宗文 (1991) Songdai caoshizhen yanjiu 宋代草市镇研究[Study of town in song dynasty. 福州: 福州人民出版社
18. Skinner. Zhongguo nongcun de maoyi yu shehui jiegou "中国农村的贸易与社会结构" [Marketing and social structure in rural China] 第二部分[Part 2],J Asian Stud, 亚洲研究学刊 第24卷第2期(1965 年,) 第196–203页

Chapter 4
Bottom-Up Approach with Global Powerhouse: Suichang Model

Since 2010, a tripartite alliance (Suichang E-commerce Association including Suichang E-commerce Co., Ltd. and Ganjie Ltd. at Suichang) worked with local governments and service providers to explore a path of rural e-commerce development.

As city environments rapidly deteriorated and food safety became an increasing concern, city dwellers began to aspire towards the qualities of an idyllic life: having access to untainted nature, clean water, as well as the opportunity to plant their own food. Their demand grew increasingly urgent as seen in the incident of dead pigs floating[1] on the Huang Pu River in Shanghai directly leading to the conceptualization of Suichang Farm Pig brand by Taobao, Sui Chang E-commerce Corporation, and local government. Excess production capacity had led to a halt in the urbanizing process. Meanwhile, the efficiency and cost-effectiveness of the Internet has accelerated the upgrade of rural and urban SMEs. Information transparency and efficient market regulation brought by the Internet reduced transaction cost, which offer a promising comeback for the downturn economy in China. Thousands of households began to start up new business online. As the rural to urban ("upstream") of agricultural products and the urban to rural ("downstream") of industrial products, rural infrastructure and commercial facilities are being built up. This provided a way in which urban-rural integration could be achieved in the future, both keeping the rural environment intact and renew the way of organization of the rural population.

4.1 Background of Development of Ecommerce in Rural China

In 2011, in China, the main agricultural products were sold in supermarkets, their circulation had some limitations, including narrow selling channels, much intermediate links, high transaction costs and a separated supply chain. On the contrary,

[1]Penetration of hand held devices, access to internet, amount of traffic generated.

L. Zi, *Online Urbanization*, Advances in 21st Century Human Settlements,
https://doi.org/10.1007/978-981-13-3603-4_4

e-commerce had some obvious advantages, such as a wide number of consumers, unlimited locations, comprehensive information and fast circulation. Thus, online selling of agricultural products could cut costs, decrease production and transaction risks, increase the income of suppliers and farmers, promote industrial restructuring, improve competitiveness of agricultural products, expand agricultural products market and speed up the circulation of agricultural products.

This trend start in 2009, Ding Lei, CEO of the Netease,[2] announced to invest in pig farms, which was called "the Internet to the countryside". In 2012, the success of Chu oranges (a navel orange in Yunnan, named for the planter Chu Shijian[3]) was reported in Beijing. At the same time, some online agricultural stores that advocated rural lifestyles began to heat up. However, rural e-commerce platform focusing on online selling of agricultural products not yet emerged. Different online selling models appeared and the Flavor of China sector on Taobao and prepared to operate in 2011 to sell large amount of agricultural products. However, they all faced difficulties because agricultural products had no evaluation criteria, required high-standard storage and had complex fresh-keeping and logistical processes. Besides, their safety was difficult to be monitored and the production was not concentrated. More importantly, e-commerce talents and technology were insufficient.

From 2009 to 2011, the number of online stores increased considerably: every online store drove almost two farmers to become online dealers. In 2009, there were 306,000 rural online stores in Taobao.com and 450,000 farmer dealers, which increased to 380,000 and 630,000 respectively in 2010, and to 590,000 and 970,000 in 2011. By September 2012, the total amount of e-commerce transactions in rural areas (includes online purchases and online sales) were 20.9 billion RMB and the number of transacted products reached 18.62 million. The per capita income of dealers ranged from 2000 to 5000 RMB, higher than the income of those without internet access, which indicated that rural e-commerce contributed significantly to the rise of farmers' income. Some agricultural products such as nuts, tea, meat, preserves, candy, snacks and handicrafts were among the most popular products. Annual transaction analysis showed that nuts made up the largest portion in 2009 and 2010, but was replaced by tea in 2011. Besides, Jiangsu, Zhejiang, Guangdong, Fujian, Shanghai and Shandong ranked top in terms of the number of dealers and online stores, which accounted for more than half in China whereas remoted areas such as the Northwest were lagging behind. In the view of the supporting services, Taobao took up nearly 70% of the rural e-commerce market, while Paipai, Jingdong and rural information platform enjoyed small share. As for methods of payment, the third-party payment, online banking transfer and cash on delivery were the most

[2]NetEase, Inc. is a leading China-based Internet technology company that pioneered the development of applications, services and other technologies for the Internet in China.

[3]The business success story of Chu Shijian is widely known in China. After being imprisoned for seventeen years, he was released at age 85 and started farming oranges. His success is part of the larger inspiration for a growing agricultural business trend and has become a model for many entrepreneurs.

frequently used, largely preferred to postal or bank transfers. If Alibaba and Taobao tended to develop rapidly and maintain their pre-eminence on the rural e-commerce market, they had to establish a rural e-commerce system and back rural e-commerce innovation and entrepreneurship.

Alibaba and Taobao always paid close attention to the rural e-commerce development. Although the sales of agricultural products accounted for 2% of the total sales in Taobao, its growth rate was high. It implied that rural e-commerce would be an important direction for Taobao to develop further. Alibaba was concerned about the potential of e-commerce and made some related preparations. For instance, B2B department, Taobao and T-Mall became the key part that sold agricultural products online; CBU in Alibaba launched an agricultural channel of domestic products wholesale, and ICBU focused on the quotation of international agriculture wholesale. In this respect, Taobao needed to advance gradually because domestic and international agricultural wholesale had mature information platform, market rules and interest groups. However, it had some advantages due to its safe and various agricultural products that could meet the demand of the increasing middle class. It created a channel (ny.taobao.com) for ecological agriculture and the flavor of China sector (http://www.taobao.com/market/china/home.php) selling specialties from counties and villages. At the same time, Juhuasuan.com, a buying website belonging to Taobao department, explored the B2C (Business to Customer) model for bulk commodity through cooperation with offline distributors and agents whereas T-MALL actively increased food items, expanded food distribution channels and supported service providers of agricultural products. Its logistics department and planning department innovated a lot in logistics stations to offer rural residents various products by opening rural online stores and developing purchasing business. In terms of Inclusive Finance, Alipay set up rural business division to provide a financing platform for agriculture-related enterprises, which connected credit business with micro loan demand and manage credit for enterprises and individuals (Figs. 4.1, 4.2 and 4.3).

Meanwhile, Taobao villages, based on Taobao.com as the transaction platform, emerged. AliResearch conducted a study and found that by 2013, already included 15,000 online stores with 60,000 employees across 20 villages from 7 provinces. It indicated that Taobao villages developed rapidly. These villages initially focused primarily on industrial production, processing and trade, instead of rural e-commerce, therefore the innovation model on agricultural products was particularly valuable.

While the e-commerce of agricultural products cut a striking figure, it also faced some conspicuous problems. The analysis drew from Research Report on Agriculture-related E-commerce in September 2012 showed that 23.5% rural e-commerce dealers were confronted with logistics problems; 20% respondents lacked knowledge about operating online stores; 13.92% thought that they should learn how to design online stores and 11.7% had difficulties in supplying products. The root causes were imperfect professional training and rural e-commerce service systems. More importantly, safety and certification of agricultural products became bottlenecks that were difficult to break through because of diversified sources and

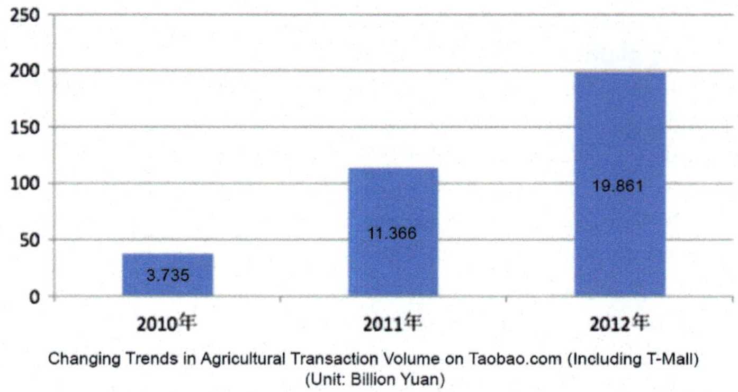

Fig. 4.1 Changing trends in agricultural transaction volume on Taobao.com (including T-Mall). *Source* Drawn from white paper on e-commerce of agricultural products, launched by AliResearch [White Paper on E-Commerce of Agricultural Products (http://i.aliresearch.com/attachment/cms_article/Mon_1301/113_5e51aa81f4a892c.pdf)]

Company	Departments	Business targets
CBU	Website operation - industrial operation -channels for agricultural products	Wholesale domestic agricultural products
ICBU	Information platform–services-agricultural products	Wholesale international agricultural products
Taobao	New agricultural development	Explore e-commerce model of green agricultural products
	The flavor of China Sector	Create market for Chinese – featured products
T-MALL	Foods	Sell foods and agricultural products
	Merchants business-merchants services	Increase operation service companies
	Logistics-planning-logistic station	Set up rural stations and develop purchasing business
Juhuasuan.com	Fresh foods	Sell fresh agricultural products
Alipay	new countryside	Convenient payment and rural financial services

Fig. 4.2 Agricultural business distribution of Alibaba. *Source* Aliresearch

special production methods. These products had complicated certification procedures with high cost and potential risks. In addition, there were few cases linked to storage, warehousing and transportation of fresh agricultural products.

Fig. 4.3 The home page of the flavor of China sector in Taobao. *Source* http://www.taobao.com/market/china/home.php

The Suichang E-commerce Association was built on this context and contribute its innovation to solve these problems of ecommerce development in rural China.

4.2 Suichang Model as a Case on the Local Level

The importance and functionality of e-commerce is shown through these local cases with local government and national ecommerce platform as Alibaba. Since local e-commerce featuring bamboo and charcoal products first began developing in Suichang between 2006 and 2010, nearly a thousand online stores have opened up for business, together with a booming express delivery industry. The sales revenue of some online stores exceeded millions or even tens of millions of RMB. Online marketing of agricultural products continues to take shape. In order to meet the development needs of e-commerce practitioners, the Suichang Ecommerce Association began to foster rural e-commerce experts for Suichang by selling their training services to the local government. In the early stages, these works were conducted under the support of the county government, especially the Personnel and Labor Bureau of Suichang County and the Communist Youth League of the County Party Committee. The latter, in order to create more jobs for unemployed young people, took the lead to partner with the Association, making the county Communist Youth League the first ever Internet-related social organization supported by the government.

4.2.1 Suichang Model with Local Government's Participation

During the development of rural e-commerce, the Suichang E-commerce Association applied the same method to integrate resources, meet requirements and constantly work out solutions to organizational and structural issues. It has trained thousands of online stores and brought them online in Taobao.com, consolidated supply, logistics, after-sale and other links into a complete production chain by involving medium- and large-scale e-commerce service providers. Therefore, uniformity of business model for small-scale Taobao stores was intentionally avoided to decrease competition between stores. In 2011, the Association established Mystore, a distribution platform, and sponsored the first Trading Fair of Online Traded Goods with the Communist Youth League Committee in Suichang County, Suichang Administration for Industry and Commerce and Suichang Private Enterprise Association. The rural e-commerce service system in Suichang County began to take shape, and an open e-commerce-based organization system was integrating with the traditional multi-layered business systems in Suichang (Figs. 4.4 and 4.5).

The government played an important role in establishing good relations between the Suichang E-commerce Association and the local state-operated banks, enabling Suichang Association to take out loans.

Fig. 4.4 Illustration of networks by Suichang e-commerce association. *Source* Author

Fig. 4.5 Pan Dongming's hometown-Bai Ye Wu village. *Source* Author

(1) localization

The flexibility of the local government was fully demonstrated when cooperating with local enterprises. The county subprefect Zhang Xiaoqiang was then an overseas returnee. Under his guidance, the county government has rallied other departments to make active preparations to embrace such a Union—an offspring of the emerging information era. They realized that this was an opportunity to develop an Internet-based industry in their county, and a new system under which a roundtable forum could be set up to involve the government, enterprises and the public so as to improve government services and strengthen supervision. In the meantime, when the government and other related departments were yet to be aware of how to deal with the transformation brought by the Internet, such a new form of civil organization deserved encouragement and support. Besides, civil organizations were needed to make up for the insufficient government resources (most of the taxes and resources must be handed in, making the local government revenue severely insufficient to complete the tasks assigned by the central government, as I have analyzed in previous chapters). This might be related to the tradition of gentry autonomy in China. As I mentioned before, Mr. Pan Dongming held a strong sense of local identity that he was always committed to public welfare; the Suichang E-commerce Association was also initiated out of concerns for public interests. The sense of identity for one's hometown and family clan has run through the whole development process of local e-commerce enterprises that by now, over 80% of the employees are locals and the enterprises have remained closely connected to local villages.

(2) Local government officer' Individual or official participation as consultant

This always finds its way into the government system—the deputy county sub-prefects, several department leaders and other civil servants who were born and brought up in Suichang are playing important roles in the Association and e-commerce enterprises and are becoming an integral part of these organizations. Deputy county sub-prefect Zhao Wenming, though not in charge of e-commerce, is a major advocator of and participator in the development of the E-commerce Association. Visiting over 200 villages, he knows his home Suichang and has a deep understanding of the local culture. I had the honor to meet him through Mr. Pan at my first visit to Suichang. Deputy county sub-prefect Mr. Zhao is willing to help everyone who could push forward the development of the E-commerce Association. It was through him that the Association and e-commerce enterprises gained access to resources in government at all levels, in other enterprises and even beyond the county. Even the executives in Alibaba were moved by his enthusiasm and showed concerns and provided support for Suichang. Mr. Zhao told us that he saw the Association and e-commerce enterprises as his own offspring. However, as far as I know, he never obtained any personal gains from them. His enthusiasm indeed originated from his genuine urge to develop his hometown and strong interest in new things. Later on, Zhao has also been involved in the direct planning of rural e-commerce. As an example, he facilitated the match-making between the Communist Youth League Committee in Suichang County, Bureau of Tourism, Bureau of Quality Supervision and the Association in 2011, as well as the cooperation with Taobao.com of Alibaba to bring online the "Suichang Pavilion" to sell local specialties in Taobao. The "Suichang Pavilion", an idea proposed by the Association to open the first government-endorsed county-level pavilion under The Flavor of China sector, has become an excellent case for the local governments to learn to jointly build produce platforms with local enterprises.

Deputy county subprefect Ye Zhaohui is another Suichang native who actively participates in the development of the E-commerce Association. On 5th February, 2013, the eco-agriculture department of Taobao, another major department under the Agriculture sector of Taobao, came to Suichang to seek potential cooperation and the two sides made a deal to host a Farm Pig Shopping Online Promotion.

(3) Local government's passion on transformation of development model

In fact, the E-commerce Association and e-commerce enterprises enjoyed substantial support from local government at each of its critical development stages in the rural e-commerce system. It happened frequently while I was studying e-commerce practices in Suichang: at 10:00 pm when we were discussing about rural e-commerce strategies with peers from Suichang E-commerce Association, the deputy county magistrate in charge of e-commerce development would always show up, though not invited. At midnight, another deputy county magistrate would join us after work. At 2 o'clock in the morning when everyone was exhausted, they were still in high spirits and decided to invite another county magistrate to discuss how to make it easier for business to deal with the government (this county has a population of over 260 thousand, with 1 county magistrate and 4 deputy county magistrates). It came as a big surprise to me. They gave very constructive suggestions, yet they were content with their role as business advisors because they respected the decision made by senior managers of local businesses. This scene is common not only in Suichang, but other counties where e-commerce thrives. I truly feel that compared with the central government, local governments are more acquainted with local conditions and more adaptable to local customs. This advantage indeed makes local governments themselves more flexible and resilient in the informatization process.

I have explained the role of local government during China's urbanization process, to some extent, local governments, if not all of them, have turned out to be real-estate developers: they purchase farmland at a lower price and sell them to developers. Therefore, profits from real-estate development become a major source for government revenue. I have also explained that under the severely defective tax-sharing regime between local and central governments, the former has no other choice but to resort to revenue of land sales. This is something different from first-tiered cities: the revenue from land sales is in a greater need of transformation, because in rural areas, there is neither rigid demand for real estates resulted (lack of population expansion), nor widespread speculative investment in real estate. Taking Suichang as an example, a county city[4] with a population of only 70,000 is unlikely to experience any large-scale growth of the real-estate industry. Another approach is to compete for an urban construction quota by developing agriculture and reclaiming barren lands, and then sell this quota to a city in need of new spaces for industry and residential housing. All of these are games between local governments and real-estate developers during a globalized resource allocation process. However, as the information technology advances day-by-day, local governments are confronting new challenges in upgrading industries. Especially for Suichang, a mountainous, less well-off place in Zhejiang with few industry clusters, water and land resources. Obviously, Suichang still has a long way to go compared with other more well-off counterparts in Zhejiang. However, it is the restrained industrial development that gives birth to such a new model that combines traditional agriculture and Internet technologies during its informatization process. This is not only a swift response to the emerging e-commerce of local enterprises and communities, but also a long-awaited opportunity for Suichang natives. The various factors for e-commerce and the Internet are in a constant process of flow. The major profits and interests of Taobao, a trans-boundary virtual space, have been settled on Alibaba, an international platform with world-leading financing and cutting-edge technology, and then been captured by Suichang. It bred a local e-commerce service platform after integrating with the Suichang society, its enterprise network, government institution and spatial distribution.

[4]In China, there is usually one city of this size that is called "county city" where the county government is based.

This is an innovative and systematically flexible mechanism of negotiation created by Suichang through consolidating the government, enterprises and rural communities into a same network. In order to coordinate local resources, provide public services, create jobs and levy taxes, the Suichang government has to face up to such a flowing business model like e-commerce, which they are unable to levy taxes on. This business lacks supervision and is unlikely to be regulated and audited by the government. Suichang government felt this deeply and observed more closely the social changes in this information era. Therefore, it made a decision to lend a hand to e-commerce and create a more enabling environment for example, the Association and government departments stipulated various guiding principles, industry regulations and provided massive training, creating a conducive environment for fair, just and targeted development. In the meantime, the county government has also included a supervision system. The government and the Association agreed to implement an online operation mechanism collectively built by the government, cooperatives, enterprises, the Suichang E-commerce Association and small online merchants. As a C2B2C operation framework that ensures food security with multiple layers of protective measures, it obtained government endorsement. It targets the three major groups of buyers for agricultural products (natives, tourists and Suichang natives living in other cities), and clearly defines the rights and responsibilities of the government, suppliers, the Association and small online merchants during the whole sales process. Such a guidance-oriented policy system and a negotiation-based industry mechanism have made possible the sustainable development of the e-commerce service system for Suichang. For example, for the foundation of Ganjie ecommerce service system, because of the financial problem of the creation of a large number of rural ecommerce service stations in village (around 20,000 RMB per one), the Ganjie company was a strategy to invite new share holders with investment and resources. The local government finally organized recourses to pay for cost of building 200 service stations in Suichang county as part of pubic service system.

4.2.2 Cooperation and Competition Within a National Platform

Suichang was therefore included into the regional, even the national market, and had access to the space of flows through Alibaba. This is the extension of a grass-rooted space of flows in the Chinese countryside. Alibaba, as the initiator and beneficiary of the nationwide network, has played an important role in the evolution of Suichang model. Alibaba represents a flowing force that has impacted a "local space" like Suichang. On 12th April, 2012, vice president of Alibaba Yu Siying, director of Taobao Business Union for Merchants Zhan Lu, director of Operation and Support Center Jia Luo, deputy county subprefect Zhan Wei, director general of Industrial and Commercial Bureau Du Weitao and Wu Huixiang from the

Communist Youth League Committee in Suichang County participated at the Suichang E-commerce Association to discuss how to build an e-commerce ecosystem for Taobao, and Suichang became the first county in Zhejiang to pilot the offline security mechanism for online merchants. On 17th May of the same year, the Public Relations (PR) department of Taobao and journalists[5] visited the Suichang E-commerce Association, Mystore and met online merchants selling Suichang specialties. From 19th to 20th July, 2012, Taobao invited other journalists[6] to visit Suichang to study the development of e-commerce and the organization model of the Association. From August to September, 2012, they also received attention from cable TV newscasters.[7] Alibaba and Taobao have widely promoted Suichang as the most representative rural e-commerce model, and issued a report titled "The Suichang Model". The Suichang Pavilion under the Flavor of China sector went online in January, 2014. On 1st August, TP Union (TaoBao Partner Union) of Taobao convened its first Joint Meeting of National Curators in Suichang. Over a dozen curators of the Pavilions in Taobao from all corners of the country joined in Suichang, among whom Mr. Pan Dongming of the Suichang E-commerce Association was elected the president of the TP Union. From then on, rural e-commerce in Suichang became the trailblazer of this nationwide industry network. E-commerce Association sometimes held divergent opinions with Taobao, from which we could notice the discrepancies between a localized social group and a national e-commerce platform when identifying and handling problems. For example, during the promotion of Juhuasuan.com, when the Service Team of Taobao was making promotion plans for farm pigs, they didn't have a good understanding of how Zhejiang people raise farm pigs. Therefore, they proposed to take photos of farmers looking after those pigs and photos of children with pigs in their arms, in order to show harmonious scenes of men and pigs and make it more dramatic. In the end, they discussed, shot and revised the photos a dozen times to reach a mutually satisfactory outcome.

However, the biggest change happened after Jack Ma, a founder of Alibaba Group, put forward the Alibaba Rural Strategy after his research and study in Suichang. The Group quickly responded to his idea by making innovations in rural e-commerce. They wanted to understand Chinese villages so they could occupy this tremendous market with 700 million population prospects. They made a strategy with a top-down approach (from province level, to county level, to village level)

[5]Xinhua News Agency, Hangzhou Daily, Metropolitan Express, Daily Commercial News, Zhejiang Dail, Qianjiang Evening News, Xinhua Net, Today Morning Express, Zhejiang Sci-Tech Report, Lishui Daily, the Youth Times, China News Service and the Market News Agency.

[6]Overseas Edition of People's Daily, Economic Daily, Beijing Business Today, Workers Daily, The Times Weekly, China Youth News, Beijing Morning Post, China Business Daily, China Business Times, China Daily, Science and Technology Daily, Tianfu Morning Post, Chongqing Commercial Daily, Chongqing Morning News, Wuhan Morning News, Guizhou Metropolis Daily, Yunnan Daily, China Information World, China Computer World, New Weekly, Kunming Finance and Economics, Yunnan Information Report.

[7]CCTV News Channel, Enlist the World of CNTV and Dragon TV of Shanghai.

that made Taobao partners from each village talk directly with famers. From the establishment of the first Taobao rural e-commerce service station in Jinjia Village, Tonglu County of Zhejiang in October 2014 to the end of 2016, such service stations have been established in around 30,000 villages in 300 counties of 30 provinces to sell and purchase goods for farmers online. Rural Taobao partnered with Ant Financial, Ali Health, Cainiao Logistics, 1688.com, the Flavor of China and Ali Trip to provide comprehensive services in rural China including financing, health care, logistics, wholesaling, marketing of rural specialties and tourism. This is a breakthrough compared to the cooperation model with rural e-commerce service providers voluntarily initiated by the county or the village, such as the Suichang E-commerce Association. A new state of equilibrium is quickly established. In providing agricultural products, for example, the Association, Suichang government, service partners and the farmers have quickly responded in an innovative way to this change. With the capabilities cultivated in the last few years in quality control, design, packaging, logistics and community marketing, the Association has rallied thousands of Wechat agencies, (most native to Suichang), and developed other direct marketing methods to sell its specialties. Let's take the grain-staffed moon cakes for example. During the mid-autumn festival of 2015, 17,000 such moon cakes were sold within 2 weeks. By 2016, after nearly 6 years of development, such an online selling system of agricultural products has further become an important resource accessible to all enterprises and organizations within a county. In the case of moon cakes, the Association and ganjie.com sold those moon cakes through a distribution platform. On the other hand, some suppliers skipped this platform and directly purchased from those Wechat agents fostered by the Association and ganjie.com. In this way, they constructed a more efficient vertical e-commerce model free of any intermediaries. Therefore, an e-commerce brand for local specialties was built, its products sold to consumers in other places of Zhejiang and even to all over the country through various Internet-based platforms.

As the ecosystem becomes established, it becomes more self-sustaining and not reliant on any one company for innovation. As a manager has said, "this is what we have been striving for in those years". They have aimed at something bigger: concentrating on building a service platform. There is much work involved in selling agricultural products online, such as distribution, e-commerce training and logistic. In 2016, enterprises in Suichang and Ganjie merged to form a new Ganjie E-commerce Co., Ltd. (Shanghai Tonglukuaijian Co., Ltd., as the major shareholder, bought back a large amount of shares), in order to integrate the online selling of agricultural products and the offline selling of consumer goods, optimize the service system, and provide a platform for rural e-commerce. The whole process from processing, design, packaging, marketing, logistics and so on, are designed to encourage rural e-commerce practitioners to make attempts, follow examples and guidelines so that suppliers and service providers could follow the trend. The participation of suppliers and service providers would relieve the burdens on e-commerce enterprises, because the staff number of service departments is greatly reduced. The staff number of the whole company was reduced from over

400 to 280, the staff size of design and packing departments was cut, while that of R&D team and training department were enlarged. In this way, these companies are able to focus on improving the functionalities and technologies, building and developing an e-commerce ecosystem in other counties, providing a platform and a benchmark, serving the whole ecosystem and creating added value in their services and optimize the whole process for more returns, rather than concentrating on some specific agricultural products.

Therefore, Ganjie E-commerce Co., Ltd., or Ganjie, proposed the three-pronged strategy that includes mobilization, digitalization and localization. In terms of mobilization, a mobile APP for e-commerce was developed based on the online agricultural products trading app Tunqin. The app is Android-compatible and can be installed in typical Android smart phones with lower prices used in rural China. In 2016, over 50% online-sold agricultural products were traded on the app of Ganjie. This system is gradually taking on the role of Wechat agents in Suichang, and is trying to build a mobile platform for agricultural products and services by improving the selling and supply chain management of such products.

In terms of digitalization, data collection and analysis for Ganjie are good examples. Ganjie and local financial institutions encourage local farming families and SMEs to make innovations and start their own businesses by providing financial products and loans. They carry out credit rating for rural business starter on the basis of data provided by Ganjie (to determine the credit record and their eligible loan quotas), with loans granted by rural cooperatives. 140 families from Suichang have been granted loans of 200 thousand RMB, the maximum amount. Rural cooperatives have more money reserves, while farmers tend to save their money in banks and don't have any access to financial management tools. The rural cooperatives in each county have deposits of at least 5 to 6 billion RMB, sometimes as much as 10 billion. It means a lot to make good use of this asset to energize rural development.

In terms of localization, apart from selling local agricultural products, the county is also building a localized network to sell industrial products offline and bring local business service system online. Take Suichang as an example. As Ganjie grows, the MRO (Maintenance, Repair and Operations) of industrial products of Ganjie is gradually separated from Taobao, the former MRO system, and such a system is being built for Ganjie. Compared with the giant MRO system of Taobao, it is not easy for Ganjie to build one for itself, and it is even harder to build a rural service system for industrial products after finishing building the MRO. In the meantime, Taobao is also faced up with a problem of localization in terms of its rural services and market, because different stakeholders have different expectations for benefits. First, users in rural areas need localized services such as home delivery of large home appliances, assembly and testing, repair, maintenance, exchanging or refunding of purchased goods. Second, there are demands from brick-and-mortar shop owners. As the e-commerce grows stronger day-by-day, shops in the county were severely impacted. For example, in Kengkou village, villagers are no longer willing to ride a motorbike for 15 min to shop in the downtown of county because of the swift rise of rural e-commerce service station. A yet-to-open large shopping mall still has many vacant storefronts to lease. It is a serious issue to help brick-and-mortar stores in the downtown of county to transform themselves. Third, the embattled brick-and-mortar stores also affected commercial properties, the real estate industry as a whole, as well as land prices, which is a major source of government revenue. At the same time, the slacking business of stores has influenced the whole real economy and tax revenues (it is still not stipulated whether to levy tax on e-commerce), therefore, local governments were worried about developing e-commerce. Though Alibaba paid large amounts of taxes for Hangzhou city local governments, there taxes had nothing to do with other local governments where their rural Taobao e-commerce station works. Localized tax collection therefore became a critical problem. This is a common challenge found in cities, counties and villages when Alibaba expands the coverage of Taobao, yet it became an opportunity for Suichang E-commerce Association and Ganjie. After long-time consideration and making attempts for many times, Ganjie has been attracting local investments to bring online its local real businesses since 2016, specific methods including partnering with local home appliances supermarket and promoting their products in rural e-commerce service stations in every village. In this way, the well-established logistics and service system of those supermarkets are put into good use to avoid the need of building same systems by itself. Of course it is unlikely for Ganjie to make it possible in a short time, nor is it easy to operate such a system. Second, it is more important to establish a localized model that is conducive to the transformation of real economy to maximize eco-collaboration and efficiency. Third, locally registered subsidiaries pay taxes to the local government and strive to become a benchmarking enterprise in its locality to create an enabling environment for local government to create jobs and make Internet-based innovations. In this way, Ganjie is able to focus its efforts on building a county-level service ecosystem, streamlining operation and quickly enriching its MRO and services, that means adopting the strategy of proximity and exerting the influences of a county to its peripheral rural areas. This is what the Association and Ganjie.com have been designed for in the initial stage: to build an Internet-based service eco-system, integrate the already-available offline services into this network to optimize online services, and achieve localization based on counties whose conditions are better understood. In 2016, Ganjie has gradually evolved into a nationwide rural e-commerce platform covering 35 counties (there are altogether over 2800 counties in China) with 4000-odd rural e-commerce service stations in place. That includes 22 county-level operation centers registered locally as subsidiaries and under the direct administration by staffs dispatched by Ganjie, and 13 are established by local enterprises who joined the Ganjie platform and received managerial and technological support. This localization strategy has delivered tangible results after being applied in those regions.

4.3 Establishment of Local Online Service System: Suichang E-commerce Association

On March 25, 2015, the county sub-prefect visited Suichang E-commerce Association and held a party with Pan Dongming, the president of the association to celebrate the 5th anniversary of the association. Just two weeks ago, the sub-prefect and several government officials came to the Suichang E-commerce Association and discussed the strategic planning of "Special Rural E-commerce District" of the county. The conversation involved principals of the association, Suichang Rural E-Commerce Co., Ltd. and Zhejiang Ganjie Rural E-Commerce Co., Ltd.[8]

As the pioneer of Suichang e-commerce model, the association was key to strengthening rural person-community and government-corporation ties. As the common wisdom goes, a strong team and a bold vision are essential to a successful corporation. President Pan Dongming was born in 1976 forty-minutes drive away from Suichang, in Bai Ye Wu, a thousand-year-old village surrounded by hills and mountains in the middle of Zhejiang Province. He always showed his attachment to his hometown and is willing to contribute to its development. Bai Ye Wu rose to prominence in the late Song Dynasty, and was expanded in the Ming and Qing Dynasties. The village faces rivers and nestles against the hills. Households on the left and right of the alleyway lead our paths up against the mountains. The traditional rural settlement patterns are preserved; the geography is such that the surroundings are higher than the inner parts. Pan's home was located halfway up the mountain as is sitting on an old-fashioned wooden armchair. His surname Pan is widely used among the 70 households in the village, being passed on for almost 30 generations (Fig. 4.6).

In addition, his passion for history and his open mind for nature determined the depth and scope of his business. Indeed, the beautiful environment he grew up in aroused his deep and strong love for his hometown, leading him to combine his interest for rural life and his love for nature by sharing this beautiful scenery through photography. He is the best example of an independent personality and innovation spirit nourished by local culture.

After graduating from university, Pan Dongming worked as a designer in Shaoxing and Shanghai, and was lucky to compete with some of the top domestic designers when he was in his twenties. There were gains and losses during these years, but they could not diminish his aim for self-realization. Thus, he co-founded a consulting firm named Shanghai Tonglukuaijian Co., Ltd. to help small and medium-sized enterprises to find a market. After a rapid development, this firm was hiring thousands of employees, making billions annual sales volume in 2014.

[8]"浙江省人社厅与赶街、遂网签署战略合作协议–遂昌网店协会" [Human resources and social security office in Zhejiang made strategic planning with Suichang Rural E-Commerce Co., Ltd. and Zhejiang Ganjie Rural E-Commerce Co]. 2015. Wdxh.Org. http://www.wdxh.org/NewsView.aspx?CategoryId=2&ContentId=1260.

Fig. 4.6 The first house built by the Pan family. *Source* Author

However, in 2012, Pan Dongming (the significant person for the firm), chose to leave and to go back to his hometown for practical and sentimental reasons. Capable people returning to their homeland and seeking the meaning of life after getting tired of metropolises is, indeed, a quite common phenomenon nowadays. This Tonglukuaijian later became one of the co-founders of rural e-commerce service stations. Therefore, we can see how Pan brought his urban experience and education back to his hometown, further increasing currency and financial flows in that area (Fig. 4.7).

In his twenties, he used the online forums to get in touch with his relatives. At that time (around 1999), the Internet was just becoming popular in China and Alibaba was just set up. Under the internet username Jiu Yulou, he made comments about his hometown's history and pointed out problems of local policies, creating a community of fans supporting him. Because he became famous in online chat group, he was involved in establishing a domestic wholesale website.

The other aspect of this story is how the local businessman can support their hometown by taking advantage of their knowledge of the area and human networks. As the local businessman rises in the local community, Pan Junyue, co-founder of the Suichang E-commerce Association, created an e-commerce association with Pan Dongming. His father was a well-known chef and good at cooking traditional cuisine and he inherited a cooking talent from his father. Pan Junyue then became a head chef at the age of 18 and was famous in his twenties and eventually laid a foundation so he could purchase agricultural products and supervise their quality. He was more gifted in business than his father. By contracting restaurants, opening a chain of fast-food restaurants and standardizing reform of catering industry, he became the first local man involved in the standardized fast-food industry.

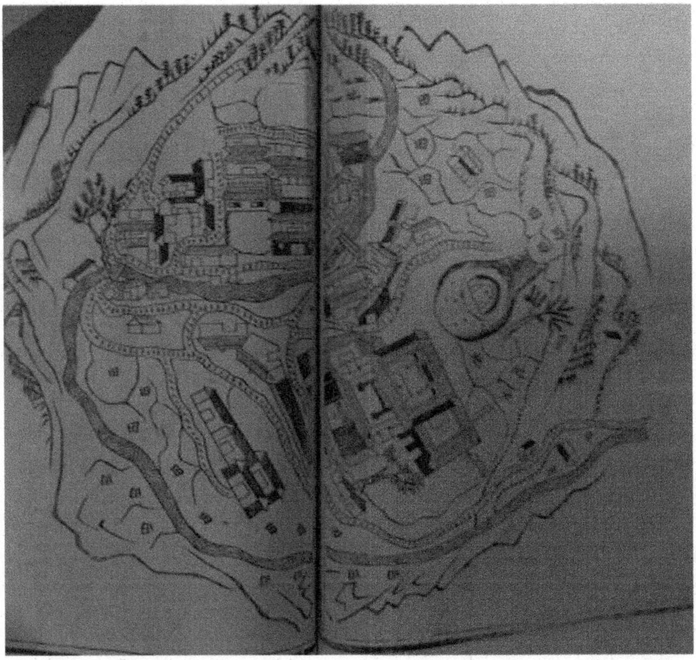

Fig. 4.7 Layout of Bai Ye Cave with houses on the left and community right and rivers. *Source* The Pans genealogy in Baiyewu

What made him even more remarkable was that he was hospitable and set up a tour pals group including members all involved in different social and economic activities in the Suichang County. This group organized like-minded friends to do online and offline activities such as traveling, gathering, photography and so on. Pan Junyue actually met Pan Dongming thanks to this network. Pan Junyue admired Pan Dongming's foresight while the latter was grateful for the sincerity and enthusiasm of the former, gradually building mutual trust and friendship.

In 2010, Pan Junyue gathered some friends interested in the Internet to establish a local e-commerce association. His motivation to use the e-commerce association as a tool to initiate a successful dynamic for the development of his hometown found its roots in his family story. Pan Dongming was elected president with a majority vote, Pan Junyue was made vice president. This association can be deemed as being the pioneer of rural e-commerce in Suichang County and even on a national scale.

The presupposition of the association was that the e-commerce was fragmented and lacked cooperation and services despite its growing scale. Pan Dongmin, Pan Junyue and his friends' ambition was to explore a set of methods to serve villages and therefore achieve co-development. The association was initiated by the Communist Youth League Committee in Suichang County, the Suichang Bureau of

Trade and Economic Cooperation, Green Rock Co., Ltd. and Wecan Co., Ltd. with 18 council members at the beginning and added members twice within a year.

The Announcement of the Second Recruitment of Council Members of Suichang E-commerce Association[9]

Suichang E-commerce Association is a non-profit social organization and its council members are volunteers. Now we have 18 council members and need more warm-hearted individuals and organizations that are keen on public welfare to join us and work on the development and construction of the association. The requirements are the following (the applicant is qualified to meet only one of them):

1. having your own online store (provide store address for check);
2. suppliers having source of goods (including manufacturers, provide company profiles, product catalogs, price list and other relevant information);
3. institutions that can provide third-party services such as lecturers, express delivery, logistics, banks, government agencies, etc.
4. volunteers in other public organizations.

The rights of council members are:
Implement the resolutions the General Assembly decided;
Decide the setting of the Secretariat;
Prepare and hold the General Assembly;
Report to the General Assembly on the work of association and its financial situation;
Elect and recall the Standing Council members;
Decide to set up branches, representative agencies and entities;
Decide inauguration and wages of the Secretary-General, the Under-Secretary-General and the principal heads of agencies;
Decide other important matters.
The council members and their online store enjoy priorities in propagation.
The association awards the online store of council members or companies some honors.
Suichang E-commerce Association
2010.7.13

[9]"遂昌网店协会第二届理事会成员扩大招聘通知–遂昌网店协会" [Recruitment from Suichang E-commerce association]. 2010. *Wdxh.Org*. http://www.wdxh.org/NewsList.aspx?CategoryId=9&ContentId=463.

The establishment of the association was only the first step, the next step was how to take full advantages of the association in order to create a sound environment for e-commerce. The key focusses of the association were about how they could integrate different forms of e-commerce and expand its scale. They thus started with cultivating e-commerce talents to achieve these aims.

The association cultivated e-commerce talents from the Suichang County for free and taught farmers how to use Alipay, open online shores and develop their businesses. They did so by opening open and customized classes for the people, including local farmers, ex-urban workers as well as disabled ones, all coming from different areas and having different experience about e-commerce. This platform aimed for communication, mutual learning and sharing experience.

The rural e-commerce in Suichang was started in 2006. At the beginning, it mainly sold bamboo charcoal products because Suichang County is said to be "the hometown of bamboo charcoal" but gradually sold other agricultural products as well.

By 2010, there were thousands of online stores selling local specialties in Suichang County and the annual sales volume eventually got close to 20 million RMB in 2010. These products would include snacks, nuts, tea, dry goods and fresh fruits and vegetables, showing that vertical e-commerce agricultural market was beginning to take shape.[10]

These e-commerce models, explored before the establishment of the association, provided experience for organizing e-commerce corporations and offering platforms for them. Of course, the focus of these practices was to learn and share experiences within the association. In this way, the association attracted capable entrepreneurs to learn from various innovation and entrepreneurial models, share practical cases and train freshmen.

In addition, a variety of operation skills and unintentional development models, such as the integration between e-commerce and public welfare, injected positive energy into e-commerce entrepreneurs. Zhu Qunwei, quitting from state-owned chemical enterprise, and Xu Zhenfeng, network engineer returning from Hangzhou to Suichang County, joined the association and became the partners. They took charge of products sales and IT project respectively.

A case of the integration between e-commerce and public welfare[11]

Xiao Tanshui was a disabled man and fond of public welfare. He aided poverty stricken students and his deed was reported by several media like *Education and Information*. He said that his action could get a double

[10]The data of Chinese Electronic Commerce Research Center shows that in 2010, the online sales of agricultural products was close to 20,000,000 RMB in Suichang County.

[11]Excerpted from Lishui Daily News, "肖潭水:不怕千人阻挡 只怕自己投降" [Xiao Tanshui: What I am afraid is myself]. 2015. Lsol.Com.Cn. http://www.lsol.com.cn/html/2015/lishuixinwen_0328/218121.html.

advantage. In an interview, the reporter saw a book named *If I Can Walk for Three Days* on a prominent position of his store. He said that this book did not sell very well after published, so he wanted to help the author because they had similar experience, thus he sold it in his online store. "I sold it at the original price and made no profit. All money earned was sent to the author," he said. Unexpectedly, the book was ordered in a large amount on the first day. "Helping him was a more satisfying thing than selling my own products."
In spite of the lack of profit, there were unexpected gain that the flow of store increased and the credibility improved. "The most crucial things for business were popularity and credibility." In other words, store owners could not make profit, but they would accumulate popularity by some promotions like seckill, giving red envelope, selling at lose and so on, which was more important.

The training got professional grass-root entrepreneurs together to teach some skills and form e-commerce entrepreneurial atmosphere. It was held 2–3 times a month. The president and council members were obligated to spare their time for the training in that the association had no money to hire full-time staff and rent offices. Taking the lead, Pan Dongming gave two half-day lectures at weekend and council members provided space for free for people who were inclined to learn. There were dozens or hundreds of trainees every time and they cherished such opportunities.

Training for online store decoration and beautifying[12]
Time: July 24, 2010
Space: 3rd Floor, Biyan Bamboo Charcoal Corporation in Shangjiang Industrial Park
Phone number: 0578-8185878
Maximum numbers of participants: 40
Other important information: application is a responsibility so you should think it over. Due to limited numbers of participants, you shall make sure to attend.
The theme of this training: online store decoration and beautifying

[12]It was collected in accordance with the website of Suichang E-commerce Association, "关于举办遂昌县网店创业培训班的通知–遂昌网店协会" [Training for online store decoration and beautifying]. 2017. Wdxh.Org. http://www.wdxh.org/NewsList.aspx?CategoryId=2&ContentId=505.

Outline:

1.1 What is the style of the store?
1.2 The name and logo of the store
1.3 Bulletin board/counter/shop classification
1.4 The name and image of the product
1.5 Product description template/personal space/shop introduction
2.1 What is store support version?
2.2 Producing store signboard
2.3 Producing decoration template
2.4 Setting the store style
2.5 Adding the counter and background music
2.6 Adding beautiful background in the products description
2.7 Using the template to design products description page.

Meanwhile, the association set up an origination named "Logistics and Trading Platform in Suichang County". It was launched in October 2010 to standardize behaviors of council members. The association began to focus on controlling online trade risks and safeguarding legal rights. Besides, it also formulated a series of specifications to protect consumer rights. More importantly, these specifications put forward a good idea to have a systematic record of online store owners, which laid a foundation for collecting and managing rural e-commerce data. They played a positive role in rural e-commerce development systematically and responded keenly to government's regulations for e-commerce.

During the training, the Communist Youth League Committee and the Bureau of Trade and Economic Cooperation, on behalf of the local government, focused on serving the young people. They also contributed to the flourishment of an entrepreneurial passion to the extent that it changed their employment intention, offering various jobs and providing low-cost opportunities for college students who returned home to start a their business. In addition, they built platforms for organizing and guiding young people and protecting their legitimate rights and interests. These acts facilitated Suichang E-commerce Association in receiving attention and support from the local government as soon as it was set up, thus giving it a precious help for organizing and supervising online stores and the whole e-commerce supply chain. Some vice sub-prefects even shared fore-running ideas about the rural e-commerce development and gave advice to the association. In the early days of the association, vice-subprefect Zhao Wenming introduced the association to the related governmental departments including the Communist Youth League Committee and the Bureau of Labor which made great effort to support e-commerce dealers, especially dealers selling agricultural products.

Notice of training for opening online stores in Suichang County[13]
Governments of villages and towns:
This training is both held by the Labor and Social Security Station and the Communist Youth League Committee in Suichang County, but was undertook by the Communist Youth League Committee, the Employment Office and the e-commerce association. The aim of this training was to support a group of young entrepreneurs committed to the e-commerce by helping them to change their employment concepts, develop more channels for employment and stimulate their entrepreneurial passion. The relevant issues are hereby notified as follows:

1. Training time and place

The training time is from August 23 to 27 and the training place is County Training Center (on the fourth floor of the County Human Resources Market building). Registration time for training is 8:30 am on August 23.

2. Trainee

People between the age of 18–60 who have recently opened online stores (they have registered online stores but need business skills in order to increase sales) and have strong will to open the online store.

3. How to apply

Please fill out the "The Recommendation and Approval form of Online Store Entrepreneurship Training Course in Suichang County" and "Summary Sheet of Trainees" and send the above materials by e-mail (gqtscxw@sina.com) or to the Communist Youth League Committee (person to contact: Mei Mingrong, tel: 8122876). The council members of the association can directly send the materials to the secretariat (person to contact: service specialist of the association, tel: 8185878) that will deliver materials to the Communist Youth League Committee. The organizer will choose potential trainees with strong will for training according to these materials and the Communist Youth League Committee will notice them.

4. Training content

Invite well-known e-commerce lecturers, general manager of Wecan Corporation as well as Chen Lihong, dealer in Taobao with four crowns, to give lectures about e-commerce and online retail, pre-service preparation and daily operation and management of online stores and so on.

---

[13]From the website of Suichang E-commerce Association, "《遂昌物流交易平台》网站管理规范–遂昌网店协会" [Notice of training for opening online stores in Suichang County]. 2010. Wdxh.Org. http://www.wdxh.org/NewsList.aspx?CategoryId=2&ContentId=470.

Meanwhile, the association invited lecturers in Taobao University to impart new thinking of e-commerce and broader perspectives to trainees.

5. Other matters

Cost: free training and appropriate accommodation subsidies for trainees in villages and towns.
Please bring ID card and daily necessities during registration.
Enclosures
The Recommendation and Approval form of Online Store Entrepreneurship Training Course in Suichang County
Summary Sheet of Trainees
Labor and Social Security Station in Suichang County
Communist Youth League Committee in Suichang County
The Suichang E-commerce Association
July 28, 2010

To make a professional training, the association cooperated with Taobao University[14] from Alibaba Group. This cooperation started to direct close relationship between the association and Alibaba Group.

The training to open online stores was successfully held in Suichang County on August 23, 2010. It broke the former training model that used to focus on vanity projects and was basically operated by the government without following the market needs. Farmers would attend the training to get subsidies instead of having a real interest in the training, which therefore made it quite useless. As the rural e-commerce atmosphere aroused by government-related departments, professional institutions, industrial organizations and entrepreneurs offered an innovated model for people. Through the government's service outsourcing, Suichang County exploited a path to foster rural e-commerce talents from all levels and filled the e-commerce development gap between urban and rural areas. Indeed, the outbreak of rural e-commerce in 2014, Suichang County model revolutionized people's conception of e-commerce, which then became quite a famous issue among households. More importantly, the multi-party integration in training provided ideas for setting up an e-commerce service platform and a system of agricultural products which would gather government, suppliers, online dealers and service providers together.

The junior e-commerce shop owners could be involved in the Association's network through a simple business model in supply chain management. However, new problems appeared after launching the training.. Most online store owners,

[14]To respond to an increasing customer and training demand, Taobao University begun to expand businesses in 2010 such as carrying out an MBA training, recruiting lecturers and online store expertise and so on. This university, being the social education and training agency founded by Alibaba Group, was looking for excellent online dealers and invited them to share their experience throughout the country and create a positive communicative and sharing atmosphere. From government to dealers and from theory to practice, Taobao University had a great contribution in the stimulation of online trading.

except those with great abilities, had great difficulties to operate well, be familiar with all links of supply, logistics and after-sales and form a product chain. When considering successful online shops, it is observed that the business models' homogenization remained high. The path to success seemed therefore quite standardized. Besides, the whole business chain needed large and medium-sized e-commerce service providers. In this situation, faced by strong providers including Taobao Service Team, the voice of store owners was hardly heard and they did not have much bargaining space. Thus, they only got low profit with losing the right to the negotiations.

As a result, Suichang E-commerce Association could make those SMEs together to adjust the process of e-commerce business. The association created the county-size e-commerce service system that put storage space of the association in Suichang County. In 2011, a dozen of council members raised more than 380,000 RMB for Suichang E-commerce Co., Ltd. with only 10 m^2 to set up the rural e-commerce service platform, launching the commercial chain of business services.

In 2014, the rural e-commerce service system was explored by Suichang E-commerce Association and Suichang E-commerce Co., Ltd. It included the following content:

First, establish quality standards and quality control system for agricultural products.

Second, establish a complete quality traceability system to supervise and control product quality.

Third, construct management system for professional supply chain centralized by Suichang E-commerce Co., Ltd. Control information flow, logistics and capital flow in the whole process of purchasing, manufacturing and selling. And integrate suppliers, manufacturers, distributors, retailers and consumers into the whole system.

Fourth, create a professional distribution chain for fresh packed food to open up the market of fresh foods.

Fifth, deeply discover and promote local agricultural specialties, which will not only improve the value of these products and increase the farmers' income, but also effectively inherit the local culture.

This system guaranteed features, quality, transportation and management of agricultural products in a comprehensive way, making it possible for high quality agricultural specialties to sale through the platform.

Everything ishard in the beginning and this system experienced a series of innovations and compromises ahead (Fig. 4.8).

Furthermore, the Association's E-commerce service platform was the fruit of combining comprehensive research with local situations. The first online products suppliers talk in Suichang County was held on February 26, 2011, led by the association and organized jointly by the Communist Youth League Committee, Suichang Administration for Industry and Commerce and Suichang Private Enterprise Association. Its aim was to draw upon all useful opinions. It advocated agricultural corporations and rural cooperatives as suppliers for the association, put

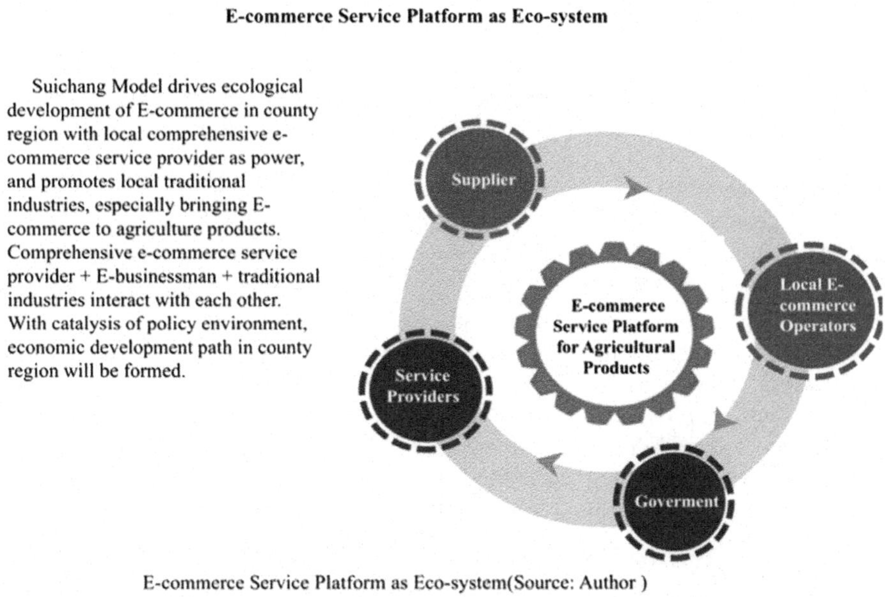

Fig. 4.8 E-commerce service platform as eco-system. *Source* Suichang E-commerce association

forward an idea that products could be distributed by thousands of local Taobao dealers and service center would provide the following services for members:

(1) Guide for opening an online store: offer guidance in terms of opening online stores and starting up a new business for freshmen, college entrepreneurs and interns.
(2) Products supply: the service center signed an agreement with many manufacturers to supply products for freshmen and entrepreneurs, as well as providing various supply channels for other dealers.
(3) Material supply: the service center customized special packing boxes, bags and fillers from manufacturers with excellent quality and reasonable price. Dealers can take use of them to decrease packaging cost.
(4) Training courses: the center will invite its own lecturers and lecturers from Taobao to hold free training.
(5) Talents recommendation: recommend capable e-commerce talents for dealers expanding business and transforming into online operation.
(6) Market information: the center will regularly organize e-commerce communication activity every month for exchanging ideas and achieving mutual development. Meanwhile, it will irregularly invite professionals, manufacturers to talk with members.
(7) Warehousing and drop-shipping: it provides solutions of storage and logistics management and one-stop service including warehousing management, processing, product allocation, mail package, dip-shipping and delivery.

(8) Financial services: financing services; investment for college entrepreneurs.

To respond this service platform for members, the association and Suichang E-commerce Co., Ltd. set up supply platform for online products called "Mystore" Warehousing Supermarket (Fig. 4.5) in March, 2011 to offer online and offline one-stop service. Members could know the dynamics of products, choose products online (download data packet), understand the price trend, complete drop-shipping, settle accounts and achieve brand promotion. It provided a unified storage, package and delivery for members and helped them to open online stores without cost and storage. The warehouse and distribution platform gathered more than 1500 kinds of agricultural products in Suichang County and the surrounding areas, which accelerated the process of traditional processing corporations to transform into the online dealers (Fig. 4.9).

These services provided opportunities of innovation and entrepreneurship for rural e-commerce talents. Until September 2010, there were 3300 individually-owned businesses in the rural area, accounting for 60% of the total number in Suichang County (5500). Due to the large spread and poor infrastructure in these areas, logistics and express companies were not willing to provide services for them. Therefore, store

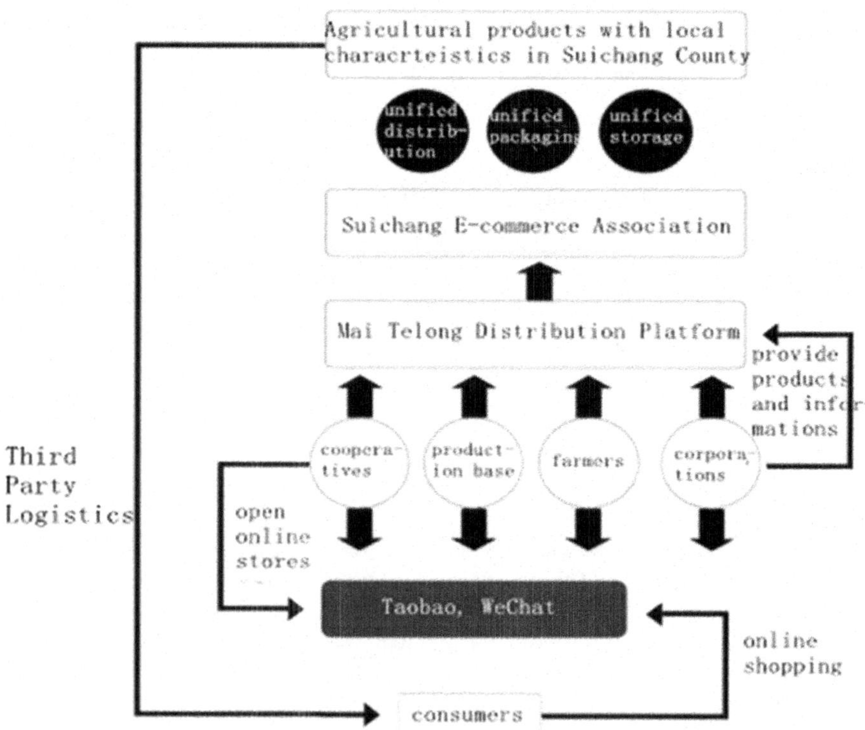

Fig. 4.9 Business process of Mei Telong distribution platform ("Mystore" warehousing supermarket). *Source* Suichang E-commerce association

owners and agencies tended to diversify business channels thanks to the Internet. However, they needed public service platform for logistics and wholesale to cut cost and increase profits. They cooperated with distributors to sell online marketable products featuring high quality, green, healthy and environment-friendly, e.g. bamboo charcoal, tea, camellia oil, organic agricultural products. In this way, the rural e-commerce talents increased, online logistics platform began to be established and some constraints like transportation and costs were removed. Besides, it was possible for the association to train and cultivate members, and even to absorb members in surrounding areas. At the same time, the administration for industry and commerce could conduct pragmatic and concentrated online supervision and vigorously develop local online economy. These practices provided a large number of job opportunities to relieve local employment pressure and tackled employment problems, business and public service.

Although it had a widespread influence and gained support from the government, the association needed innovative thinking on a governmental level to promote cooperation between the government and its people. The understanding and backing of the government was traditionally given to enterprises that created much job opportunities, attracted heavy investment and paid high taxes. However, it was difficult to tax the rural e-commerce dealers because of the immature tax mechanism for online business. Meanwhile, the online entrepreneurship made fewer contributions to the employment than large industrial and mining enterprises, let alone attract investment. Thus, few e-commerce corporations could meet the investment and taxes demand defined by traditional indicators. Pan Dongming summed it up by saying: “2010 is a milestone for e-commerce development. Therefore, I hope that the Suichang government will understand the significance of developing new economy and not miss this excellent opportunity.” In this year’s government report, the China Premier Wen Jiabao has put forward plans to strengthen infrastructures like logistic systems and vigorously develop e-commerce. In this context, the Suichang government was praised for giving more support to e-commerce.

In fact, iResearch pointed out that China’s online transactions increased by 120% in the first quarter of 2010, accounting for less than 3% of Chinese transaction volume.[15] Even though this figure was too low compared with those in Europe and the United States, China was still in the initial stage of e-commerce.

What advantages from local government enabled Suichang to be an e-commerce demonstration county in that time? In places such as Chengdu, local government made great contributions to support local e-commerce companies with the current situation (Figs. 4.10 and 4.11).[16]

[15]China’s online transaction reached 160.8 billion RMB in the fourth quarter of 2010 (On January 13, 2011, Su Huiyan, an analyst in iResearch): The latest statistics made by iResearch showed that China’s online transaction reached 160.84 billion RMB in the fourth quarter of 2010, an increase of nearly 35 billion RMB in comparison with the last quarter with 27.4% growth.

[16]“成都市政府鼓励引进电子商务全国三强” [Chengdu government encouraged e-commerce as top 3 in China]. 2010. It.Sohu.Com. http://it.sohu.com/20100610/n272688255.shtml.

Fig. 4.10 First meeting of online products suppliers. *Source* Suichang E-commerce association

Fig. 4.11 Staff of the first meeting of online products suppliers. *Source* Suichang E-commerce association

With cooperation with different departments from local government, the rural e-commerce service system came into being. The association offered free training and management consulting for local e-commerce entrepreneurs and provided value-added services (e.g. taking photos for online products, packaging and designing). Meanwhile, some entrepreneurs were willing to attend the Mystore distribution platform to coordinate products supply with suppliers, be responsible for warehouse, provide logistics and drop-shipping with the help of logistics companies and discuss about comprehensive entrepreneurial services like credit and loans with Youth League committee, Bureau of Labor, Bureau of Commerce and banks.

In the form of wholesale, Mystore warehouse coordinated suppliers and logistics offline, as well as helping them to sell products in large quantities online. The online products were mainly local specialties and foods from local mature companies with low price and large quantity. The warehouse would offer members high-quality information, preferential sales policies, delivery services, third-party logistics and regular training for free. Guided by the government and funded by the public, the association was moved by win-win cooperation dynamic.

Opening online store had nothing to do with status and education, and only needed computer and an internet connection. It offered opportunities for online sales of agricultural products (Figs. 4.12, 4.13, 4.14 and 4.15).

Fig. 4.12 Mystore went into operation. *Source* Suichang E-commerce association

Fig. 4.13 Mystore went into operation. *Source* Suichang E-commerce association

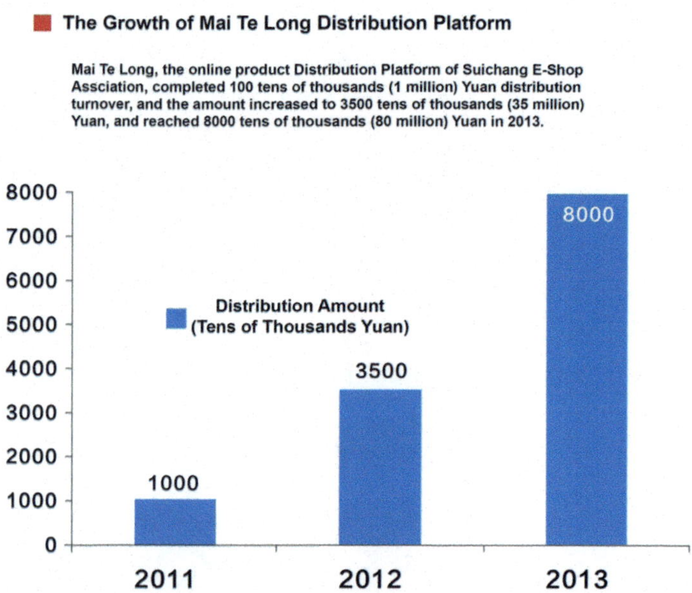

Fig. 4.14 The development of Mystore. *Source* Suichang E-commerce association

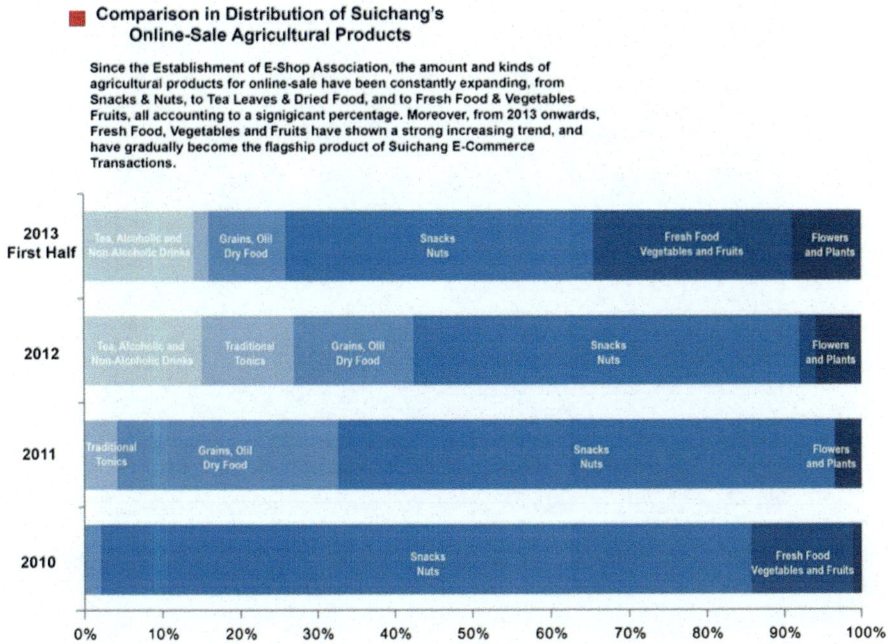

Fig. 4.15 The distribution of Suichang's online-sale agricultural products. *Source* Aliresearch

4.4 Cooperation with the Alibaba Taobao E-commerce Platform

The association, as a comprehensive service platform for e-commerce innovation and entrepreneurship, attracted Alibaba and Taobao's attention. The association and Mystore were committed to solving these problems and helping farmers sell agricultural products online.

On November 8, 2011, Yu Siying, deputy general manager of Alibaba, and Ni Liang, chief inspector of Information Security Department of Taobao, visited the association, which provided a larger e-commerce platform for the association and Suichang E-commerce Co., Ltd.

The original intentions of service center for young entrepreneurs, association service center and Mystore were to train online dealers and provide them with one-stop services, including counseling, design, package, supplying, delivery and logistics. Meanwhile, the governmental departments across all levels reached a consensus on supporting rural e-commerce, supervising online agricultural products, preventing the inflow of unsafe food and developing rural e-commerce (Fig. 4.16).

In addition to the effective online entrepreneurship supported by the association, Yu Siying, the vice president of Alibaba, was concerned about monitoring the

Fig. 4.16 Suichang E-commerce association and service center for young entrepreneurs. *Source* Author

quality of agricultural products with local government, improving food safety and breaking through certification limitations. Suichang explored solutions to these common problems of rural e-commerce. Its exploration provided the model case for Taobao to set up rural e-commerce service system as well as the cooperation opportunity between Alibaba and Suichang E-commerce Association, Suichang E-commerce Co., Ltd. and the local government.

On April 12, 2012, Yu Siying and leaders from different departments of Alibaba visited the Suichang e-commerce association again. This time, Zhanlu, inspector general of Taobao business division for dealers, and Jia Luo, inspector general of operation support center also came. Their talk focused on substantial cooperation of establishing Taobao e-commerce system in local areas. On May 17 of the same year, Taobao signed a contracted with Suichang government, and Suichang became the pilot county of the offline security mechanisms for online dealers in Zhejiang Province. Besides, Suichang E-commerce Association became the impellor of this cooperation and the core of work in the future.

The Suichang government cooperated with Taobao to make preparations for the Suichang Pavilion, the only county-level pavilion in "the Flavor of China Sector.com" from Taobao.com. The online pavilion was designed to not only to facilitate the sale of local specialties, but also include local and life services. Since they signed a cooperation agreement at the beginning of 2012, Suichang Pavilion was put on the agenda in October. On October 1st, as operators of the pavilion, the association and Suichang E-commerce Co., Ltd. set up a project team that included a group for attracting investment and a promotion group. They actively prepared and wished to launch the pavilion within 60 days. At that time, they only had

20 employees working round the clock, so Pan Dongming recruited some fresh graduates in Lishui College. However, they did not have basic knowledge and experience about the pavilion and could not work efficiently.

As mentioned above, Alibaba.com and Taobao.com expanded their business on rural e-commerce and established online pavilions under "the Flavor of China Sector.com". In 2012, they cooperated with the Chinese Agricultural Media to collect agricultural products in Hunan Province. This activity covered 33 brands with 5.87 million hits within four months and the sales reached up to 400 million RMB. This experience was a real exploration for selling local agricultural specialties online. By the end of 2012, they had opened four province-level online pavilions. They could connect local governments, suppliers and online dealers with Taobao.com. In this way, Taobao discovered more specialties through suppliers and created an industrial chain that included supply, quality control, logistic and after-sales services. It could also ensure and supervise products quality by local governments, and urge the governments to support the rural e-commerce. Meanwhile, operation service providers were responsible for sales and promotion such as channels, marketing plan and customer service system. They had the status of a third partner as they would incubate, develop local specialty products and coordinate small and medium-sized sellers to help them expand. This platform was in charge of customer flow, such as product libraries, management model for products, sellers and so on. In addition, local governments expected to discover more agricultural products with the help of Taobao.com and improve agricultural product prices. More importantly was to support local online dealers to promote employment. Zhang Xiaoqiang, sub-prefect of Suichang County, and Du Xinglin, the secretary, emphasized the urgent issue of youth entrepreneurship and connected rural e-commerce with government departments (Figs. 4.17 and 4.18).

Fig. 4.17 Zhang Xiaoqiang surveyed Suichang E-commerce association and Mystore. *Source* Suichang E-commerce association

Fig. 4.18 On September 29, 2011, Zhao Wenming and other officers of governmental departments held a coordination meeting on opening Suichang Pavilion. *Source* Suichang E-commerce association

On September 29, 2011, Zhao Wenming as well as other leaders of governmental departments held a coordination meeting on the opening of the Suichang Pavilion. He was a native of this region and received professional training in finance and management. After taking office in Bureau of Statistics and Finance and traveling around almost all the villages of Suichnag county, he gained a steady working experience and an in-depth understanding about conditions in Suichang. On October 22, the project leader of Taobao.com visited the association, discussed about the preparations of the pavilion with members and attended mobilization meeting. On October 31, project members of the pavilion probed into related issues in conference room of Taobao.

The biggest differences between members of Taobao and the association was the positioning of Suichang Pavilion, because only the agricultural products with Quality Standard could enter the pavilion in order to ensure food safety. However, most agricultural specialties in Suichang had no Quality Standard as they were made by passed down processes. Tian Shu, the project leader of the Flavor of China Sector in Taobao, as well as Zhao Wenming and Pan Dongming discussed a new operation model for these products that integrated government, cooperatives, enterprises, platform of the association and online dealers. It was an operation framework that possessed government support, focused on food safety with a multi-layer protection and targeted three groups of consumers (locals, tourists and Suichang people from other areas). In addition, it clearly defined the rights and responsibilities of government, suppliers, the association and online dealers during the process of pre-sale, in sale and after-sales. For example, the joint guarantee of five households ensured that farm pigs were free-range ones.

The second difference was the price. Taking chicken as an example, Suichang government suggested high price to increase farmers' income, while Taobao hoped to cut prices to create brand equity. The association finally cooperated with Taobao in the way of subsidizing farmers.

During this process, Ye Zhaohui, a vice subprefect, took charge of the sales of these products on Taobao platform. He paid much attention to quality control and marketing strategies, demonstrating that he understood the original intention of the association to promote win-win cooperation. The pavilion was an experiment in creating local brands funded by the government and seeking customers on the internet. It was also a combination between a low price strategy and customized marketing of agricultural products.

Through the coordination with suppliers and online dealers, members who entered the pavilion were selected and trained. Later, representatives of some governmental departments participated in a meeting with the theme of establishing quality control center and planned to set up special expert base for quality control. In the afternoon of December 6, He Weining, Pan Dongming and some representatives visited Taobao, talked with Yu Siying about related issues of Suichang Pavilion and set up leading group that were led by He Weining. The "Suichang Pavilion" that sold local specialties in Taobao.com was officially launched on January 8. Its products contained agricultural specialties and some tourism products such as tickets and hotels.

The Suichang Pavilion, as a fruit of the cooperation between the association and Taobao, was the first step for the Suichang model to reach a national level. This e-commerce community became an effective and transparent platform of sharing information. It gathered elite and grassroot people and facilitated communication among people of all ranks and classes. Most of the curators came from rural areas and had shared the same ambition to improve rural people's life.

The association's cooperation with Taobao was not based on a sustainable development plan, so it turned to cooperate with S.F. Express to meet the needs of VIP customers from markets with mature fresh distribution like Hangzhou and Shanghai. It sold 2000–3000 chickens through S.F. Express and the sales volume increased nearly tenfold. In addition, as S.F. Express needed to cut costs and increase profits, it transited from a conventional logistic to fresh distribution by probing into a set of processes for fresh food, including planning, acquisition, processing, storage, distribution and customer feedback and maintenance (Fig. 4.19).

The attempt to build an online industrial chain for "Suichang Farm Pig" was originated from the incident in 2012 when dead pigs were floating in the Huangpu River (in Shanghai), which was reported as the typical food safety problem. At that time, consumers in Shanghai, Jiangsu and Zhejiang were scared to talk about this incident. However, Pan Dongming perceived a strong thirst for high-quality agricultural products behind it. He talked about his ideas with senior managers of Taobao.com and received a favorable response, so they planned to sell Suichang farm pigs online. This cooperation gave full play to advantages of government, the

Fig. 4.19 Quality control process of agricultural products. *Source* Suichang E-commerce association

association, members, suppliers and service providers, and was a trail on quality control and supply chain for fresh food (Figs. 4.20, 4.21, 4.22 and 4.23).

The exploration of fresh food purchasing, quality control, logistics, online sales and after-sale service laid a solid foundation for the association and Suichang E-commerce Association to become pioneers on fresh food e-commerce. More importantly, the fresh agricultural products e-commerce became a nationwide transparent platform for sharing information. Sellers often gathered together to share experience and made common progress. In addition, the traceability system of agricultural products played a role in reconstructing consumers' confidence in food security, especially in online fresh food. It also became the key part in creating smart supply chain of agricultural products (Fig. 4.24).

To those cases, how to transact agricultural products online and establish mutual trust between urban buyers and rural sellers?

In online transaction, e-commerce enterprises like Alibaba built mutual trust between city dwellers and achieved transaction integrity through Alipay, a third-party who supervised the return of goods for any reason. These transactions were restricted to industrial products with unified standards, industrial inspections and testing systems, which were sound foundations for mutual trust between buyers and sellers. However, standards still lacked for most agricultural products.

Fig. 4.20 The promotion event of Suichang farm pigs. *Source* Suichang E-commerce association

Fig. 4.21 Taobao.com promoted Suichang farm pigs in April 2013. *Source* Suichang E-commerce association

For instance, there were no complete and workable standards to scientifically inspect organic food in China. Besides, it was difficult to inspect local specialties and realize standardized control. The answer was to establish a smart supply chain that included production, packaging, storage, transportation and sales (Fig. 4.25).

The smart supply chain for online selling of agricultural products included seven parts:

First, establish an agricultural quality standard system to unify standards in the following inspection and supervision.

Fig. 4.22 Juhuasuan.com promoted Suichang farm pigs in April 2013. *Source* Suichang E-commerce association

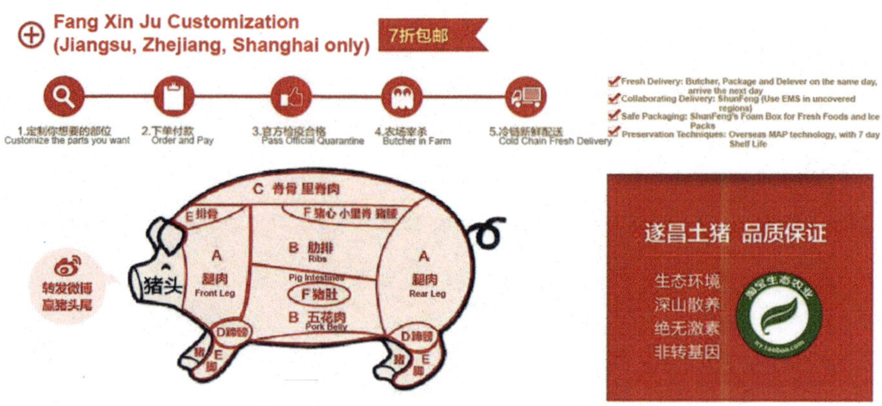

Fig. 4.23 The page on Juhuasuan.com. *Source* Suichang E-commerce association

Second, establish an agricultural product information, management and reservation system. This system would reduce unsalable products by producing in a customized way.

Third, establish an agricultural products quality traceability system that could monitor production, storage, transportation and sales, and trace a specific sector.

Fourth, establish cold storage warehousing system to ensure the quality and freshness of agricultural products. Taking Suichang farm pig as an example, local e-commerce dealers cooperated with S.F. Express to store and transport pork by mature technology of vacuum pumping and cold storage.

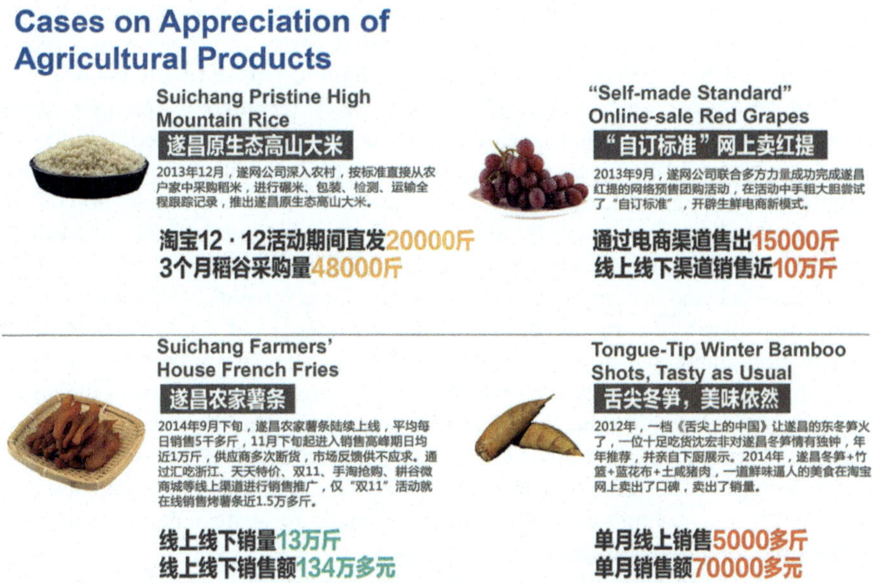

Fig. 4.24 Cases on appreciation of agricultural products. *Source* Suichang E-commerce association

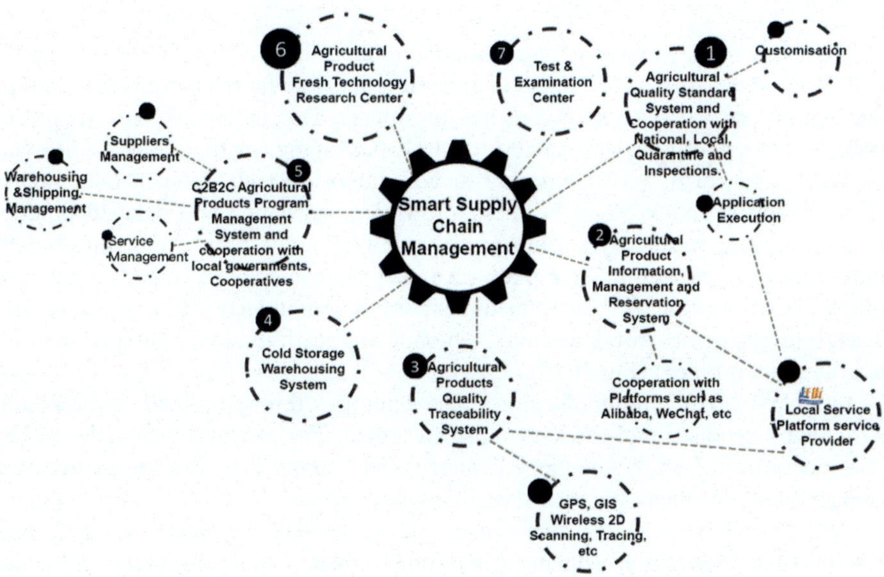

Fig. 4.25 The smart supply chain for online selling of agricultural products. *Source* Suichang E-commerce association

Fifth, establish an agricultural products program management system. It could manage records, backup the warehousing and delivery information and receive after-sales feedback, which facilitated the suppliers to realize timely control.

Sixth, establish an agricultural product fresh technology research center. Different agricultural products required diverse storage temperature, humidity and time, which should be determined by experiments. In addition, foreign advanced technology and experience could be innovated and used as a reference to conform to local situations. For example, the association once used ice bags to fresh red grape during transportation, but it was not suitable to loquat.

Seventh was the test and examination center. Governments across all levels and enterprises should be involved in establishing strict and hierarchical test and examination standards. In this regard, Taobao.com, Juhuasuan.com and Suichang E-commerce Co., Ltd. cooperated with Suichang government to monitor the quality of local agricultural products and punish suppliers who provided substandard products. Though it was an innovation, it only played a simple role in management and was hard to be promoted throughout the country. The Farm Pig Shopping Festival gave an opportunity for the government to realize the risk of being responsible for product quality.

All of those processes of smart supply chain help to solve a problem about how to make the large e-commerce platform (Taobao.com), the local e-commerce platform (Suichang E-commerce Association) and the local government (Suichang government) be accountable to consumers. Furthermore, with this smart supply chain, the association launched an application to sell agricultural products, realizing direct communication between farmers and consumers to further establish mutual trust.

Most online businesses of agricultural products in Suichang County adopted C2B2C model. The first "C" refers to local suppliers like farmers, rural cooperatives and companies, while the second means consumers. The middle "B" corresponds to rural e-commerce processes (quality control, packaging, marketing strategies and distribution), which were connected to consumers through Taobao.com, mobile sales platforms and WeChat business. However, inaccurate and delayed product feedbacks were written by consumers because they could only communicate with personnel of local e-commerce platform rather than interacting directly with suppliers. This situation was an impediment to their mutual trust to some extent. Therefore, the association launched the mobile application called "Tunqin" in order to solve this problem (Fig. 4.26).

In March 2015, this application came into use, through which farmers sold agricultural products and consumers placed orders. The products were delivered to consumers by the above-mentioned smart supply chain. It built a bridge between farmers and consumers for their direct communication.

With good results of cooperation between Alibaba and the Suichang E-commerce Association, Alibaba group tried to make a Suichang as a good model of county-level e-commerce service. Professional research institutions began to concentrate on Suichang County. On September 10, Professor Wang Xiangdong, director of Information Research Center of Chinese Academy of Social Sciences,

Fig. 4.26 The home page of Tunqin application. *Source* Suichang E-commerce association

and Chen Liang in AliResearch visited Suichang County and studied its rural e-commerce model. They gave counsel and guided its development to a larger and higher level. Moreover, Liang Xiaochun, the director of aliresearch center, praised the influence of the association, Suichang E-commerce Co., Ltd. and Mystore on rural e-commerce and put forward "Suichang Model". He investigated this model with other experts and issued a wide-reaching report named "Suichang Model" (Figs. 4.27, 4.28 and 4.29).

On July 31, 2012, reporters of CCTV News Channel visited the association. Later, Chinese network television and Dragon TV reported it in succession. These reports played a key role in popularizing rural e-commerce and Suichang Ecommerce Association. The fact that the Suichang government was widely respected by the media thanks to its long-term support for rural e-commerce contributed to spread this positive opinion about e-commerce.

Moreover, the experience of rural e-commerce was not only recognized by some institutions in Suichang County, but also duplicated in other areas. As early as 2012, the secretary of Fenshui Town in Tonglu County visited Suichang Ecommerce Association. Two years later, the subprefects of Hongsi County in Jiangsu Province and Qingshen County in Sichuan Province visited the association

Fig. 4.27 Professor Wang Xiangdong and Chen Liang visited Suichang and researched its rural e-commerce model. *Source* Suichang E-commerce association

Fig. 4.28 On May 31st, 2012, Mr. Ren, member of the association, showed his online stamp store to the members of Alibaba public relations department

as well and were impressed by this example in rural e-commerce development. As the association regularly shared the difficulties and opportunities it encountered when developing e-commerce, its experience became a steppingstone to the formation of a nation-wide online and offline community that was keen on rural e-commerce development.

Fig. 4.29 Lin Sihao, member of the association, interpreted the business conditions of his online store that sold local specialties to reporters. *Source* Suichang E-commerce association

4.5 Establishment of Ganjie[17] Rural E-commerce Service Station

In rural areas, products introduced from cities were more expensive and the release of new products were delayed with many fakes. Therefore, e-commerce conglomerates and online store owners were all concerned about how to make rural people enjoy convenient shopping like urban residents. Although T-Mall set up online stores in rural areas to increase rural purchasing agents and solve hard-to-buy problems, their development pace was unsatisfactory due to three main problems.

The first problem was how to deliver products from counties to villages. Logistics companies made various attempts to develop logistics in villages, but all failed because there were few packages to cover the transportation cost.

The second concern was about the suppliers and marketing channels. It was hard to open home appliance stores that required thousands of square meters and large investments in rural areas due to scattered settlers.

The third issue was about the restrictions to rural online shopping. The rural residents were mainly children and middle-aged people. Most of them were not accustomed to online shopping and online payment, and did not trust the credit system in paying before receiving products.

To popularize online shopping, the association launched the “Ganjie” program with retail departments and supermarkets in order to buy online products on rural

[17]In March 2014, the Suichang Ecommerce Association Set up the Rural E-Commerce Service Station- Ganjie Ltd.

consumers' behalf. It offered express baskets and computers for these stores and promoted online buying of industrial products by store owners.

In March 2014, the Suichang Ecommerce Association set up the rural e-commerce service station-Ganjie Ltd. The first Ganjie rural e-commerce service station was set up in Wuchu village with only dozens of households. Wuchu village was chosen because it was the farthest village from the logistics center. The association knew that if they could supply Wuchu, they would prove that they could provide services to any village within the county. The association started in the way of freely providing computers, liquid crystal display, showcases and express baskets for retail departments. Storekeepers would help villagers to buy products online while selling their own products. Meanwhile, it planned to establish rural e-commerce service center in Suichang County to make it the hub of logistics transfer and information exchange between cities and villages. However, in practice, logistics between counties and villages was a challenge. Rural consumers in remote areas had to wait a long time before receiving products and the logistics costs were high. Thus, the head of service center and personnel in the association, Suichang E-commerce Co., Ltd. and Zhejiang Ganjie Rural E-Commerce Co., Ltd. discussed ways to improve delivery frequency and cut single logistics costs. For the remotest villages, product packages were distributed to service stations in the nearest village and villagers working in the county were entrusted to deliver products to their villages when they returned home. As for relatively remote villages, product packages would be delivered by bus to reduce costs. In a word, they adopted various methods to realize low-cost logistics between county and villages. Zhejiang Ganjie Rural E-Commerce Co., Ltd. was responsible for transporting products to service stations if packages were large or villages were willing to pay for delivery. The logistic cost was 2.5 RMB (0.4 USD) for nearest villages, while the cost was split by the number of packages for the more remote villages.

Based on the research of rural e-commerce service stations in Yewu village, we will further discuss how villagers take advantages of the regenerated spaces. Rural e-commerce service stations of Yewu village were one of the first online purchasing agencies that were transformed from traditional village shops (Figs. 4.30, 4.31 and 4.32).

The rural e-commerce service station of Yewu village was built by villagers by following the traditional construction styles in Jiangsu and Zhejiang. The second floor is used as classrooms for cultural lessons and for e-commerce training (Source: the author).

There are over 70 households residing in Yewu village. The village shop is transformed into a rural e-commerce service station after sparing 6 m^2 for a computer, a TV screen, a shelf and two express delivery baskets, and being fully covered by free Wifi. Li Xue, the proprietress of the e-commerce service station in Yewu village is not a native, but her husband was born there. After working many years in Wenzhou City, they decided to return to open a breakfast stall. One year ago, however, she shut down the grueling breakfast stall and transformed it into a rural e-commerce service station, whose facilities are provided for free by Zhejiang Ganjie Rural E-Commerce Co., Ltd. and are subsidized by local government.

Fig. 4.30 Yewu village. *Source* Google map

Fig. 4.31 Distant view of Yewu village. *Source* Author

Li Xue was proficient in using computer when working in the city, and received further training. Therefore, she can help villagers purchase daily necessities with ease and collect surplus agricultural products from other farmers, which are purchased, quality checked, packaged, and transported by Suichang E-Commerce Co., Ltd. to be sold to other places via the e-commerce platform. In 2014, the family of four had 16% of its income from the business of rural e-commerce service stations and related revenue (Figs. 4.33, 4.34, 4.35, 4.36 and 4.37).

Fig. 4.32 The rural e-commerce service station of Yewu village. *Source* Author

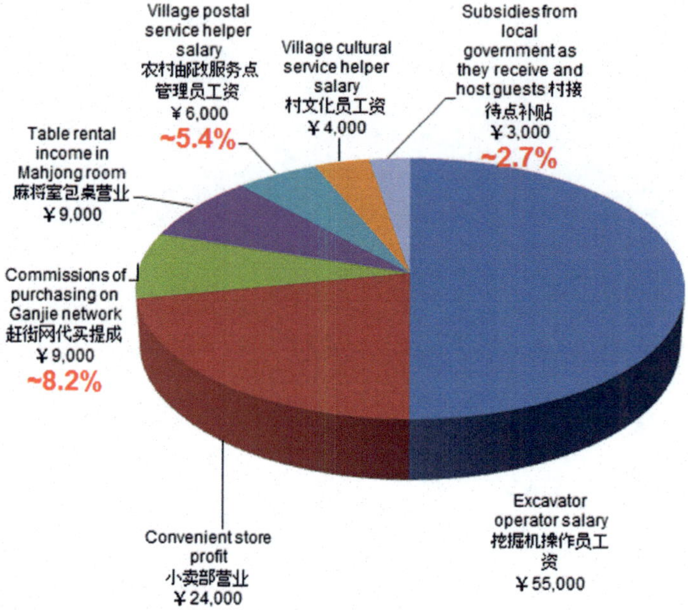

Fig. 4.33 Sources of income of Li Xue's family. *Source* Author

Fig. 4.34 Li Xue, a purchasing and selling agent, in rural e-commerce service center in Yewu village. *Source* Author

Fig. 4.35 Rural e-commerce service center in Yewu village. *Source* Author

After the reconstruction of house, the rural e-commerce service station in Yewu village boasts more comprehensive functions. The retail department covers an area of more than 80 m^2, three rows of stocking shelves covering 20 m^2, the counter 5 m^2, mahjong parlor 15 m^2, storage room 15 m^2 and the break room being a space for children activities, such as doing homework, playing mobile games and

Fig. 4.36 The square dance contest was held in the basketball court in front of the rural E-commerce service center that served as a busy backstage. *Source* Author

Fig. 4.37 The evening school classroom on the second floor of the rural E-commerce service center in Yewu village. *Source* Author

watching TV. Behind the retail department is a village restroom. Outside the door of the retail department is a large awning with a logo of the rural e-commerce service station as well as a table and chair where villagers can chat and enjoy the sunshine. Both sides of the door were covered with online-shopping advertising, with the QR code for rural e-commerce and the WiFi account and password for Internet access. Outside the grocery store is a standard basketball court and some parking spaces, with a few notice boards on one side. At the same time, there is an exterior staircase connecting the square to the evening school with an area of 30 m^2 on the second floor. Each week, some evening classes are held here, such as computer science and other training classes. Not long ago, the village head requested that the second floor of Li Xue's house be transformed into an evening school. In return, the village head promised her that the relevant fees would be included in the village budget and after ten years the second-floor space would be returned to Li Xue. At the entrance of the main road of the village and at the end of the basketball court, is a pavilion and a cultural hall (500 m^2), which became the busiest place in the village working in tandem with the grocery store. Thus, choosing the site for the rural e-commerce service station and space reconstruction have become a typical case. The grocery store has been an activity center for villagers to play mahjong, chat with each other and watch performances (such as the festival party and entertainment performances to advocate family-planning policy) in the cultural hall. Children also have their own activity space here, such as playing mobile games. In this process, the rural e-commerce service station becomes a popular place for villagers. The most typical case is the square dance contest (Fig. 7.34) in Sanren Village. More than a dozen groups got together in the public basketball court outside the center to take part in the contest. Many costumes were bought through the rural e-commerce service station, where also became the dressing room on that day. Li Xue serves as an agent for villagers and actively takes part in the public affairs in the village, resulting in the service station gradually becomes the community center of the village. Apart from that, Wechat groups were set up and Li Xue, resembling a volunteer village official, makes an active effort in delivering the messages and village notices through social media platforms. The cultural hall added a new function, besides holding village conferences and entertainment performances. Each season, Suichang E-commerce Association and Zhejiang Ganjie Rural E-Commerce Co., Ltd. would come here to promote rural e-commerce products. Even president of Unicharm Co., Ltd. once came here to hold a promotion campaign, vividly demonstrating that through rural e-commerce, Yewu Village is profoundly influenced by globalization (Figs. 4.38, 4.39 and 4.40).

By May 2015, Ganjie was materialized and publicized in 15 counties in Zhejiang Province, settling up altogether 15 county-level operation centers and around 1500 village-level service stations (Fig. 4.41).

Meanwhile, Ganjie also gained experience to meet villagers' demand. As a result of rural e-commerce, the villagers adapted their behaviors. Therefore, we can see how e-commerce affects the daily life in the villages.

First, rural consumers got used to planned online shopping and would for example buy large bags of detergent in advance.

Second, rural consumers often followed suit. They would gather to buy fashion clothes at the price of about 100 RMB to get discount.

Fig. 4.38 Rural e-commerce promotion campaign in the cultural hall of Yewu village. *Source* Suichang E-commerce association

Fig. 4.39 Villagers are reading newspapers, rural E-commerce news, in the cultural hall. *Source* Suichang E-commerce association

Third, they introduced a seasonal promotion of agricultural fertilizers. Tea growers would then order fertilizer plant with home delivery service 10 days in advance.

Fourth was the promotion time. As consumers were generally willing to shop online at 8 p.m., shopping activities were launched at that time.

Fig. 4.40 The secretary of a village writing on blackboard to encourage villagers to buy online products with the help of service stations. *Source* Suichang E-commerce association

Fifth, online house-building business would become popular. With the help of online customized building materials, rural people could build homes with lower costs and higher level, which advanced the development of local tourism.

Finally, Ganjie expanded its market in rural areas with an incredible speed.

4.6 Online Service Integrated with Rural Culture

Agricultural products were closely related to the rural culture, highlighted during the promotion of these agricultural products, agriculture and handicrafts. Embracing plain rural culture, traditional agricultural products, characteristic artworks and unique production methods not only improved the value of agricultural products, but also recognized the value of farmers' way of life and work. Previous agricultural products' online selling would always focus on the product itself rather than its cultural value. Farmers would become important lifestyle disseminators if e-commerce and the media could tap culture behind the products.

Indeed, the whole society underestimated agricultural development and the value of agricultural products and traditional handicrafts. In the past, the government promoted urbanization in the way of establishing industrial parks and making a requisition of rural lands and cheap labor, which exerted massive effect on traditional values and social systems. As a result, children and aged people were left-behind in rural areas, and rural cultural values were abandoned. Meanwhile, farmers got very modest profits from agricultural products because they would be

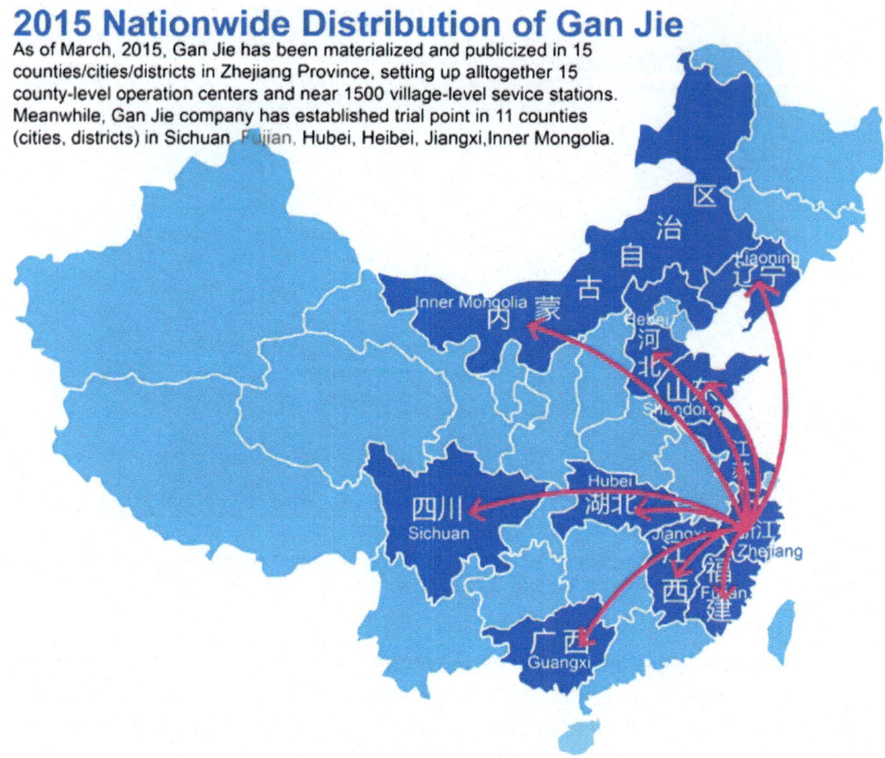

Fig. 4.41 2015 nationwide distribution of Ganjie. *Source* Suichang E-commerce association

deprived by middlemen. Therefore, a growing number of farmers began to use excess pesticides and fertilizers to increase outputs and make profits, which resulted in the above-mentioned mutual distrust between rural and urban areas. To improve agricultural products' image among consumers and therefore promote the rural culture, agricultural products had to be improved. To do so, farmers were encouraged to improve their production methods by following rural traditional values. As agricultural products' value was significantly improved, consumers accepted to pay a more important price for these products and handicrafts. The inclusion of the Internet in this process contributed to make consumers discover cultural values of these products, being also promoted by the media to finally form a new business model (Fig. 4.42).

In 2013, Zhang Shuyan led members of the Natural Community to take example from its plantation and rare handicrafts, and to follow his attempt to recreate the value of grapefruit while protecting the environment. They injected feelings and emotions to the packaging of the grapefruit. After one year of record and recreation, the Natural Community launched the artworks under the name "At the Beginning of the Heart". It contained hand-made story series of people and events in Cangnan

Fig. 4.42 An artwork named "At the beginning of the heart". *Source* The natural community

Fig. 4.43 The member of natural community working in the plantation. *Source* The natural community

County, a blank notebook, a bamboo knife made by craftsmen from Yi County to cut grapefruit and the micro-film of farmers planting grapefruits. They presented the production values of the grapefruit and rural handicrafts, which were promoted by sharing them on WeChat, which contributed to make it gain social approval (Figs. 4.43, 4.44, 4.45, 4.46 and 4.47).

Except for artistic creation of agricultural products, traditional handicrafts were also embedded in these artworks thanks to the contribution of Zhang Shuyan and

Fig. 4.44 The ripe Gusang grapefruit. *Source* The natural community

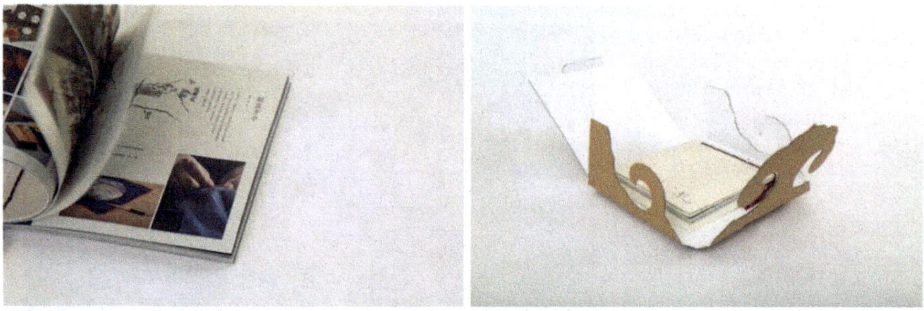

Fig. 4.45 The first volume of series. *Source* The natural community

Fig. 4.46 The notebook. *Source* The natural community

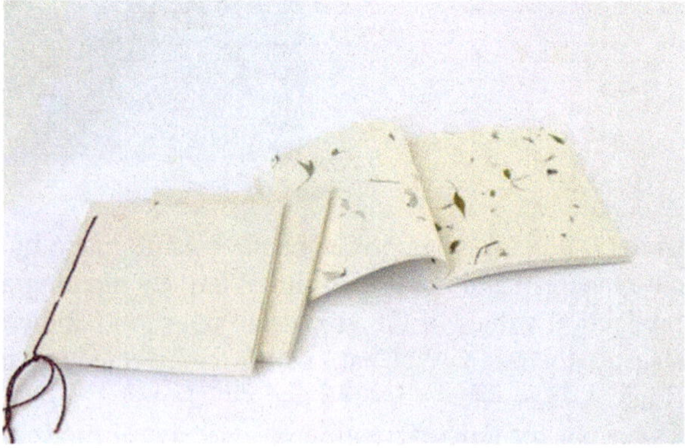

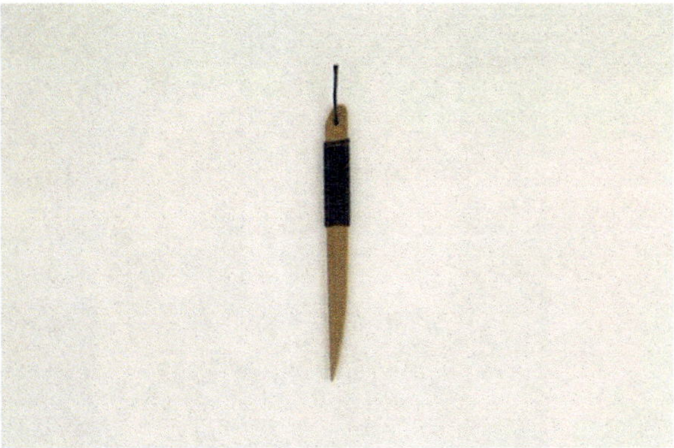

Fig. 4.47 A handmade bamboo knife. *Source* The natural community

Zuo Jing people. Zuo Jing promoted local culture and architectural concepts to help villagers to value their traditional culture by reconstructing buildings in villages and opening a bookstore. In 2010, he sponsored a national activity that sought professional handicraftsmen to make a map by traditional skills, the first promotion and inheritance activity of rural handicrafts. Another pioneer in this respect was Huang Yongsong, a professor of Taiwan University. He spent several decades exploring traditional handicrafts, recorded and published them on journals to propagate them to the whole world. Affected by Huang Yongsong, Zhang Shuyan devoted himself to inheriting handicrafts.

The Natural Community used micro-film and characters to record and display the stories behind the works and popularized products and their culture through new media like micro-blog and WeChat, creating a new business model for agriculture and product promotion.

In 2014, Zhang Shuyan met Pan Dongming and discover that they were sharing the same attachment to their homeland and tried creating a new product that could be used to promote values of agricultural products, culture and handicraft through the Internet. The Natural Community was responsible for designing products, while Suichang E-commerce Co., Ltd. took charge of products collection, storage, quality control, delivery and packaging. At the end of 2014, the final works of the Natural Community—"Plain Food" was launched, which included Liangshang Tea, dried sweet potato, paddy and rice. These products were packaged by handicraftsmen (Figs. 4.48, 4.49, 4.50, 4.51, 4.52 and 4.53).

This new business model for agricultural products' promotion was practicable in Suichang County and even in the whole nation. The rural culture behind the agricultural products would be a keystone for urban-rural integration.

Fig. 4.48 Plain food. *Source* The natural community

Fig. 4.49 Wood cut and rubbing. *Source* The natural community

4.7 Regeneration of Farming and Local Community

Qinnonggu Eco-agricultural Demonstration Garden, beside Yewu Village, is another example of upgrading rural space by e-commerce.

The integration between traditional agriculture and rural economy and social organization and modern technology promotes the upgrading of space functions, which also leads to the improvement of industry and service. As an example, Qinnonggu Eco-agricultural Demonstration Garden beside Yewu Village, is partnered with Suichang E-commerce Association to promote farming and country tourism online (Figs. 4.54, 4.55 and 4.56).

Suichang E-commerce Association, Suichang E-commerce Co., Ltd. and cooperatives mutually negotiate and strive for win-win situations. Grassroot

Fig. 4.50 Farmers dried sweet potatoes. *Source* The natural community

Fig. 4.51 The paddy. *Source* The natural community

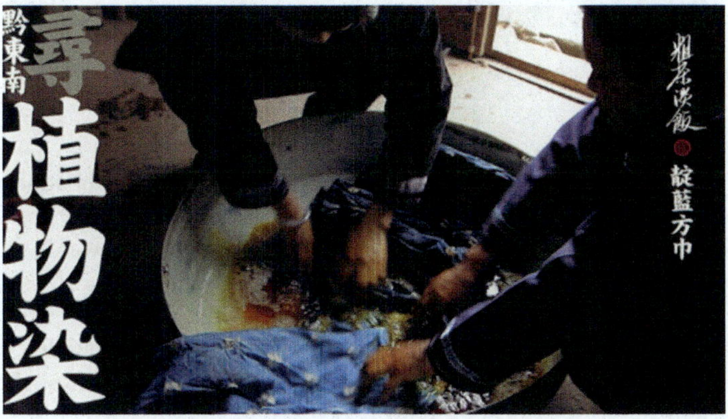

Fig. 4.52 Blue hand towel dyed by plants. *Source* The natural community

Fig. 4.53 Original new year figures. *Source* The natural community

Fig. 4.54 Rural guesthouse facility in the Qinnonggu eco-agricultural demonstration garden. *Source* Author

organizations, such as village committees, are in charge of coordinating managing and putting forward a series of regulations, such as credit system, namely, "the five-household joint guaranty" policy, and government reward and punishment system. Suichang E-commerce Association and Suichang E-commerce Co., Ltd. purchase products from cooperatives and discuss the payment methods. They provide cooperatives with a loan after selling goods online. Actually, the development of cooperatives in Zhejiang Province is at the forefront throughout China and some family farms cooperate with cooperatives, through which the resources are integrated and the production technology is improved by mutual complement.

Fig. 4.55 The photo of Ma Yun, Zhou Chunfang and the author in the Qinnonggu eco-agricultural demonstration garden. *Source* Zhou Chunfang

Fig. 4.56 Tea plantation of the Qinnonggu eco-agricultural demonstration garden. *Source* Author

Family farms also actively join in the eco-sphere of rural e-commerce and take advantage of the reform of rural production mode in the new era.

Some rural cooperatives have also tried to build vertical e-commerce platforms, but most of them ended up turning to Suichang E-commerce Association, Suichang E-commerce Co., Ltd. or Taobao for career opportunities. The reason is that rural e-commerce needs enough products as a fundamental basis, while rural cooperatives are generally made up of one village. So they will not be able to cover the demand of products for the whole year's e-commerce business, so as to support a professional e-commerce team. There are e-commerce teams that originally were rural cooperatives, but they grow to professional team very quickly. With suppliers from all over the county, it has combined products far beyond their only product line. For example, there was a winter bamboo shoots cooperative named "Maitanweng". Soon it became an e-commerce platform with dozens of computers that sells hundreds kinds of local specialties and industrial products with its own brand. Other cooperatives are more suitable for the mode in which they collect products from farmers (some farmers in Taobao Village contract the land to others in order to focus on online selling. So generally farmers would not sell the winter shoots directly online), and transport them to Suichang E-commerce Association and Suichang E-commerce Co., Ltd. for online selling.

Take as an example, Zhou Chunfang, 52 years old, once was a village director in Yewu Village, Suichang County, which gave her a good knowledge of village situation. She organized "Suichang Minqing Farm Produce Professional Cooperatives", which had a specific operation scope written on the person's legal business license. The cooperatives provide members with the sales channels and planting technique for bamboo, tea and bamboo shoots as well as consultation services. Apart from that, the cooperatives also offer various services, including machine cultivation, crop protection, irrigation, crop harvest and other techniques. Besides, cooperatives purchase production materials for its members. Cooperatives partner with Suichang E-commerce Association and provide farm produce to the association.

In 2013, Zhou Chunfang's cooperative helped farmers transport thousands kilograms of winter shoots to Suichang E-commerce Association and Suichang E-commerce Co., Ltd. for free. His cooperative, now as a "company + cooperative + farmer" product base, has 168 member households. The cooperative has twice invited experts to provide bamboo, vegetables and tea training for its members in Kengkou Village. It also manages the members' organic fertilization, pest control and purchase of pesticide as a whole, in order to guarantee product safety. The organic fertilizer they use includes pig manure, goat manure, cattle manure, biogas from the pig farm, organic fertilizer produced by factory, rape seed cake from oil-pressing mill. Organic fertilization helps improve the quality of white tea, as well as the price to 282 RMB (41 USD) per kilogram, which motivates more farmers to join the cooperative. Zhou Chunfang sets a standard in tea market, gains the price-decision right and explores more chances for the members. Usually, the cooperative would confirm the amount and price with purchaser one day ahead. There was one household successfully sold tea valuing several hundred thousand

RMB. Afterwards, Zhou Chunfang established Qinnonggu Entertainment Travelling Company with the theme of "Qinnonggu Agriculture Demonstration Park". His farm has hence developed into the Top 5 demonstration sightseeing farm in Lishui.

Cooperatives also adopt information management and build food safety and quality tracking system, in order to build their own brands. For example, Zhou Chunfang has installed network cameras in Bamboo Mountain and Tea Mountain. Each camera can cover a circular area of 200 m, supervising the fertilization, weed control and packaging. Customers can also track the whole production process by scanning codes, which would help on branding. Suichang E-commerce Association is now exploring how to present the customers the real field by GPS on the phones, so that the customers can be assured with the quality and the brand can be built. This will largely depend on the industrialization, as well as the cooperation between cooperatives and rural E-commerce platforms.

With the platforms such as family farm and Suichang E-commerce Association, villagers gradually fit into the network of production and daily life, which in turn contribute to space updating. The environmentally friendly tea garden becomes the popular holiday destination for local people. Parents and children come to see the tea planting with new technology and experience digging bamboo shoots by themselves. A demonstration ecological experience farm hence grows rapidly. Meanwhile, to better serve the increasing visitors during holidays, Zhou Chunfang built 5 rooms to cook for travelers, and started the experiment on bamboo tube wine. Now the farm has more than 20 guest rooms and one meeting room that holds 50 people. The pricing has risen to more than 200 RMB.

While planning and working with the villagers, we gradually blend in the communities. At the same time, as the main force of this construction, villagers designed their own local space landscape and homestays. Their understanding of the village's value evolves and the whole community unites together, showing great vitality and energy. Cheqian Village in Dayou Town, 1 h drive away from Suichang city, is an example of the combination of rural e-commerce, rural travelling and rural construction. I am the volunteer planner of Cheqian Village and have engaged in their space updating and industry upgrading.

May 2014, I was taken to Cheqian Village in Dayou Town, a village that is 1 h drive away from Suichang city. The village party secretary (the leader and manager of a village) Fan Jianwu was worried about how to motivate the villagers to develop rural travelling and agricultural products.

After becoming friends with Fan Jianwu, I realized it is important to start with industry that can directly benefit the villagers, such as agricultural specialties and travelling, because the purpose of the space designing and construction is to help the village develop and regenerate sustainably. Fan agreed with me, but other villagers didn't believe that an average village like that could make money out of travelling business.

Thereupon, Fan joined the local China Youth Travel Service, and contacted local travel agencies. His wife also started to produce local specialties such as fermented bean curd and Zongzi (a kind of traditional Chinese rice-pudding), and sell them on

Wechat and Taobao. In 2014, their effort began to take shape and attract customers from Hangzhou, the capital city that is 4 h away from Suichang. These all laid a base for the future combination of agricultural products and travelling.

Starting with 7-day trip for the elderly (60 RMB or 10 USD) per day, with accommodation covered), this village attracted more and more retired civil servants and teachers. The beauty of the village was known by more and more people through their photos. Then, we cooperated with Zhejiang Daily and held a Photography Festival. We also provided colleges and universities in Hangzhou a wonderful site for landscape painting. The conversation between villagers and tourists gradually changed their way of thinking. They gain the service awareness and confidence in their handicrafts and specialties. The villagers even volunteered to support tourists photographing and public activities. In the meantime, they can display and sell their own products. Fan also works with an internet company and operates Cheqian Village's official account on Wechat, on which tourists can order local specialties and accommodation. Villagers now are very willing to take e-commerce and rural trainings, and I am honored to organize such trainings for them (Fig. 4.57).

Fig. 4.57 We provided rural e-commerce training for Cheqian village in Dayou Town. *Source* Fan Jianwu

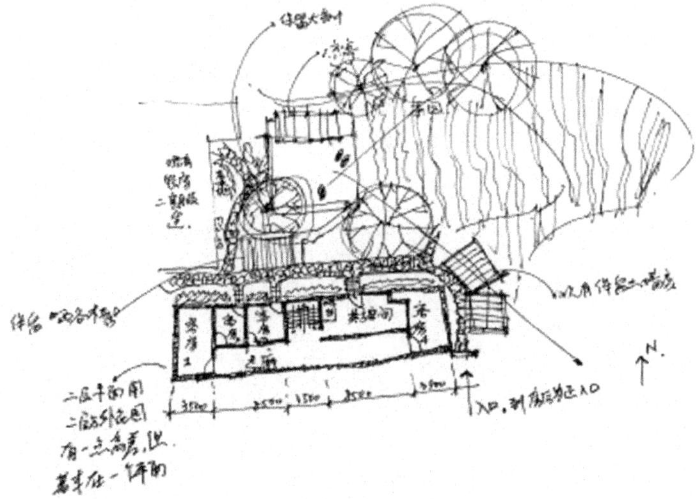

Fig. 4.58 The design of the homestay by me. *Source* Author

In the middle of October, 2015, Fan, craftsmen and I together decided the positioning of each view in this village, and made some suggestions on the project. In the end, we chose this school to be the spot of homestay. We hoped to find a mode that local villagers can build and operate by themselves, in every aspect including space construction. We discussed with the villagers with sketches all the time. After explaining the general design plan and space layout, we would let them talk with the workers and inspire them to find their best construction plan (Fig. 4.58).

It went more smoothly than we expected. The villagers were highly motivated. They even created clear concrete and made use of the traditional skills of mud wall building. This homestay opened in June of 2016. Meanwhile, construction budget was issued by county government to improve the mountainous road up to the village and set special sight for photographing. Then every household committed to the staged transformation plan. With plan, labor and money ready, the transformation proceeded very fast.

We are planning to build an online-offline agricultural centre and homestay on the spot of the obsolete warehouse. With two years of effort, we have seen this village of 800 households becoming a combination of agricultural specialties and rural traveling. From the end of 2015 to early 2016, more than 50,000 Zongzi were sold. The new homestay increased the room price from 60 RMB per day to 280–580 RMB per day. The 9 rooms are of different kinds and different levels, but they will all be booked during holidays. The internal construction also inspired more residents to join in.

The villagers in Cheqian Village are full of energy and ambition. I think this is what we expect for rural construction. The goal of space construction ultimately is to boost the residents' spirit, which is to say community cohesive force. Villagers now care more about their rights and rural policies. They volunteer to take part in discussions and activities that matter for both individuals and communities, striving for government's policy and financial support on road and irrigation projects (Figs. 4.59, 4.60, 4.61, 4.62, 4.63, 4.64, 4.65, 4.66, 4.67, 4.68 and 4.69).

Fig. 4.59 Snow view of Cheqian village. *Source* Fan Jianwu

Fig. 4.60 Agricultural products of Cheqian village in Suichang County. *Source* Fan Jianwu

Fig. 4.61 Renovate the facade of a derelict primary school in Cheqian village of Suichang county by setting an entrance at the back and building a cloak bridge by virtue of the slope to connect to main and guest rooms. *Source* Fan Jianwu

Fig. 4.62 Renovate the facade of a derelict primary school in Cheqian village of Suichang County by setting an entrance at the back and building a cloak bridge by virtue of the slope to connect to main and guest rooms. *Source* Fan Jianwu

Fig. 4.63 The staircase built in 1960s is kept and joined with home-made lamps and bonsai racks after a lot of talking with villagers. *Source* Fan Jianwu

Fig. 4.64 Building a shared space to show some folk arts instead of seeking guest rooms. *Source* Fan Jianwu

Fig. 4.65 Building a shared space to show some folk arts instead of seeking guest rooms. *Source* Fan Jianwu

Fig. 4.66 Using local materials for home-made bonsai racks. *Source* Fan Jianwu

Fig. 4.67 Designing an outdoor tour route to blend in the scenery. *Source* Fan Jianwu

Fig. 4.68 A guest room of Yunxian Zhai, a B&B. *Source* Fan Jianwu

Fig. 4.69 The second-story corridor closed. *Source* Fan Jianwu

4.8 Online Service Ecosystem

The formation of Suichang rural e-commerce platform model of service was mainly divided into three steps: exploration, improvement and upgrading. This whole process was also an exploration for various factors of urban and rural co-development e-commerce-wise.

To be specific, the exploration phase included the following practices. The establishment of the Suichang E-commerce Association that could train and serve local online dealers corresponds to the first step of this industrial chain of service platform—that is to say the exploration step. Later, the association got into service industries such as storage, warehousing and photography, and became a bridge connecting suppliers and Taobao operators for the sake of communications between urban and rural people and sound operation of online stores. Meanwhile, it cooperated with logistics companies and gained financial and policy supports by training and providing services. This phase emphasized on cultivating rural e-commerce talents, laying a solid foundation for Suichang e-commerce development. The rural online stores increased from 500 in 2010 to more than 1000 in 2015. At the same time, local service providers grew in number and training for e-commerce suppliers were popularized. This platform also played an important role in transforming the thinking of government officials. These practices contributed to Suichang model 1.0 (Fig. 4.70).

The second phase was the improvement step. Despite the previous e-commerce training, this platform added agricultural products e-commerce services, including the standardization of smart supply chain, quality inspection system, professional supply chain management, quality traceability system, packaging and distribution of fresh products, the promotion of the value of local agricultural products and on

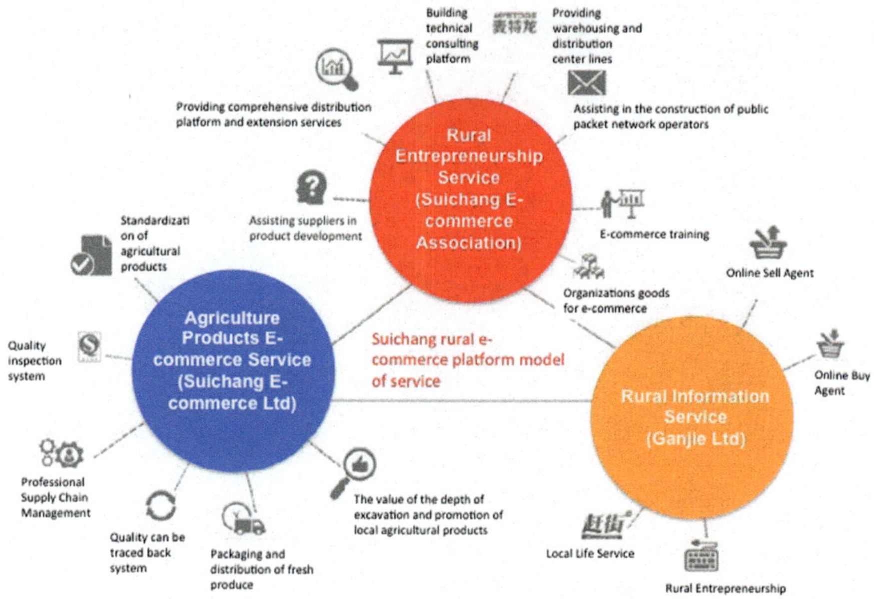

Fig. 4.70 Suichang pattern 1.0: this phase helped to take shape of rural e-commerce atmosphere in Suichang County. *Source* Suichang E-commerce association

Mystore. The essence of smart supply chain was the logistics system between urban and rural areas, which was improved by the efforts of Suichang E-commerce Ltd. and Zhejiang Ganjie Rural E-Commerce Co., Ltd.

In terms of rural information services, Ganjie Rural E-Commerce Co., Ltd. set up online sell agents and online buy agents, provided local life services and established information data platform that covered local information and urban-rural comprehensive information. In addition, it collected mass data of the smart supply chain, which was conducive to county-level improving e-commerce system.

In 2015, the previous Suichang pattern was ungraded to 2.0. This phase mainly contained upgrading of key factors of training and agricultural products appreciation, such as supply chain management service, marketing systems and market services. It improved the logistics system and information exchange system between urban and rural areas, and developed the core competitiveness of rural e-commerce.

As for the consumptive products depreciation system, it improved the urban-rural logistics system, Ganjie service station system, convenience service system and post-sale service system, as well as a new payment system to help local e-commerce entrepreneurs to gain a loan. In summary, this phase was to upgrade the flow of labor, logistics system and information flow system and be involved in capital system. It supported the business and public system of rural-urban co-development and urbanization online-mobile, increased local job opportunities and transformed the concept of government and local people on rural e-commerce (Fig. 4.71).

Suichang e-commerce eco-system development can be deemed to be the fruit of an integration between rural markets and new media, especially the Internet and mobile Internet.

Development of the association marked that it played the role of agricultural products e-commerce suppliers to explore the way of connecting rural suppliers with the market. Meanwhile, Ganjie service stations were set up in villages to help villagers to buy products online, providing them online services so they could sell their agricultural products and monitor products quality.

Suichang County was the only one case in which a new urban-rural relationship was made thanks to the Internet. The Internet smoothed the flow of information, products, means of production and labor, promoted the market and industry development, increased job opportunities and contributed to a new urbanization. Meanwhile, Suichang County set a good example to poverty-stricken counties. There were more than 2800 counties in China, while poverty-stricken counties accounted for 21%. Until March 2015, over 30 county governments sent delegations to Suichang to learn from its experience.

The cooperation between Alibaba and local e-commerce platforms prompted a new e-commerce form that covered four aspects. First, the international Internet giants like Alibaba improved rural e-commerce infrastructures through Tabao.com. Second, local e-commerce platforms coordinated suppliers, service providers and e-commerce corporations offered comprehensive services for local people. Third, farmers and rural cooperatives concentrated on innovations of production

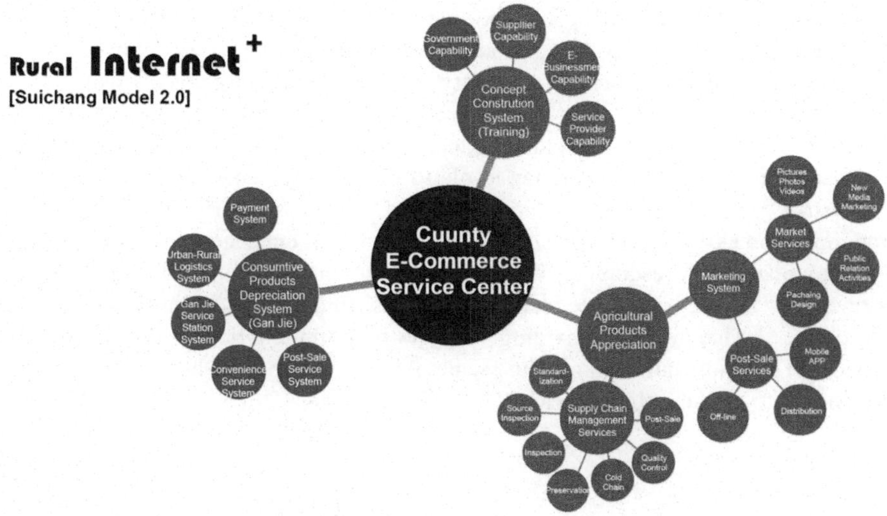

Fig. 4.71 Suichang model 2.0. *Source* Suichang E-commerce association

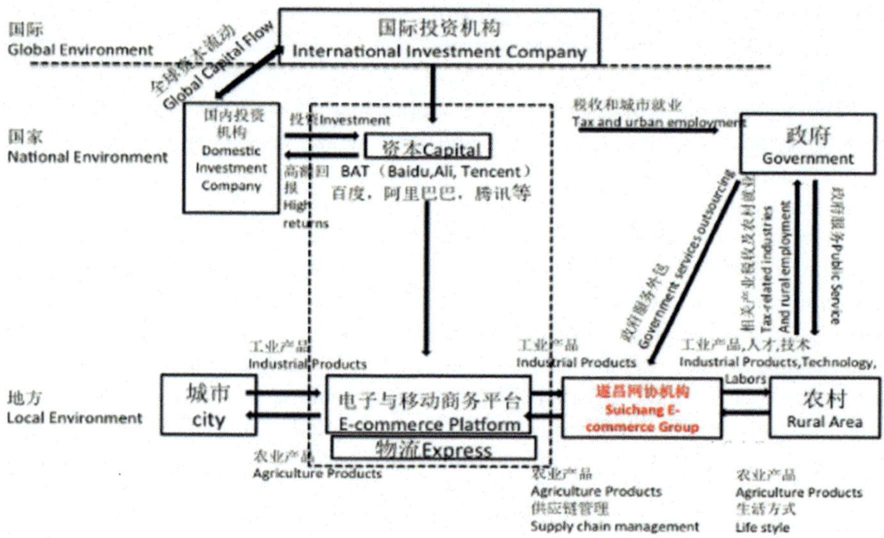

Fig. 4.72 The urban-rural resources flow of Suichang model. *Source* Author

technologies and agricultural products. Fourth, the local government formulated the supporting policies and provided subsidies and appropriate supervision to balance the interests of all parties. Each performed its own functions, making it possible to form balanced business eco-system.

This business eco-system brought about distribution and flow of new urban-rural factors. The international and domestic capital flowed to Baidu, Ali and Tencent (BAT) through investment companies, which were used to establish local e-commerce platforms and promoted logistics development. Meanwhile, local e-commerce platforms introduced urban resources to rural areas and collected rural agricultural products. Besides, county government cooperated with local e-commerce platforms to offer agricultural products and services that were made use of by rural people to sell better products to city dwellers (Figs. 4.72 and 4.73).

In summary, the local e-commerce platform adopts an eco-system approach to link urban and rural resources and inside and outside supports while serving as important forces to help Internet-based organizations enter counties and villages and organize rural resources. The county government and local organizations partner with local e-commerce platforms under such a model to form a commercial and public service system, providing villagers with more agricultural products and services. To region and even national scale, Alibaba group have been inspired from this model to create online service (Chap. 5).

Fig. 4.73 Timeline of development of Suichang ecommerce association. *Source* Suichang E-commerce association

References

1. "浙江省人社厅与赶街、遂网签署战略合作协议–遂昌网店协会" [Human resources and social security office in Zhejiang made strategic planning with Suichang Rural E-Commerce Co., Ltd. and Zhejiang Ganjie Rural E-Commerce Co]. 2015. Wdxh.Org. http://www.wdxh.org/NewsView.aspx?CategoryId=2&ContentId=1260
2. "遂昌网店协会". [Suichang E-commerce Association] 2010. Wdxh.Org. http://www.wdxh.org/Default.aspx
3. "遂昌网店协会第二届理事会成员扩大招聘通知–遂昌网店协会" [Recruitment from Suichang E-commerce association]. 2010. Wdxh.Org. http://www.wdxh.org/NewsList.aspx?CategoryId=9&ContentId=463
4. Cheng Lihong's webstore. www.taobao.com
5. "肖潭水:不怕千人阻挡 只怕自己投降" [Xiao Tanshui: What I am afraid is myself]. 2015. Lsol.Com.Cn. http://www.lsol.com.cn/html/2015/lishuixinwen_0328/218121.html
6. " 《遂昌物流交易平台》网站管理规范–遂昌网店协会" [Notice of training for opening online stores in Suichang County]. 2010. Wdxh.Org. http://www.wdxh.org/NewsList.aspx?CategoryId=2&ContentId=470
7. "成都市政府鼓励引进电子商务全国三强" [Chengdu government encouraged e-commerce as top 3 in China]. 2010. It.Sohu.Com. http://it.sohu.com/20100610/n272688255.shtml
8. "阿里研究院发布《遂昌模式研究报告》-资讯-阿里研究院". [*Report on Suichang Model*] 2013. Aliresearch.Com. http://www.aliresearch.com/blog/article/detail/id/18391.html
9. White Paper on E-commerce of Agricultural Products (http://i.aliresearch.com/attachment/cms_article/Mon_1301/113_5e51aa81f4a892c.pdf)

Chapter 5
Top-Down Strengthening: Alibaba Rural Strategy

On July 21st, 2014, in the bamboo forest of Qinnong Valley in the Zhejiang Province, a bucket of unique local bamboo wine was laid on the ground, waiting for a short man—Jack Ma—to crack it with a bamboo hammer. With a big smile on his face, he rested his hands on his hips and bowed slightly, looking at the wine with childlike wonder. After a little while, the bamboo bucket was cracked with a loud "bang" and the fragrance of wine flowed freely into the air. Jack Ma laughed out loud, bursting with pride. He was holding wine cups and chatting merrily with all present, lauding the flavor of the wine.

Two months later, Jack Ma freely gave the opportunity of ringing the bell in the New York Stock Exchange (NYSE) to eight of his clients. The ringing bell broke the record of financing in the Wall Street.

It was the shared aspiration for Jack Ma and Suichangers, with the help of rural e-commerce, to bring a livelihood as good as, or even better than that in urban areas to rural people without leaving their hometown.

The Suichang Model can be viewed as a product of multiple factors: firstly, Jack Ma, together with such international internet magnate as Alibaba, worked together to improve the infrastructure facilities of rural Internet business. Secondly, such local e-commerce platforms as Suichang E-commerce Association went further into villages and households, thus mobilizing and organizing local suppliers (family farms and cooperatives), service providers (local logistics providers) and small- and micro-rural e-commerce enterprises to provide integrated services for local communities. Thirdly, local family farmers or rural cooperatives produced specialized agricultural products, redoubling their efforts in improving production technology and product innovation. Finally, local magistrates of Suichang County Party Committee formulated policies in favor of the development of local rural e-commerce to coordinate the interests of multiple parties, offered appropriate government subsidies to the industry and provided moderate supervision. Thus, as each performed its own function, a subtle commercial ecological balance was taking shape.

The seed of innovation had been widely spread across the soil of rural e-commerce of Alibaba Group ever since Jack Ma's Suichang journey. Alibaba

L. Zi, *Online Urbanization*, Advances in 21st Century Human Settlements,
https://doi.org/10.1007/978-981-13-3603-4_5

Fig. 5.1 The author was lucky enough to exchange ideas and share opinions on the *Proposal of Rural E-commerce Promoting Urban-rural Integration* with Jack Ma who was in his rural investigation and research in Bamboo Forest Village, Suichang. *Source* Author

announced its Rural E-commerce Strategy with 10 billion RMB invested to establish 1000 county-level operation centers and 100,000 village-level service stations. It was designed to invest into villages directly by opening dialogues top-down with farmers with Rural Taobao Partner of each village as an intermediary, thus penetrating the massive rural markets with over 700 million potential clients. Since the first Rural Taobao e-commerce service station was launched in Jinjia Village, Tonglu, Zhejiang Province on October 29th, 2014, rural e-commerce service stations, designed to provide proxy purchase and sales online services for farmers, had been established in 3667 villages in 102 counties across 18 provinces by August 30th, 2015. Relying on Anti Jinfu, Ali Health, Cainiao Logistics, 1688, Taobao Features of China and Alitrip, Rural Taobao has successfully provided integrated rural services with financial business, medical care, logistics, wholesales, agricultural specialties sales and tourism included.

The vision driving the business operation of Alibaba Rural Taobao and its seventeen operating departments in villages is to bring about the talents cultivation of rural e-commerce, deliver rural microfinance and ultimately realize a type of new urbanization.

The top-down Alibaba Rural Strategy led by Jack Ma personally and the bottom-up practice of Rural Taobao the past several years will undoubtedly impact the Chinese urban-rural structure (Fig. 5.1).

5.1 Alibaba Rural Strategy: Globalization with Local Participation

Taobao, Rural Taobao and other business departments of Alibaba have unified their efforts towards the rural development strategy put forward by Jack Ma and built an "aircraft carrier" for online services. This carrier indeed represents the flowing powers within—it does not belong to any village, county, city, province or any country. On the contrary, it represents a stream of flowing power in the information era brought about by the powers of globalization and Internet-based enterprises,[1] who have achieved networked and globalized financing and operation and whose influences have directly reached out to villages by passing the authorities of the state, the province, the city and the county.

Alibaba's Rural Strategy was shaped according to some main trends:

5.1.1 Social Reputation

As one of the main leading Internet companies of the world, Alibaba tries to build a milestone of their social responsibility in China.

Alibaba tried to fill the gap of services between urban and rural areas. When we are discussing the Alibaba Rural Strategy, we mean that the villages are pulled closer to the world through online services. On one hand, many more products can be put on the market at home and abroad with the help of platforms provided by Alibaba. On the other hand, many more rural residents can get easier access to the same benefits as citizens in large cities, for example, enjoying the high-quality products with affordable prices. For instance, it would be easy to get fake products from local rural shops. We might find fast-cooked noodle such brands as Master Li or Master Wong but not the real brand Master Kong.

The television is another example. In the counties, if you choose to buy a TV in the physical stores, rather than online shopping, it will cost you RMB1000 more. Now, thanks to the sales promotion of LeTV in rural Taobao, you can buy a TV just at a price of RMB1600. It is especially true when it comes to services. It is fairly difficult to establish a layered system of health care right now. However, with the help of rural service stations and rural Taobao Errands, distance health care stations can be built. By uploading the information data of patients in rural areas with intelligent health care equipment, we can make the video diagnosis possible. Besides, on-line entertainment and education are also seeing great development. Along with the Rural Teachers Program put forward by Mr. Jack Ma, the online education is carried out in rural areas as well right now. All of these moves will bring better services and more products to the villages.

As the Chinese proverb goes, "Give a man a fish and you feed him for a day; teach a man how to fish and you feed him for a lifetime". In the course of selling rural products on the online markets, initiative actions of rural e-commerce

[1]On Oct 1999, Goldman Sachs, Investor AB and Singapore TDF (Technology Development Foundation) invested $5 million in Alibaba. Before long Softbank CEO Masayoshi Son offered $20 million to Alibaba. In the second half of 2003, Alibaba received another $82 million from Softbank, Fidelity Investments, Granite Global Ventures (GGV) and TDF. In 2005, Alibaba sold a 40% stake, or $1 billion to Yahoo. In 2007, Alibaba listed in Hong Kong. In 2012, it Alibaba dropped plans for Hong Kong listing. In Sept 2014, Alibaba made its long-awaited Wall Street debut and acquired more financings from global sources.

practitioners play a tremendous role. Entrepreneurship is then a key element of Alibaba's influence over the rural communities ecosystem. For instance, during the 2016 Double-11 Shopping Festival in China, the sales of raw and fresh agricultural products grew nearly tenfold. It is quite difficult to ensure the supply chain of raw and fresh agricultural products. When the sales are enjoying a dramatic growth, the on-line selling of other rural specialties will be easier. People are then surrounded by many more entrepreneurial opportunities, including means of online services, microfinance and other models of consumption introduced into their villages.

In the health care field, Ali Health, Wuhan Downtown Hospital in Hubei province and Jointown Pharmaceutical Group[2] have established rural distance medical pilots.

Villagers can log in the On-line Hospital on the website YAO.TMALL.COM. They can get access to the registration and diagnosis services. At present, on-line hospitals provide diagnosis services of 13 medical detection departments, including gastroenterology, endocrinology, Chinese medicine and dermatology departments. Apart from this, electronic prescriptions will then generated. Dispensed by Ehaoyao On-line Pharmacy, a sub-branch of Jointown Pharmaceutical Group, orders of medicine will be gathered and sorted in the storage center in Wuhan. Next, the medicine will be wrapped in parcels and delivered to the counties. Through Rookie Logistics, the parcels will then be delivered to villages.

In the Ngari region of Tibet and Shigatse of Lhasa, Alibaba public welfare fund, jointly working with the Peking University People's Hospital, also initiated a distance medical care program in these areas.

If patients get a serious illness, the program makes it possible for patients to find matching medical resources in counties and even in cities.

Of course, it is reasonable to make a combination between medical care and the insurance and borrowing. This may help to avoid some diseases caused by poverty. Early detection means that you can get treatments at an initial stage so as not to make things worse.

Now, the greatest challenge may lie in how to fulfill the practice of electronic prescription diagnosis. The traditional medical system is relatively conservative. That's the major problem. The technology is not a thorny issue anymore. However, what we see right now is still at a stage of trials.

5.1.2 Expanding Customer Volume

With a large number of residents in rural China, Alibaba wants to get much more users from this group in order to engage in its business and its ecosystem.

[2]Jointown Pharmaceutical Group Co., Ltd. mainly operates products of Western medicine, Chinese traditional medicine and medical devices; it is a large-scale enterprise group focusing on clients of medical institutions, wholesalers and retail pharmacies and providing information, logistics and other value-added services.

For example, employment is a very important aspect. From the latest Taobao Village report released in 2016, an estimated number of 840,000 jobs was generated by 1311 Taobao villages.

In terms of rural Taobao, it might solve employment problems for at least ten thousands of families. There are 30,000 (2018) Rural Taobao ecommerce service stations, which means that several ten thousands households of families are operating the business. By the way, not all of them are full-timers. Moreover, multiple Internet platforms, local rural e-commerce practitioners and service providers in China will make increase by ten times. Besides, the sellers who sell agricultural products on Alibaba platforms have reached a number of at least 900,000 (2016).

5.1.3 Building a Logistic System as Infrastructure

For e-commerce practitioners, the key still lies in the construction of the logistics line, especially the last kilometer. For Alibaba, this can be a large-scale presence, and it can be regarded as a combination of services and a plan to expand its business. Rural Strategy proposes rural residents enjoy the same delivery services as citizens.

This kind of co-construction has evolved quickly into a system composed of several different parties, including Rookie Logistics (logistics service platform belong to Alibaba), local logistics companies, service providers, governments and local communities.

For Alibaba, the whole process has not been only about logistics, and it is designed to optimize the service system in an all-round way. Just to take rural logistics business provided by Rookie Logistics as an example, over 2015, the network has successfully covered more than 300 counties. The haulage time between cities and counties should be controlled within 48 h while the time between counties and villages should be within 24 h. Of course, in western regions, we will face more challenges, so we have to take the local conditions into full consideration and we are looking forward to local innovative models.

Meanwhile, Alibaba cooperated with local governments, especially county level government. For example, each county level government has input money and labor, for instance, granting one or two million for each of villages as transportation subsidies.

About communities, I learned that some villagers would take initiative actions to tackle the problem. For instance, the servers in the e-commerce service stations will, by taking turns, go to fetch parcels in counties every day. Besides, villagers who need to come back home every day can also help with it. It is also necessary to give full play to some unused transportations, including long-distance buses for delivery services in some remote mountain villages.

Actually, they are quite similar to traditional ways of local communities in China. In history, in rural areas with canal system of Jiangsu and Zhejiang provinces, when peasants drive their boats to go shopping at downtown, meanwhile, they often ask the neighbors all along the river if they are in need of something. If so, they will help to buy some daily necessities for them. The Internet has just revived this kind of help and assistance relationship. It can be said that the so-called sharing economy is closely related to this tradition in villages.

Furthermore, nowadays, empowered by big data analysis, they are well positioned to make more precise predictions on the demands. I found that big data was useful for analyzing demands of rural residents and ensuring more accurate judgments. This might be also helpful in filling up the shortage of infrastructure facilities and ensuring better delivery services and satisfaction of demands.

In fact, they are incorporating it into a larger system of technology, or in other words, Internet global facilities. For instance, when we incorporate it into the data calculation of Rookie Logistics, SkyNet (logistics data), EarthNet (storage and logistics centers) and HumanNet (service stations), how can we further optimize the configuration and the system of express sheets? In every village, Taobao Village Errands are more than just one individual. Supported by the data provided by Taobao and even Alibaba departments, they can get instant access to the demands of villagers. In this respect, they might do a better job than village chiefs or even cadres in counties. They are able to observe what is going on in neighboring villages, counties and even provinces. What's more, big data analysis will be helpful in improving their sales, client managements and making decisions.

At the same time, they also play a role as data collectors and analysts, which in turn provides feedback to the background database and forms a forward cycle.

In this way, more targeted services will be offered in the future in the field of on-line finance, on-line health care and other sectors.

Everyone has his or her own perspectives on the targeted poverty alleviation. They are quite different. On the basis of big data, the widely applied new technology can be really conducive to identifying poverty population and causes. In this way, these people in poverty can benefit a lot from the on-line services. However, there should be some premises, like existing data for analysis and network infrastructure facilities. Some first-hand researches are needed to be conducted on these projects. We will need some more time but the overall direction is right.

5.1.4 New Innovation to Benefit Their Existing Business Model

For example, in the field of finance, it is commonly known that in the period from 2015 to 2018, Ant Financial was set to invest 1 billion RMB to show its support for more than 100,000 Village Errands through the product of Taobao Village Shopkeeper. Among the investments, some are also devoted to serve as the loans for Taobao Village partners. Some of the partners are college students who returned to their hometown to start their businesses. The loans can be used as the advance working capital for villagers online shopping. But how to make convenient process of application for microloans?

In 2016, MYbank president, Mr. Yu, invited me to pay a visit to Junying Village in Xiamen Province. In Junying, I had the chance to check upon the online application system of microloans.

MYbank, the Ministry of Public Security and the NCF Group[3] have been working together on this project. They adopted the technology of online personal identity verification. For instance, instruments are used to scan the face of villagers and then link it to the online identity card system. In this way, rural residences can directly apply for microloans.

Such inclusive financial innovations can bypass some restrictions on online financial services by the Central Bank of China. At that time, this solution became an institutional innovation under technical and policy conditions. This way facilitated new attempts for Alibaba's online financial services.

In many rural areas, Taobao Village Errands are operating Wangnong (Famer's) Loans business. Besides, under the guarantee of Taobao Village Errands, villagers can apply for microloans through Ant Finance.

Although the Village Errands get a commission, they still keep cautious. Based on the consumption data and observations in daily life, they are empowered to find who has the potential to start his business in villages. They crave for a win-win situation by jointly working with talents from all walks of life, like stock farming, crop farming, tourism, handicraft industry and so on.

Therefore, Outlook of Alibaba Rural Strategy is delivering urban online services to residents in rural China, and gets 20% residences in rural China access to Alibaba service and its ecosystem from 2014 to 2019.

As an international organization listed on Wall-street, Alibaba's rural strategy faces some problems. Its two main challenges are: (1) How to create an ecosystem between Alibaba Rural Strategy with local rural ecommerce platform? (2) How to maintain the balance of interests between Alibaba Group, local governments and center government in China?

About the first question, take the relationship between SEA (Suichang Ecommerce Association,) and Alibaba Group as an example, from 2010 to 2014, Suichang Ecommerce Association and their business network based on Taobao. com from Alibaba, but from Oct 2014 to 2017, when Alibaba Rural Strategy was launched, there was competition between SEA and Alibaba. For example, SEA have to start their own supply chain out of Taobao.com ecosystem, because there is a voice from Alibaba about stopping cooperation between Taobao and SEA. But after 3 years practices of Alibaba Rural Strategy, the director of Rural Taobao (a department of Alibaba Group who leading the Alibaba Rural Strategy) found that it was very hard to handle the business in county and village levels with limited human resource, public relationship and other resources, because of huge scale

---

[3]NCF Group, based in Beijing and serves the entire country. As part of its globalization initiatives, is a comprehensive FinTech services group.

(around 2800 counties with more than 900 thousands of villages), diversity and unbalance development in China. One of solution of this challenge is close cooperation with local rural ecommerce platform again. As a mile stone, in Nov 2017, Alibaba invested around 8 million US dollars on Ganjie (Part of Suichang Ecommerce Association), to be its second biggest share holder. With this cooperation, SEA could be empowered by Alibaba though not only investment but also ecosystem system of supply chain, technology and so on. Meanwhile, SEA helps Alibaba to handle local partner's treatment, local public relationship, local service ecosystem, innovation of local business model and supply chain and so on. It's a good example to explain latest adapt cooperation between Alibaba and local rural ecommerce platform.

But, to the second question about the cooperation between Alibaba Group, local governments and center government in China, a long term vision should be drawn. In China's complex political context from local government level to central government level, it's very difficult to make a general vision and implementation strategy.

From late 2014 to early 2015, Jack Ma led delegations to visit provincial secretaries and county sub-prefects, and received positive responses. In just a few months, Alibaba signed strategic cooperation agreements with governments in nearly 20 provinces, autonomous regions and municipalities directly under the central government. The rural development strategy received strong support, and authorities at provincial and municipal levels have played significant roles in rallying these flowing forces. From the county-level ecommerce summits that have been held for several times and the willingness and readiness of governments at all levels, we can tell how eager they are to be a part of it. This also shows how local authorities at the county level and at the village level respect and appreciate the opportunities brought by Alibaba.

The cooperation between rural Taobao and government focuses on addressing the problems arising in the process of rural e-commerce and relevant industrial development. In pushing ahead with the cooperation with enterprises, a wide range of business had been carried out with a mutual trust tie built. With the collective efforts of Rural Taobao and county-level governments, "four sets of projects" have been formulated and "two sites" have been divided. The first one referred to the "first-leader project". A leading group consisting of officials from relevant administrative departments was established to promote the new concept of Rural Taobao across all branches, reconsider the development direction of departmental benefits, coordinated the business group model featured by rural Taobao industrial products downstream and agricultural products upstream, and more importantly, to bring out a batch of officials equipped with e-commerce knowledge and innovative thinking and a specialized local e-commerce team. The second was propaganda program. With the help of village broadcasting, blackboard, wall paintings and other grass-root level publicity methods, Taobao can appear in every aspect of villagers' life. The third referred as the training program. County-level leaders would attend the 3-day county magistrate training class offered by Taobao University in Hangzhou, and in addition to field research, county-level officials

Fig. 5.2 The Changshan county government intends to localize Rural Taobao by giving too much guidance, an idea not recognized by Alibaba Group. *Source* Author

would also participate the training in local areas or carry out investigation and researches related to Rural Taobao. In some counties with rapid development in Rural Taobao, even township-level officials were required to attend training. The fourth was a set of e-commerce operation project outlining the implementation strategies (including motivation schemes) for long-term development. For example, county-level operation centers and local governments worked out a plan to build learning mutual-aid groups.

During its localization process, the Rural Business Unit of Alibaba is both collaborating and competing with local governments. While Alibaba depends on the local authority to implement strategy, local governments are also a source of risk. They may use Alibaba's resources in order to pursue their own interests and vision. Therefore, Alibaba needs to keep firm control over the departments and divisions at all levels in its rural development strategy, while flexibly dealing with local issues, without being overly controlled by local governments or assimilated by local relations. In a word, Alibaba's top priority is to ensure that partners and local service teams put the objectives of Alibaba over local government interests (Fig. 5.2).

This delicate relation is also seen in the case of Changshan county, as we have discussed before. In July, 2015, Changshan introduced the first standardized rules regarding county-level e-commerce—*Development Specifications and Evaluation*

Standards of Rural E-Commerce.[4] The Changshan county government proposed to "localize Rural Taobao" and build a Rural Taobao system that was controlled by government at all levels. As the most important component of its strategy, government-based localization instituted a four-tiered tutoring system. That meant that each Rural Taobao partner at the village level must be supervised by four tutors—one from county government as the chief tutor in the county level, official leaders in townships as the second tutor, village secretary as the operating tutor as third one and e-commerce enterprises as the fourth tutor. A responsible person of Rural Taobao in Zhejiang stated that this was only the wishful thinking of the local government; it was worth learning it didn't reflect Rural Taobao's ideas regarding its future development. This case is found in many regions. Being too closely involved with local authorities will make Rural Taobao prone to problems. Conflicts of interest arise when the relatives and friends of local government officials send files or seek personal connections to be a partner. If they actually made it, Rural Taobao would have access to more resources and progress its work more smoothly with local governments and communities, as Changshan government encouraged the whole family to participate in the service station for rural e-commerce. Nevertheless, in this way, grey zones will abound, which is in stark contrast to Alibaba's corporate culture that champions open, fair and transparent competition. In the meantime, in order to create sales in a short time to make a good beginning for rural e-commerce service stations, local governments will finish their procurements online through the village-level rural e-commerce service station. For example, the county government of Changshan explicitly stipulated that official goods must be purchased online in principle, and materials of village construction projects should also be purchased online, as a preference.

Ideally, the local government (county level and village level) have to face challenges and cooperation with digitalization. The local government supported cooperation between Alibaba Group, local ecommerce platform and Rural Taobao Partners by investment and buying their services (e.g. ecommerce training for local residents and ecommerce service stations at village level) and founding of database. With the data collection and analysis through local scale, the different departments of local ecommerce platform scan catch key issues of industrial transformation through local and big scale of trends of online services and provide better infrastructure, public services and investment context. Unfortunately, without deep understanding of data and online services and a shortage of professionals on digitalization area, some local governments usually just focus on the data of this new industrial transformation with political benefit (e.g. good results of rural ecommerce help the county mayor or director of this department to get support from high authority), and try to expand the rural ecommerce with kind of political movements without logic of marketing system.

---

[4]"农村电子商务"常山标准"出台-中国国际电子商务网" [Rural e-commerce with "Changshan standard"—China International Electronic Commerce Network]. 2015. Ec.Com.Cn. http://www.ec.com.cn/article/ncds/201509/5358_1.html.

Meanwhile, this conduct fails to agree with the vested interests of local government, for offline enterprises that once depended on government procurement to develop and thrive were severely impacted. Voices against Rural Taobao were heard everywhere then, blaming the latter for not paying taxes to local governments and crashing real economies.

These are the challenges that the "flowing forces", with Alibaba's Rural Taobao at its core, have encountered during its localization in the information era. However, judging from the rapid development of village-level e-commerce service stations of Rural Taobao, none of these problems have suppressed the strong momentum of it. Here we should be aware of the strong support from the provincial government, municipal government to the county government. Mo Wenjian, a well-known practitioner in rural e-commerce, once said that: "the county subprefect can quickly get promoted if they support rural e-commerce". Indeed, governments at local levels need to find a new approach to industrial upgrading, and poverty alleviation through rural e-commerce. This was given much importance by the central government, and became the key to improving their performance. Against such a backdrop, rural e-commerce is strongly backed by governments at all levels—from 2015 to 2018, supporting policies have been introduced in those areas, and Alibaba delegations, visited many provinces, and Taobao University has played a significant role in deepening the understanding of rural e-commerce and bringing forward those supporting policies.

List of policy papers that were introduced by local governments in terms of rural e-commerce:
Sichuan Province
2015.5.22—*Opinions on Promoting E-Commerce Development in Sichuan Province.*
Jiangsu Province
2015.8.11—*Opinions on Supporting E-Commerce in Starting Businesses and Creating Jobs.*
Guangxi Zhuang Nationality Autonomous Region
2015.5.28—*Notification of Printing and Distributing Action Plans of Rural E-Commerce from 2015 to 2017 in the Region.*
Zhejiang Province
2015.4.29—*Key Points of Developing E-Commerce in Zhejiang Province in 2015.*
Fujian Province
Key Points of E-Commerce in Fujian Province in 2015.
Jiangxi Province
Opinions of Jiangxi Provincial Committee of the CPC's Rural Work Committee and Business Office of Jiangxi Province on Stepping up Rural E-Commerce Development in Jiangxi.

Hubei Province
Notification of Implementing E-Commerce Training Program for the Young People in Rural Areas of Hubei.
Chongqing
2015.3.6—*Notification of Commerce Administration of Chongqing Municipality about Printing and Distributing Action Plans of Bringing E-Commerce to Rural Areas in Chongqing Municipality.*

Source The author.

This has again created delicate relations between the central and local governments, whose roles have evolved during informatization, despite the fact that rural e-commerce is integrating swiftly with local governments and organizations (provinces, municipalities, counties, towns and townships, villages), and that the central government is competing for more power of guidance and leadership on the stipulation of policies, regulations and rules and the allocation of funds. The central government wants to take control of the whole process of informatization and be able to formulate emergency plans.

List of policy papers that were issued by the central government concerning rural e-commerce from 2014 to 2015:
【The State Council】
2015.8.7—*Opinions on Accelerating Transformation of Agricultural Development Patterns.*
2015.7.9—*Several Opinions on Using Big Data to Strengthen Service of and Supervision over Market Players.*
2015.7.4—*Guiding Principles on Actively Promoting the "Internet+" Action Plan.*
2015.6.21—*Opinions on Supporting Migrant Workers and Other People to Return Home to Start Businesses.*
2015.6.20—*Guiding Principles on Promoting the Sound and Rapid Development of Cross-Border E-Commerce.*
2015.6.1—*Guiding Principles on Pressing Ahead with the Pilot Project of Rural Community Development.*
2015.5.7—*Opinions on Vigorously Developing E-Commerce and Moving Faster to Foster New Engines of Economic Development.*
2015.4.3—*Decision on Deepening the Comprehensive Reform of Supply and Marketing Cooperatives.*
2015.2.1—*Several Opinions on Speeding up Agricultural Modernization by Strengthening Reform and Innovation.*

2015.1.22—*Opinions on Guiding the Sound Development of Rural Property Rights Exchange Market.*
2014.12.8 *Opinions On Further Mobilizing All Sectors of Society to Contribute to Poverty Alleviation and Development.*
2014.11.21—*Opinions on How to Guide the Orderly Circulation of Rural Land Management Rights and the Development of Appropriate Scaled-up Operation of Agriculture.*
2014.9.12—*Medium and Long-term Planning for Logistics Development (2015–2020).*
2014.4.24—*Several Opinions on Serving Agriculture, the Rural Areas and Farmers by Financial Development.*
2014.1.20—*Several Opinions on Deepening Rural Reform in an All-round Way and Accelerating Agricultural Modernization.*
2014.1.25—*Opinions on Innovating Mechanisms and Steadily Promoting Rural Poverty Alleviation and Development Works.*
【The Ministry of Commerce】
2015.7.24—*Notification of the Ministry of Commerce on Releasing the List of Model E-Commerce Enterprises from 2015 to 2016.*
2015.7.21—*Opinions on the Implementation of Intelligent Logistics and Distribution System.*
2015.7.13—*Opinions on Carrying out Comprehensive Demonstration Work of Bringing E-Commerce into Rural Areas in 2015.*
2015.4.3—*Key Points of E-Commerce in 2015.*
2014.2.20—*Notice on the Promotion and Application of National Business Information and Public Service Platform for Agricultural Products.*
2013.11.21—*Opinions on Promoting the Application of E-Commerce.*
【Ministry of Industry and Information Technology】
2012.3.27—*The 12th Five-Year Plan of E-Commerce.*

Source The author.

On October 9, 2016, Chinese President Xi Jinping stressed at the meeting of the Political Bureau of the CPC Central Committee that “we should accelerate the independent innovation of network information technology, promote economic development by digital economy, strengthen the network management, improve security and defense capabilities in cyberspace, promote social governance through the use of network information technology, increase Chinese people’s say over cyberspace and power of rule-making, and make strenuous efforts toward achieving the goal of making China an Internet power".[5] This is the unequivocal attitude of the highest decision-making department of the central government toward the role of Internet in national and social governance.

In the meantime, local government adopts another strategy to confront challenges in the information era: build an information bank. Through this approach, it can closely monitor and respond to local communities, so as to check and balance the flowing powers (Alibaba and other organizations). Building a local information bank for rural e-commerce is an attempt worthy of our expectation. Alibaba is building an information bank that covers localities and the whole country by sourcing various data from consumption, loans, medical care, elderly care, etc., and reaching out to local government departments. By sharing data with local governments, Alibaba and other conglomerates make their data collection process legitimate. They aid local governments to monitor and manage local affairs and lay solid foundations for their decision-making. "Smart City"[6] and "Graphical County Governance"[7] are the most prominent examples of their efforts. From the perspective of central government, the data that Alibaba has collected from different regions is more comprehensive, timely and efficient than central authorities, and it has more powerful data analysis capabilities. The central government is actively preparing for a national data center (Fig. 5.3).

Localization is also an integral part of Alibaba's rural strategy. Let's take the Rural Taobao business unit for example. Its major driving forces derive from the Ironclad Chinese Suppliers Group. The responsible person of the Group, regional chiefs and coworkers in cities and counties all share strong sentiments towards their hometown. Most of them are raised in rural areas, volunteer to work for Rural Taobao and go back to their hometown to develop rural e-commerce. They are more familiar with the place where they grow up, and they have local connections. Most importantly, they need to recruit 100 thousand rural Taobao parters capable of running service stations in full time. This job entails a firm grasp of government-business relations and indigenous culture. Currently, rural Taobao is introducing a new business model with "service" at its core, and is committed to let

---

[5]"习近平:加快推进网络信息技术自主创新 朝着建设网络强国目标不懈努力-新华网" [Xi Jinping: Accelerate independent innovation of network information technology Make unremitting efforts towards the goal of making China an Internet power]. 2016. News.Xinhuanet.Com. http://news.xinhuanet.com/politics/2016-10/09/c_1119682204.htm.

[6]Alibaba and Ant Financial launched an "urban services" module. Centering around the innovation-driven development strategy, Alipay focuses on applying payment, data and other technical capabilities to specific scenarios in the smart city. Alibaba will make mobility and data capabilities more accessible to those institutions that are involved in the construction of smart cities.

[7]"The Graphical County Governance" is a big data-based and visualized economic analysis tool that targets at governments and their departments at all levels. It relies on a powerful cloud computing platform and big data analysis capabilities. By mining Internet-generated and government data, it can generate a pattern with comprehensive indicators including population, rural areas, consumption and e-commerce development, and export this pattern in a highly visualized way to provide a clear overview of local economy and people's living conditions.

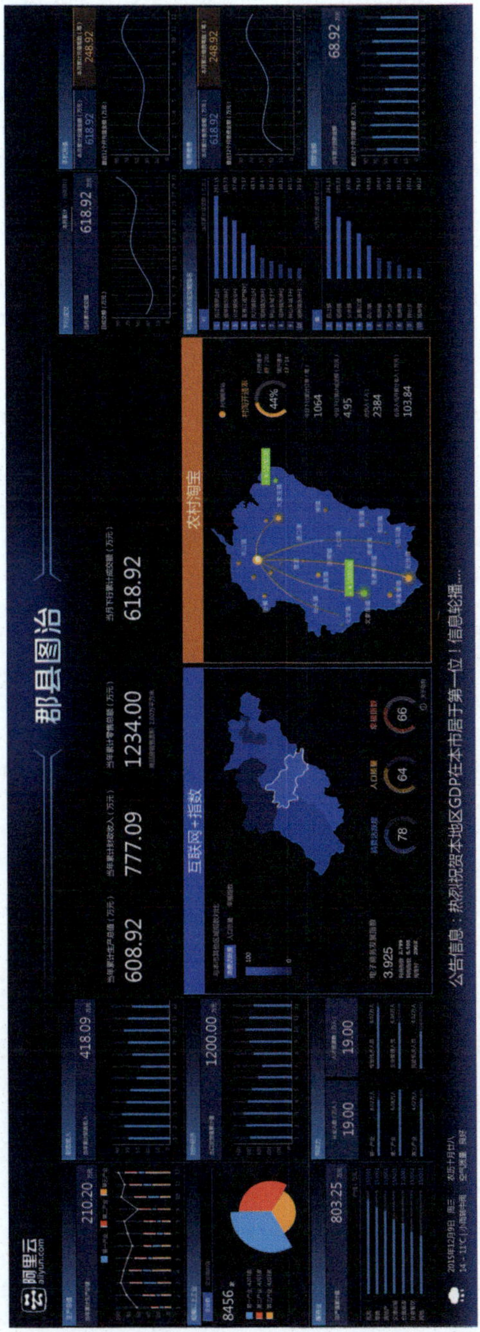

Fig. 5.3 Information displayer of Alibaba's "Graphical County Governance" 9. *Source* AliReaerch and AliCloud (https://data.aliyun.com/visual/yuntu-jx)

Alibaba's whole service system go deeply into rural areas. To make this attempt deliver, partners of rural Taobao should be more grass-rooted. Alibaba leverages its platform as a globalized Internet giant and fully integrates local resources. This process is bound to confront with indigenous culture and ideology. Another example to illustrate this point is the "Rural Culture Festival" held in Kunming by rural Taobao, Alibaba. By utilizing the network of more than 16 thousand rural service stations, rural Taobao enriches country life, develops local culture and boosts the tourism industry.[8] And it takes a further step to make the urban-rural cultural exchanges a pivot of strategic importance. These efforts result in the flow of ecological culture.

The central government is, however, put in a disadvantageous position, because the data that Alibaba has collected from different regions is more comprehensive, timely and efficient than that of the government, as it also has more powerful data analysis capabilities. It is evident how eager the central government is to acquire more data. Grasping and using network data by establishing database has become an important premise for national and social governance. Thus, in the information society, the Internet has penetrated the traditional top-down governance system that once prevailed in the central and local governments, the urban and rural areas are making strides towards a new stage that features new types of localization, community recognition and regional reconstruction. Manuel Castells has noted that local and regional governments with more flexible market players had remained closely related to their identity foundation, they were more adaptable to the flow of powers in various forms and the governance pattern in the information era. The executive power of the state bureaucratic system is likely to be replaced by more flexible local governments, market and social powers. Local governments will be involved in the regional restructuring process and govern local communities through inter-regional cooperation and competition.

5.2 Establish of Alibaba Rural Strategy

Zhang Yong, the then CFO of Alibaba, announced Alibaba Rural Strategy to establish 1000 county-level operating centers and 100,000 village-level service stations with 10 billion RMB investments for the ultimate realization of new urbanization after his signing of strategic cooperative agreement with Zhejiang Province on October 13th, 2014. However, people in the industry really doubted how the rapidly expanding urban e-commerce magnate achieve its new rural ambition. The industry had several questions:

[8] "我们筹备几个月,只为给你呈现一场完美的乡村文化盛宴!" [Rural Taobao: Several Months' Preparation to Present A Feast of Indigenous Culture]. 2016. Mp.Weixin.Qq.Com. http://mp.weixin.qq.com/s?__biz=MzAxNzI5NjI0MA==&mid=2650283494&idx=1&sn=3b6e101c94837e91b8b0ce90ff595c27&scene=5&srcid=0804ASTWWnaUiD2Kmue1Ekfc#rd.

Primarily, how to bring out a batch of front-line staff familiar with rural e-commerce business in a short time?

Secondly, is the main purpose of the rural strategy a stock market strategy for Alibaba's listing in New York?

Thirdly, how can the rural strategy link with the organizational framework of Alibaba, a corporate listing in America? How can such a group complete relevant business re-engineering and resources inclination disposition in line with rural strategy in a short time?

Alibaba had launched a quick layout in response to the first question and created a new department. Employees from the "China Suppliers Iron Army" from Alibaba Wholesales Marketplace (B2B business division) were given the opportunity to choose whether to join the new endeavor Rural Taobao.

"China Suppliers Iron Army" refers to the direct selling team of China suppliers services introduced by Alibaba Group in 2000. As a "ground troop" under Alibaba Group's canvassing for introducing e-commerce B2B model to SMEs, "China Suppliers Iron Army" provided foreign trade e-commerce services for SMEs in China, which laid a solid foundation for the initial development of Alibaba Group.

On October 15th, the second day after Alibaba's announcement of its rural strategy, Jack Ma together with Peng Lei, Alibaba CHO and Sophie Wu, president of Alibaba Wholesales Marketplace, attended the commemorative activity for senior employees of China Supplier Division who had been working for Alibaba Group for more than 10 years. At the ceremony, Jack Ma addressed his first speech since Alibaba's listing in NYSE in September where he again mentioned Alibaba Rural Strategy as an earnest request for mobilizing colleagues to join in the rural revolution:

"The electric cookers currently sold in Supply and Marketing Cooperatives, as I see in Lishui, Zhejiang, are expensive, old-fashioned and of poor quality, while what we sell on Taobao are cheaper and with good quality. What we are thinking about is to sell urban products to rural areas and then sell rural products to urban cities, which is of considerable significance. It is our job to spread our understanding of Internet, Internet knowledge and urban civilization across any small village. Nothing is more meaningful than this undertaking, because we will then renovate the life of thousands and thousands of people", said he in all earnestness.

By then, "China Suppliers Iron Army" emerged as the main driving force of rural strategy from the team taking charge of the founding of Rural Taobao. The system was divided into two major areas (Northern areas and Southern areas) with appointed directors in each province directly governing several cities and counties. Most employees from this division were born in villages, retained in cities as a result of education and entered into Alibaba Group. Many of them volunteered to Rural Taobao, regardless of the difficult conditions and limited labor. As the division was newly set up, having not yet earned profits, the employees who switched departments experienced a decrease in income despite increased responsibilities and longer working hours. For example, In Heilongjiang, a province with 13 sub-provincial administrative units, 19 county-level cities, 47 counties, 69 districts, 464 towns, 480 townships and 9157 villages, only 10 people were initially appointed to implement the project of Rural Taobao, thus the workload is evident. The backbone of Rural Taobao consisted mainly of elderly employees, ranging from 30 to 40 years old. As they returned to the once familiar countryside, they were full of motivation and could quickly assimilate into local governments and get along well with local villagers.

As for the second question on whether the main purpose of the rural strategy is a stock market strategy for Alibaba's listing in New York? In an interview in the small hours of "Double 11" day of 2014, Lu Zhaoxi mentioned that "600 million rural users may bring out another Taobao and another Alibaba".[9] From October of 2014 when Alibaba announced its rural strategy to March of 2015, the team, under the leadership of Jack Ma, had signed strategic cooperation framework agreements at an unusual rate with over 10 provincial and municipal governments. The reasons that rural e-commerce has been laid out rapidly are as follows:

First and foremost, rural e-commerce boasts a huge market potential because of the low starting point. According to statistics, the county commodity consumption reached 5 trillion in 2013 (724 billion USD) and the first half of 2014 topped 4.9 trillion (710 billion USD). Meanwhile, the total trading volume of agricultural products entering wholesales market annually totaled 3 trillion (434 billion USD), among which that of green vegetable accounting for 362 billion (52 billion USD). However, Chinese rural users only contributed a mere of 5 billion RMB (724 million USD) in the "Double 11" day of 2014 on the platform of Alibaba Group whose market share dominates 80% of the Chinese-commerce market. Furthermore, the order of purchasing urban products in rural areas only accounted for 10% of the total trading volume and the sales volume of agricultural products on the Alibaba e-commerce platform in 2014 was about 50 billion RMB (7 billion USD), less than 2.5% of the 2 trillion (289 billion) more online sales volume of Alibaba Group at the same year.

In addition, rural e-commerce will help to mitigate the scarcity of product and services as well as hollowing-out problem in China's rural areas. It provides an opportunity to break out of the stalemate of unbalanced development as a result of China's urbanization for the past 30 years. It remains as the shared aspiration for business magnates led by Alibaba, governments of all levels, local e-commerce new farmers, local household farmers and cooperatives, rural migrate workers, college-educated, and ordinary farmers to deliver a better off livelihood equal with that in urban cities for villagers and people in small towns. As economist Zhou Qiren put it, "A vast majority of people are distributed in county and rural levels and 65% of China's total population holds rural household register. A large number of rural residents moving to cities and towns actually left the counties".[10] Based on the target put forward by the World Bank in 2015 that is delivering the fruit of

[9]"陆兆禧现身直播间 6亿农村人将创造另一个阿里". [Interview with Lu Zhaoxi, 600 million rural users may bring out another Taobao and another Alibaba] 2014. Zjnews.Zjol.Com.Cn. http://zjnews.zjol.com.cn/system/2014/11/11/020351463.shtml.

[10]"周其仁:让互联网惠及更多人" [Zhou Qiren; Let Internet benefit more people]. 2014. News. Ifeng.Com. http://news.ifeng.com/a/20141022/42264895_0.shtml.

poverty alleviation and common prosperity to 40% of the moderate and low-level income groups, China shall focus on lifting elder people, children and young people (the main force of production) lacking of technology know-how, accounting for 45–50% of county and below population dominated by moderate and low-income group, out of poverty. To materialize the goal of delivering the livelihood equal with that of urban residents to rural people, it is essential for Internet and rural e-commerce to leverage their power and resolve serious social problems result from hollowing-out in rural areas at the meantime.

The magic of Internet and rural e-commerce has radiated from urban cities to rural areas, bringing in services and consumption with brisk labor demand in rural areas short of young workforce. Rural e-commerce has mobilized an increasing number of people to bring benefits and services to more people. In addition, it plays a vital part in integrating the urban-rural information, logistics, talents and capital channels. There are still over 70% (hundreds of millions of) of rural residents without access to the Internet, let alone e-commence.

Finally, just as the "Click-and-mortar" mentioned by Jack Ma at the Hanover Conference in Germany, rural e-commerce provides an exciting opportunity for rural infrastructure construction.[11] Jin Jianhang, president of Alibaba, pointed out precisely that "counties and towns in China are as prosperous as Europe, while villages are as poor as Africa".[12] It is urgent to include county-level economy into the coordination and overall planning of metropolitan integration. Serving rural residents and bringing out rural e-commerce + beautiful countryside has emerged as the orientation directed by China's county-level economy as well as the Alibaba Group, and the docking of county-level economy with the potential market of 2 billion global online consumers in the future. Looking forward, the three strategies of Alibaba Group, internationalization, big data, as well as Alibaba O2O (Yintai and Suning Commerce Group), it is evident that the integration with rural public infrastructure, commercial infrastructure and logistics infrastructure will further boost the asset price of rural resources (land and other and fixed assets).

How to integrate rural strategy with the organizational framework of Alibaba, a corporate listed in America? How can such a group complete relevant business re-engineering and resources inclination disposition in line with rural strategy in a short time? That is related to the theory of bringing forth the new through the old in Taobao and other e-commerce platform. Accordingly, Jack Ma and CEO Zhang Yong took the command personally to integrate resources. In addition to a Rural

[11]"马云:未来的生意将是C2B模式 - 财经 - 中国日报网" [Jack Ma: the future of business is the model of C2B]. 2015. Caijing.Chinadaily.Com.Cn. http://caijing.chinadaily.com.cn/2015-03/16/content_19824786.htm.

[12]"阿里巴巴总裁金建杭:美丽乡村 + 农村电商,再造中国农村-资讯-阿里研究" [Alibaba president Jin Jianhang: beautiful rural + rural electricity business, rebuilding China's rural areas]. 2015. Aliresearch.Com. http://www.aliresearch.com/blog/article/detail/id/20537.html.

Taobao Business Division, a Virtual Business Division was set up with the collective efforts of 17 business departments under the coordination of Rural Taobao, with the shared commitment to promote Alibaba Rural Strategy. The strategy can be outlined as follows:

(1) Offering college students the opportunity to become entrepreneurs in their hometown

The number of college students enrolled for rural Taobao partners reached 18,000 in 3 months from the program initiation in the early of 2015 to May. Participants were from 32 counties, with at least 500 students enrolled in each county. These well-educated young people will take the role of leader of future. According to Sun Lijun, one of the directors of Rural Taobao, over 1000 Taobao Village e-commerce service stations had been set up during the same timeframe. What's more, one of the rural Taobao partners, a young man in Bingchuan, Yunnan province, gained over 13,000 RMB (1884 USD) in the month of April 2015, and there were another dozens of partners earned 5000 RMB (724 USD) per month. By September 2015, 4 out of 37 rural Taobao partners in Xinxian, Henan province earned over 10,000 RMB (1449 USD) in the first month.

The target set up by Sun Lijun was to help 10–20% of these college rural Taobao partners gain an annual income of more than 10,000 RMB (1449 USD). It was the core objective of Rural Taobao to foster a favorable employment and entrepreneurship for young college returnees as Sun said. Rural Taobao was just the beginning. In addition to infrastructure and platform, the monthly group sharing, communication and training among the rural Taobao partners in town and county level has brought opportunity for common development.

(2) Young people encouraged to become entrepreneurs in their home town

There is a great advantage in mobilizing more young people equipped with education and new ideas to carve out new business in their hometown and to popularize e-commerce and agricultural technology. This can be done in a scientific manner so as to cultivate pioneers in casting off poverty and achieving prosperity in rural areas.

First, farmers were equipped with technology know-how and organizational management skills. Taking Shouguang as an example, the application of gaseous fertilizer, temperature controllers, ozone sterilization and other high-tech equipment helped to save both time and labor for farmers. The greenhouses covered an area of 800,000 mu (533.3 km squared). The rural e-commerce, urban-rural information flow as well as the efforts of young returnees from cities are elements for new agriculture. They provide strategic guidance in many areas including market research, production project approval, agricultural materials allocation, information management, personnel organization, quality control, supply chain, logistics, network marketing and feedback.

According to the *Shouguang Daily* newspaper on September 9th, 2015, Zhang Wenguang[13], a young greenhouse planter of Hualong county with a 14-mu greenhouse and an investment of 700,000 RMB, could generate 400,000 RMB per quarter even after the deduction of fertilizer and labor force costs, completely making back his investment in two years. Therefore, he, together with a group of other aggressive villagers with long-term sight, knowledge and brain, started to invest this undertaking. Zhang Wenguang admitted that he desired to take a lead by investing a large sum of money that encouraged villagers like him to become prosperous through agricultural equipment development. Once villagers "tasted the sweetness", the path to prosperity would become widely accepted. Thus, cooperatives and agricultural enterprises were organized so that villagers could easily grasp the business opportunities for agricultural development in a new model featured by modernized management and scientific research.

Alibaba Rural Strategy is designed to enable villagers start new undertakings and bring forth new ideas without leaving their hometown. By improving online platform systems, Alibaba has successfully provided capital, information channels and marketing platforms for rural entrepreneurs. A comprehensive platform with industrial products downstream and agricultural products upstream has been established. On top of the rapid growth of Taobao and Rural Taobao, the "Brand Products Going Countryside" campaigned by T-mall pushing forward in April 2015 had also generated agreeable results with over 10,000 domestic brands enrolling for the project. Looking at the agricultural products upstream platform, Mobile Rural Taobao O2O model, together with Taobao, T-mall and Juhuasuan, has been launched.

(3) Through rural e-commerce services centers, other Business Division of Alibaba can help to provide local services for villagers

Let's imagine this scene: if a rural elder comes to a city to see a doctor, he can book a railway ticket, bus ticket and hotel in Alitrip, and his medical appointment in advance of his visit. In terms of providing cheaper mobile phone fee payment, the next step will be to open up the operation points of Ali Telecom, a department of Alibaba, through rural Taobao partners, thus bringing the benefits of complete Internet infrastructure services to villagers. That being the case, people in rural areas can also enjoy more economic telecommunication and data traffic services and contract phones services provided by the various telecommunication companies. Besides, villagers can close a deal online and receive products via delivery services, which is particularly convenient for villagers without access to urban offline direct-sale store services.

---

[13] "农业发展需要有胆有识的年轻人 _寿光评论_新闻中心_中国寿光网" [Agricultural development requires a young man with knowledge]. 2015. Sgnet.Cc. http://www.sgnet.cc/news/201509/11/639279.shtml.

(4) Leveraging the cooperation with local government, Alibaba Rural Strategy is designed to achieve the layout of the rural e-commerce ecosystem

The cooperation between rural Taobao and the government focuses on addressing the problems arising in the process of rural e-commerce and relevant industrial development. With the collective efforts of Rural Taobao and county-level governments, four sets of projects have been formulated and two sites have been set up. The first one referred to the "first-leader project". A leading group consisting of officials from relevant administrative departments was established to promote the new concept of Rural Taobao across all branches, reconsider the development direction of departmental benefits, coordinate the business group model featured by rural Taobao industrial products downstream and agricultural products upstream, and more importantly, to bring out a batch of officials equipped with e-commerce knowledge and innovative thinking and a specialized local e-commerce team. The second was a propaganda program me. With the help of village broadcasting, blackboard, wall paintings and other grass-root level publicity methods, Taobao can appear in every aspect of villagers' life. The third project is referred to as the training program. County-level leaders would attend the 3-day county magistrate training class offered by Taobao University in Hangzho. In addition to field research, county-level officials would participate in the training of local areas or carry out investigation and research related to Rural Taobao. In some counties with rapid development in Rural Taobao, even township-level officials were required to attend training. The fourth was to set up an e-commerce operation project outlining the implementation strategies (including motivation schemes) for long term development. For example, county-level operation centers and local governments worked out a plan to build learning mutual-aid groups of 5 or 6 township-level rural Taobao partners to be appointed in each town. Mutual-aid groups competed with each other monthly, thus inspiring each partner. Teams with high performance would be awarded with certificates and bonuses, and excellent individual partners would be awarded with additional prizes. By leveraging the power of government credibility and influence, the first-tier partners were encouraged consistently to work for the further development of e-commerce.

To realize communication with governments from the top-down, Rural Taobao sets a principal person system with Rural Taobao managers governing the nation-wide business, under which there are regional, provincial, city and county managers, who may communicate with their counterpart governments. Procedures for cooperation between Rural Taobao and government are: reaching a preliminary agreement, signing Letter of Intent, preparing four programs and two sites (setting up project leader teams and implementation teams at different government levels, formulating publicity programs, finishing initial training, working out operation mechanism and implementing sites for Rural Taobao in counties and villages) and decorating sites by Rural Taobao and relevant departments of Alibaba.

5.2.1 Creating a Transportation Network

The last kilometer issue from county to village will be solved by the transportation network with the cooperation between logistics platforms covering under county-level places set up by Rookie Logistics and county-and village-level logistics companies.

Logistics from county to village has always limited the development of the rural e-commerce. Rookie Logistics, which has traditionally combined YTO Express, STO Express, ZTO Express and Yunda Express, has become the major provider of e-commerce logistics in urban areas. No uniform logistics can be found to support districts within a county, especially the smaller ones. Take Suichang County with a population of 260,000 which includes 70,000 living in the county area for instance, local private logistics companies which are mainly consisted of National Postal System and those established by formers employees of the above-mentioned three expresses. They become outsourcing agencies to several logistic companies and operate in a low-cost and low-profit way. Even so, the logistics from county to village is still hard to solve, provided mainly by the National Postal System with subsidies from the government. As there are less delivery bags in villages, packages and mail will often only be sent when delivery bags accumulate to a certain degree to save costs, which incurs a long-period of delivery and an inferior experience for farmers. As Mr. Zhou Qiren, an economist, pointed out, “A scale-size economic model can be found. Although villages have access to modern communicating technologies thanks to the telecommunication and internet infrastructure have developed rapidly nationwide, especially in eastern part of China, the logistics in villages still finds it hard to achieve economies of scale”.

Studies should focus on how to make urban area’s logistics to radiate into the rural area and support logistics from county to village when its size is relatively small. “Without logistics, rural e-commerce can’t find basis for development,” added Mr. Zhou, “In turn, rural e-commerce companies can’t provide enough orders to support logistics. The issue is just like whether chicken lay eggs first or eggs hatch chicken first, which is still unresolved”. Rural Taobao and government’s solution is to let government subsidize for three months, which will be RMB 100,000 per month for a county. This subsidy, combined with the e-commerce system which promotes downside industrial products advocated for several months, will increase rural e-commerce companies’ orders and logistics orders, thus breaking the deadlock. The cooperation between Rural Taobao and local government and to let government change its thinking patterns are hard to realize. Meanwhile, the logistics in villages will bring more prosperous development to local logistics companies and create more job opportunities.

As the most important of Alibaba’s rural strategies, their human resource development efforts aim to attract and cultivate talents who will innovate and create businesses in rural area. Rural Taobao, the important key to Alibaba’s rural strategies, expects to seek balance among demands of rural residents, rural society and local government, to realize a win-win situation and change the rural appearance. Rural Taobao promotes cooperation between college students returning to their hometowns and local talents who will become young partners of Alibaba Group and spur the development of rural e-commerce and relevant industries.

5.2.2 *Impact on Villages*

The innovative and change-embracing characteristics of Rural Taobao Business Unit are beyond everyone's expectations. "Since June 2015, number of orders from Rural Taobao has been over 10,000 which are achieved through rural partners who do online shopping for local residents", said Zhang Yong, CEO of Alibaba Group, at the 2nd County-level E-commerce Summit held by Tonglu, "Various products have been purchased by rural residents, including four 65-inch colored TV sets. The consumption range in rural area is so immense that it is beyond our imagination". "One resident bought most of construction materials online to build his house", he added, "One day we found 5000 trash cans were bought by one area. Why would this happen? It is because this area intends to change the city image by putting trash cans on the streets. It's a kind of government purchase, but the efficiency and cost-saving effect are too obvious to be omitted. This is a mirror reflecting economic changes in rural area brought by e-commerce".[14]

Meanwhile, farm products are being sold online. On August 4, 2015, Rural Taobao cooperated with Ju Taobao for the first time to sell nine counties' farm products online. The transactions within 72 h was over 5 million RMB (0.74 million USD). 50,000 bundles of corn produced in Mengzhou, Henan were sold out just in 37 h.

E-commerce has not only facilitated products, however, but also land-leasing arrangements between farmers and city families. Through e-commerce city families can essentially "lease" land from farmers to ensure greater food security and gain access to fresh food. 436 mu[15] rice field (which yields 260,000 jin[16] ecology rice) were leased online through "Ju Land" by over 2100 city families which would be supplied fresh produce every month in certain quantity. Additionally, this will also generate tourism opportunities for these villages.

In Linan, Zhejiang Province, many chicken raised in hills were ordered for the coming spring festival and 130,000 eggs were sent to over 2500 families in three months. Also, over 21,000 customers ordered sweet potatoes to be yielded on 100 mu of lands who will receive them within one month. Rural Taobao partners will organize people to reap these products, supervise their qualities and pack them for delivery.

---

[14]"阿里巴巴CEO张勇:把农村的机会留给创业者-资讯-阿里研究院" [leaving opportunities in rural to entrepreneurs]. 2015. Aliresearch.Com. http://www.aliresearch.com/blog/article/detail/id/20536.html.

[15]667 m 2 per mu.

[16]500 g per jin.

Unlike Suichang who operates in a single county, Rural Tabao's resource management works on a national scale.

5.3 Rural Taobao Partner Strategy

Rural Taobao partner strategy means to establish county-and village-level rural e-commerce service centers. Those county centers provide services such as operation management, logistics, infrastructure construction, training of Rural Taobao partners, etc. However, those partners are not workers but preliminary partners of Alibaba, that consist of college students, entrepreneurs returning to their hometowns, and local creative talents capable of innovation with adventurous spirit. They gain profits from goods commission after becoming Rural Taobao's partners, receiving Alibaba's training and resources, and serving the rural market based on the platform provided by Alibaba. The whole rural ecological system will be activated by cultivating a batch of leaders, who have their own thoughts, creativity, dreams and missions in this process.

Promotion of the Rural Taobao partner strategy provides basis for the Rural Taobao in the following ways:

Firstly, it brings infrastructure hardware investment. One weakness of rural e-commerce is the lack of hardware equipment and their operators. As most of rural residents cannot do transactions online via computers, Rural Taobao provides factories, offices, computer equipment and other infrastructure facilities needed by workers and logistics in county service centers. Besides, it provides internet-connecting device to those centers, including computers, promotion materials, which consists of a uniform VI design. Those facilities are similar to those of e-commerce centers set in counties and villages by "Gan Jie" of Suichang.

Secondly, it innovates rural comprehensive services. Through the Rural Taobao service center, more farmers will experience comprehensive service, buy industrial products sold only in cities, and enjoy convenient lifestyle. Through this center, Alibaba may promote its partner Ant Finance, loans, and more financial services among farmers and rural economy.

Thirdly, it activates rural e-commerce ecology. It can cultivate local e-commerce ideas and change local residents' thinking patterns with local ways of doing things.

The case of He Shenxin, Rural Taobao partner of village-level Rural Taobao service center, Shijiju Village, Sihong County, Suqian City, Jiangsu Province, marks people's zeal in participating in Rural Taobao.

Typical Case of Rural Taobao Partner[17]

He Shenxin, Rural Taobao partner of village-level Rural Taobao service center, Shijiju Village, Sihong County, Suqian City, Jiangsu Province, was tired of working in Nanjing, Shanghai and other large cities before participating in Rural Taobao established in his hometown where he desired to settle down to take care of his parents.

On June 5, 2015 when the service center was open, the trading volume of this center topped at 510,000 RMB, creating a new national record. On the event of home appliance festival in Tmall on June 18, this center's trading volume reached 200,000 RMB, ranking third nationwide with the average trading volume being over 10,000 RMB. Mr. He, an admirer of Jack Ma, desired to participate in Rural Taobao to create his own business. Before the opening of this center, Mr. He trained other workers and partners of Rural Taobao until 11o'clock of the evening. Afterwards, he continued to acquire shopping demands and decided to create a new record on the opening day of this center, aiming at proving himself. For the past 20 days before the opening of this center, he worked very hard and slept for only three hours per day. The working team of county Rural Taobao covering the Sihong County provided consultation service to Mr. He 24 h a day which moved local partners and ignited their passion. Mr. He learned new products, did considerate preparations, and collected local residents' demands on the Taobao Home Appliance Festival held on June 18. He always answered local residents' questions in a clear and professional way and offered professional solutions to their shopping demands and outstanding issues.

Meanwhile, the local government paid high attention to Rural Taobao and made efforts to propagandize it. The whole of Sihong County was marked by promotional banners of Rural Taobao on streets and walls. Mr. He advertised it in his own ways. Before the Taobao Home Appliance Festival, Mr. He promoted it in streets and alleys on a tricycle equipped with radio loudspeakers and distributed flyers. The hot weather made him sweat, but in just 10 days, Mr. He had distributed two rounds of flyers to the whole village so as to let all residents participate in the money-saving festival. It, indeed, brought benefits to villagers. For instance, one grandpa was interested but confused by this flyer, thus he asked his son to consult detailed information, including ways of saving money through shopping online and home appliances' after-sale services, at the center. This grandpa bought an air-con at last, but still had many concerns. But when the air-con was delivered to and installed in his house, his concerns dissipated and took many more flyers to voluntarily promote Rural Taobao to his friends. After the center's opening, Mr. He, his wife and his sister worked together to serve villagers to improve

[17]"宿迁日报:贺沈新创业有"三坚"" [Suqian Daily: the key to the pioneer of He Shenxin]. 2016. Sihong.Gov.Cn. http://www.sihong.gov.cn/art/2016/12/26/art_30_319384.html.

the service rate. During the Festival, he hurried to make orders for villages at 12o'clock of the evening. Because of this, his two-year old child had to have dinner after 12o'clock, but Mr. He thought it was worthy because he could teach fighting spirit to his child. For left-behind elderly people, Mr. He provided door-to-door services; for illiterate villagers, Mr. He installed home appliances in accordance with instruction manuals. Many villagers thought Mr. He's work was worthless, yet Mr. He climbed hills to deliver goods to villagers' doors. However, when villagers invited him to have meal with them, offered him a glass of water and trusted him, Mr. He proved his value and was welcomed by other villagers.

He transformed Ding Talk (a platform that facilitates coordination among small and medium sized companies) into a social media platform where Rural Taobao and local residents communicate. On this platform, Mr. He can send messages, local residents can receive phone calls, and enjoy 100 min of free phone talk. Local residents prefer to "Ding" others instead of talking them face to face, which is really convenient and money-saving. Mr. He expects to work closely with local residents and become their steward and financial planner to bring benefits to them in the future. He also hopes to sell his village's featured products to other parts of China and the world so as to help other create business and realize common prosperity.

Under this system established by Alibaba, villagers will become full-time partners and enter into the rural economy as the local agents. Alibaba has limited human resources. Therefore, Rural Taobao's partner strategy has gained initial benefits in aspect of the urban to rural ("downstream") industrial products and developing finances in the rural areas, but it has weakness in the rural to urban ("upstream") of agricultural products which hinge on produce quality control. In fact, Alibaba has been trying to establish a Taobao with Chinese characteristics, work with the local government and solve farm produces' quality supervision issue by utilizing rural cooperatives in village and local governments. For example, activities of Rural Taobao on Ju Taobao at August 7 2015, the quality control was followed the way of Suichang Ecommerce Association (Chap. 4). But because Rural Taobao's upstream of agricultural products are from different counties, it's very hard to build a standard immediately. However, it has encountered numerous difficulties. Based on the industry model built by Alibaba, Rural Taobao intends to control farm produces' quality through working with its partners.

Rural Taobao's partners endeavor to establish a new ecology which includes e-commerce platform, local government, village partners and local residents.

Cases of the Rural to Urban ("Upstream") of Agricultural Products[18]

5 million turnovers for Rural Taobao in three days: Rural Taobao launched activities on Ju Taobao for the first time between 10:00, August 4 and 9:59, August 7, 2015.
For example:
Linan, Zhejiang province
Every order you make online will bring one baby chick to Shizi Mountain in Linan. After 150 days of being raised in mountain, the baby chick will become a delicious dish in Spring Festival.
Meanwhile, thousands of chicken on hills will lay 130,000 eggs in three months which will be sent to 2500 families.

Linan, Zhejiang province
100 acres of Xiaoxiangshu (literally translated as small sweet potato), raised by spring water and famous for its powder and sweetness, were bought by 21,274 customers.
In the following one month, partners of Linan Rural Taobao will dig out 100,000 jin of Xiao Xiangshu (literally translated as small sweet potato) and send them to these customers.

*Qixia, Shandong province
Nearly 1100 apple trees were subscribed and adopted early.
When they are ripe in the middle of October, top grade apples will be sent to their masters across the nation. Ecologically planted, freshly picked up, secure and delicious fruits are only provided by Ju Fruit Garden.

Huazhou, Guangdong
Mr. Yao, a Rural Taobao partner in Guanqiao Town, was excited yet stressed. He could just sell 10 orders per day after selling red orange for over half a year, for many customers don't understand it. However, he sold about 800 jin of red orange equivalent to 12,954 bags of 60 g, which shocked him. Together with other five partners, they stored goods, served as customer services personnel and delivered bags, making the rural service center a major ground. It also introduced the local health care product representing Huazhou culture and health maintenance philosophy to other parts of China.

[18]Rural to Urban Agricultural Products Promotion, Rural Taobao Official Wechat Account: https://mp.weixin.qq.com/s/AMMi66G74u1HYV4p-ixLTg.

Yushan, Jiangxi province
After introducing Rural Taobao, Yushan has been searching and exploring ways of selling farm products online, which once admired professional TPs who can sell 4000 Zongzi (rice dumplings) in one order.
However, this time they sold 10,857 bags of brown sugar manually made by local farmers, which made every one realize that Rural Taobao would become a major place to create infinite possibilities.

Peixian, Jiangsu province
As a traditional health care plant, Niuqiyang is less known to others. The primary producing area of Niuqiyang, which was sold 2337 bags, has a chance to bring health to others.

Huoshan, Anhui province
As the top magic medical herb, Shihu, which was once only enjoyed by nobilities, is used by ordinary people today.
Mihu, the most valuable variety of Shihu, has been sent to 5453 families through Rural Taobao, becoming a noble plant in urban citizens' families.

Tongyu, Jilin province
Thousands acres of Sunflower Garden have become a famous tourist spot in Tongyu. Sunflower seeds which are round, fresh and crisp have been a famous farm produce that many people in Tongyu are proud of. 3220 customers have bought 1.6 ton of sunflower seeds, who will enjoy "sunflower king" sought by local agricultural planting experts and Rural Taobao partners which are planted in better places in a natural way and scientifically processed.

Xiangtan, Hunan province
Picking lotus seeds under numerous lotus leaves is a great pleasure. Lotus seeds produced in Xiangtan, hometown to Chairman Mao, are top of four great lotus seeds and praised as tribute lotus seeds. 5851 orders make Xiangtan government which just sign cooperation agreement with Rural Taobao feel excited and brightened (Fig. 5.4).

Fig. 5.4 Nearly 5 million turnovers for Rural Taobao in three days after selling special farm produces on Ju Taobao. *Source* AliResearch

5.4 Inclusive Finance in Villages

Ant Financial Services invests in micro-enterprises, especially micro-enterprises trading farm products, which contributes largely into Alibaba's competitiveness of its rural strategies. Since its day of establishment in 2014, Ant Financial Services has been devoted to a vision, which will open cloud computing, big data, credit system and other lower bottom platforms, and popularize mobile financial services in third and fourth tier cities.

In September 2014, Mybank (owned 30% by Ant Financial Services) was officially authorized to become one of the first five private banks in China. In 2015, Mybank asserted that it's "the first bank based on the independent and controllable core system" and it "will not do business with more than 20% of high-valued clients". Instead, it will focus on inclusive finance. Rural finance has become an important part of Alibaba's rural strategies.

Rural finance has been a hard bone to crack, limiting rural economic growth. In the past urbanization process, no financial capital flow could be found in rural areas, creating uneven development and enlarging the gap between rural and urban areas. This kind of uneven development damages the common environment, ecological crisis and isolation in rural and urban areas and leads to society hollowing in villages and fragmentation in urban societies.

When township enterprises grew rapidly in 1980s and 1990s, villages were gradually urbanized. However, due to township enterprises and other kinds of agriculture industries, services industry encounter growing difficulties in financing and fail to engage in globalized production network, causing it to wither dramatically.

It has always been difficult for small-scale peasant economy to participate in the global capital flow system since the founding of the PRC, while the emergence of rural e-commerce has successfully linked it to international and regional capital operation and production division through BAT[19] and other global financing channels. Up to now, the use of Internet in rural areas will upgrade the entire rural industrial chains in the context of general overcapacity in China's industrial production. As the Chinese saying goes, "Provisions should be arranged before an army is mobilized", rural finance will become the vanguard of rural internet with the reorganization and orderly development among the vast rural markets. That will become the important pivot for Alibaba to cooperate and compete with and with other Internet companies in China and even global Internet giants.

The advantages of establishing rural financial system through the internet are obvious. Alipay, Yu'E Bao, Zhaocai Bao, Ali Microloans, Zhima Credit, Credit Investigation, Insurance, Financial Cloud Computing below Ant Financial Group extended into the fields of payment, foundation, insurance, bank, credit investigation, Internet financial management, equity-based crowd-funding as well as financial and IT system services.

[19] Baidu, Alibaba and Tencent.

As we all know, Alipay is targeted at the trust problems in e-commerce transaction. Furthermore, the Alipay 9.0 with social and loan functions launched on July 8, 2015 helped villagers get accustomed to loans. It can be seen that countryside was the strategic pivot of Ant Financial. Ant Financial will fully support Alibaba rural strategy by providing services for more than 600 million rural residents.

As a result, the rural strategy of Ant Financial was as follows:

First, support the "One Thousand Counties and One Hundred Thousand Villages Plan" (establishing a rural e-commerce service system covering 1000 counties and 100,000 villages with an investment of 10 billion RMB), and link financial products to farmers through rural Taobao partners.

Second, provide financial services products on the rural Taobao online platforms.

Third, develop inclusive finance in poor rural areas and cooperate with government and global financial organizations. For example, Ant Financial worked together with World Bank and granted 500 million loans to female entrepreneurs in rural areas in 2014.

As of July 2015, actual urban and rural users of Ant Financial exceeded 350 million and Alipay wireless client payment transactions hit the largest proportion in among all wireless payment platforms with an annual growth of about 30%. By far, Alipay has over 53 million rural users and 30 million rural mobile users. Over the past few years, Ant Financial has provided a total of 13.3 billion loans for over 580,000 small and micro enterprises, established partnership with more than 2300 rural financial institutions nationwide and started to push ahead businesses with 2000 of its partner intuitions, such as pushing links of Alipay and Zhaocai Bao.[20]

The first task is to expand financial services to the fast-growing rural online shop services. As a result of the emergence of rural e-commerce, the development trend of the future rural finance is featured by resources conservation, production organization intelligence and younger rural e-commerce practitioners.

With rural e-commerce as its starting point, Ant Financial provides different services in accordance with the reality of rural Taobao partners and general rural online shops.

First, Ant Financial will invest 1 billion RMB to support 100,000 rural Taobao partners in the form of Rural Taobao Shopkeepers Fund, with which college returners can apply for start-up loan credit. Villagers can also use it as revolving fund for online shopping. As for those suspicious of online shopping, they can choose cash on delivery. Furthermore, compensation in advance is also accessible for unsatisfying products. As of July, 2015, over 1500 rural Taobao partners have gained credit.

Second, financing, finance management and other basic services are also accessible for rural e-commerce practitioners on the mobile App of E-Financial Shopkeepers.

---

[20]"拆解网商银行:最不像银行的银行" [Network bank: the most-unlike-bank bank]. 2015. Antfin.Com. https://www.antfin.com/newsDetail.html?id=57b2cb44e059e41b67e00a06.

Third, with the help of rural Taobao partners and rural Taobao online platforms, financial services related to agricultural capitals will be developed to help farmers solve capital turnovers problems in agricultural production and expand production. Meanwhile, as rural finance partners, rural Taobao partners will participate in the promotion of Internet finance management. In 2014, Yu'E Bao brought an income growth of 700 million RMB for rural residents. Villagers only need to provide ID card, copy of registered permanent residence and fill in a form about loan purposes, to apply for network loans with rural Taobao partners, which is acceptable for most villagers who have never borrowed money from bank. Zhao Jihua, a farmer from Baijing town, Tonglu County, Zhejiang Province, was informed to have received 20,000 RMB in his bank account through a short message only two days after he submitted his application for a small loan with the help of rural Taobao partners. No mortgage and guarantee were required.

Fourth, Ant Financial will be promoted in the county and village level. Jiande County and Tonglu County in Zhejiang Province will be the first "Alipay Counties" where traffic violation information query, hospital registration, utilities, social insurance and public accumulation fund inquiry, tuition payment and other public services included in the "City Service" on the Alipay phone app. On September 20, 2015, the Ant Financial cooperated with businesses in the ancient city of Lijiang, thus giving birth to the first "no cash" city in China and greatly lifting its business services.

Fifth, the big data cloud computing services of "Smart City" finance will be built into the financial services system in the county and village level. New breakthroughs will be made in the urban-rural trust value system based on "faithful farmers".

At the same time, Yu Shengfa, president of MyBank, said that Ant Financial will finance a total of 20 to 30 billion capitals to support Alibaba Rural Strategy between 2015 and 2018.

5.5 The Urban-Rural Layout of Cainiao Logistics

On November 11, 2014, the total transaction volume of Alibaba broke the record of 36.2 billion in 2013 with 57.112 billion in a mere 24 h, 10% of which were contributed by county level and below residents. That is, quite a few goods have flowed to rural areas in addition to those transferring between cities. To understand the layout of Cainiao Logistics in rural areas, we must first figure out the logistics operation model of Cainiao Logistics.

Alibaba Group took an initiative to establish the Cainiao Logistics Technology Co., Ltd. on May 28, 2013. From Cainiao official website, it is define "taking a collaborative approach to logistics". As an "innovative data platform drives efficiency in China's logistics industry by connecting e-commerce companies with players along the logistics chain to enable end-to-end solutions", their goal is "to realize delivery anywhere in China within 24 h, and across the globe within 72 h".[21]

As the supporting platform of the whole back end of Alibaba Group, Cainiao Logistics, together with Ant Financial, constitutes the iron triangle of transaction, logistics and payment. Cainiao Logistics, other nationwide freight warehousing and logistics services companies and even customs work together to tackle the 30 million package of Taobao every day. Since the establishment of rural Taobao, Cainiao Logistics has also provided support for its logistics system.

"Space Network", "Geological Network" and "Human Network" have been built to support the huge logistics system.

The Space Network is a cloud processing terminal on the Cainiao Big Data Platform that integrates and intensively processes all data included in Alibaba e-commerce system, network business, logistics, Cainiao terminal and consumers. Space Network is designed to enable data access and data matching nationwide and beyond, while the Geological Network works to provide demand forecasting, inventory planning, logistics coordination and supply chains visualization services.

(1) Demand forecasting: demand analysis of regional markets made based on big data to help businesses forecast demand, mainstream product categories, sales volume in the district so as to deliver products to the logistics centers of the Geological Network before transaction is made.
(2) Inventory planning: the inventory for the offline warehouses of logistics centers. Excessive distribution and wrong products categories will lead to excess inventory and overstock. Therefore, it is necessary to work out scientific inventory planning based on market demand and big data analysis.
(3) Logistics coordination: It refers to a digital report to guide and coordinate logistics express companies based on the real time sharing of logistics data. Through screens similar to traffic flow diagrams, express companies can monitor the situation of specific sites and lines in their logistics networks.

When it came to the performance of Cainiao Logistics during the Double-11 Festival, Tong Wenhong, COO of Cainiao Logistics mentioned that Cainiao Logistics pooled together 14 main express companies, 617 core branches, 3000 main lines, 50,000 sites, 1200,000 couriers and countless orders and its job is to enable the smooth flow of the network.

(4) Supply chain visualization services: in the ideal state, a comprehensive supply chain service platform with the ultimate goal to enable the whole supply chain visualization services ranging from demand to inventory, from order placing to storage and operations, from offline operation to online coordination, and distribution.

[21]Cainiao Network Overview, Sep 2016, https://www.alizila.com/wp-content/uploads/2016/09/Cainiao-Factsheet.pdf?x95431.

"Geological Network" receives the data from "Space Network" and strives to make same-day delivery services accessible in any area of China with the cooperation with Shentong, RMBtong, Zhongtong and Yunda. Under the collective efforts of the "Geologic Network" team, 5 to 8 core logistics centers have been established in Tianjin, Hangzhou, Guangzhou, Zhengzhou and Wuhan. Furthermore, offline warehouses have also been put into place. By setting up branch warehouses nationwide, logistics costs have been reduced, warehouse and distribution efficiency has been promoted.

In addition to improve the efficiency of couriers form express companies, "Human Network" also works to establish offline entity services system. For example, Cainiao Station was established under the cooperation with entrepreneurial students in colleges and universities, Green Town and China Vanke and other community properties, C-store and other convenience stores. A terminal public services network covering major cities in China has taken shape via social synergy. At present, over 180,000 stations are distributed across the country, enabling comprehensive life services. Looking forward, it will be a door-to-door nationwide logistics delivery network.

Ultimately, the layout of Space Network, Geological Network and Human Network will lead to logistics optimization. Taking Beijing as an example, some possible products have been delivered to offline warehouses in advance before the Double-11 Festival based on the forecasting of Space Network. In addition, Space Network will process all logistics data to assign tasks for express companies such as STE Express, YTE Express, ZTE Express and YDE Express. In this way, same-day delivery becomes a reality.

As you can see, the Space Network, Geological Network and Human Network of Cainiao Logistics have offered a lot of inspiration and supports to the online and offline strategic layout. The key to rural logistics lies in inadequate online shopping orders in the first place. As more consumers shop online, companies will be able to distribute packages at lower costs. Currently, the absence of home delivery services imposes restrictions on the online shopping of rural residents.

As a matter of fact, some local e-commerce platforms and local logistics platforms have worked out some experience. For instance, the model of Suichang "Ganjie" rural e-commerce services station shed a new light for the development of delivery services in counties and villages. The logistics department subordinated to "Ganjie" can provide logistics services in counties and villages by charging 3 to 5 RMB (0.4 to 0.7 USD) for each order, and many shop owners also provide free package pickup services for villagers. Furthermore, several shop owners take turns to provide package pickup services in a logistics route or may ask those villagers working in towns and cities to pick up some packages in their way home. Actually, these solutions grow from the soil of the countryside, and can be referred to as the genuine sharing economy. With the support of national logistics system of Cainiao Logistics, rural Taobao logistics will have the opportunity to be supplemented and upgraded in a systematic manner.

Fig. 5.5 Distribution map of Cainiao Logistics' delivery sites, which covered over 746 dispatching center and 180,000 distribution sites to collect and deliver packages. *Source* AliResearch

The core of the warehouse and logistics center established in Tonglu lies in the fact that rural county-level logistics centers were set up in logistics nodes. The warehouse and logistics center is not only a warehouse, but also the hub for goods transport of the whole rural e-commerce in the near future.

Cainiao Logistics reaches to counties and villages across the country to bridge the logistic gap between urban and rural areas. During the Double 11 shopping spree in 2016, logistic service providers covered over 746 dispatching units and 180 thousand distribution sites nationwide, to form a logistic network that extended from east to west. Rural Logistics under Cainiao also built a logistic network that linked counties and villages (it covers 28 provinces, autonomous regions and municipalities, including 450 counties and 18,000 villages). Logistic hubs are also available in rural Taobao's county-level service stations, where Cainiao Logistics joins hands with local counterparts to better serve villagers. By far, Cainiao Logistics has established partnership with dozens of express companies (Fig. 5.5).

Cainiao Logistics and Rural Taobao strive to work together with governments at all levels to build a national rural logistics network, to accomplish the essential mission that express and logistics companies are unable to complete.

With the cooperation of government, logistics subsidies will be accessible to provide a favorable environment for the development of rural e-commerce so as to engage in local logistics enterprises and encourage local entrepreneurship.

Apart from the above mentioned department businesses, Ali Micro Store (mobile App), Taobao "Feature of China", Taobao University, Alibaba Cloud and so on invested by Alibaba Group are all included in the rural strategies of Alibaba Group.

On April 14, 2015, Alibaba Group launched a mobile App named Micro Store, or Xiaopu. Micro Store was initially regarded as a rival of Wechat Business in the WAP APP.[22]

"Feature of China" has always been an epitome of Alibaba's exploration of "agricultural products going upstream".[23] "Feature of China" started in 2012 when Taobao rural market worked together with provinces, cities and some counties to set up specialized websites and cooperated with local operators to sell local agricultural products on the platform of Taobao.

Taobao University has cooperated with e-commerce training operators at all levels to offer training classes for county magistrates in rural areas. The future development of county economy will benefit from talents dividends. Therefore, a comprehensive talents system is indispensable. Government officials, operators and third-party services providers and cooperatives have the opportunity to introduce rural e-commerce in their hometowns.

Alibaba Cloud provides the digitalization services for nearly all businesses of Alibaba to back up its rural strategy. Meanwhile, county-level Internet platform and e-commerce platform have also started to apply Alibaba Cloud services.

---

[22]According to the economic operation condition of communication industry in September 2015 released by Ministry of Industry and Information Technology, domestics mobile call volume has maintained negative growth on a year-on-year basis for a successive 9 months, while GPRS has been doubled during the same timeframe. In September, mobile Internet access volume reached 3900,000 G, setting a record high. The aggregated volume of January to September topped 27,900,000 G, showing an increase of 99.4% on a year-on-year basis. GPRS reached 25,000,000 G and has doubled for a 9 months in a row.

[23]In 2010, "One Newspaper, One Store" was launched to promote online stores through offline newspapers. In 2012, Xiao'er Team of food department started to promote "Feature of China". Since then, the platform has gradually received attention within Taobao. By 2013, the portal of "Feature of China" appeared on the front page of Taobao and then on mobile Taobao. Shortly, as a wide range of cities in different provinces started to open online stores on "Feature of China", the platform has gained recognition from the government. Because the performance growth of "Feature of China" is not the fastest, it is hardly to be regard as the main push in activities featured by fierce internal competence such as "Double 11 Day" and "Double 12 Day". However, "Feature of China" has been received due attention as it is an essential link in Taobao's exploration in developing rural business. Before rural Taobao was established, perhaps "Feature of China" was the only branch in Alibaba Group that has established relatively close partnership with local governments. Later, the partnership between "Feature of China" and local e-commerce platform has evolved into the trilateral partnership between "Feature of China" on the one hand and local government, local e-commerce platform on the other hand. Just take the Quzhou Feature Store as an example. Quzhou Feature Store was opened in September 2014 after local government took a lead to submit an application to open a feature store. As the online sales windows for the agricultural products in Quzhou, Zhejiang, the feature store is operated by Quzhou Boontown E-commerce Co., Ltd, a local e-commerce platform. There are six divisions under the store, namely Kecheng, Qujiang, Longyou, Jiangshan, Changshan and Kaihua. Each county offers a feature agricultural product that can fully demonstrate the distinctive characteristics of the county. Over 60 online stores specialized in agricultural products have been launched in the first batch, consisting of over 500 superior feature products with 10 geographical indication products, 6 organic products and 8 green products. The launch procedures of all these products are exactly the same with that in Suichang Stores.

In summary, this evidence demonstrates that Alibaba rural strategy has applied diversified paths, which will continue to contribute to the exploration of online service on a national scale.

5.6 Reflection of Alibaba Rural Strategy Case

Despite the inherent "flowing" feature of Alibaba's rural strategy, it is constantly integrating with local organizations and social relations and continuously adapts itself to local demands. Take Rural Taobao as an example, there are as many as thousands of applicants during the recruitment of partners for Rural Taobao, with acceptance rate kept at around 5%. By June 2016, more than 1000 partners, or over 8% of Rural Taobao partners around the country had their incomes exceeded 10 thousand yuan. Among those 10 thousand villages that implemented the Rural Taobao strategy, 107 disabled people are registered in the system, whose monthly income remained at around 5000 yuan.

Furthermore, by collaborating with partners of Rural Taobao, Ant Financial offers tremendous financial services and petty loans. As mentioned before, from 2015 to 2018, Ant Financial introduced a financial product to fund shopkeepers of Rural Taobao program. Under this project, it invests 1 billion yuan to help 100 thousand partners of Rural Taobao. The money will be used either as credit for partners including university graduates who intend to start their own business, or as buffering funds for villagers who purchase online. In addition, there is another program, Agri-loan 2.0 that allows farmers to mortgage their harvest and grants them agricultural insurances so that they have access to procurement funds. On 18th, Jun. 2016, MYbank, a subunit to Ant Financial, piloted its remote ID authentication technology in Junying village, Tong'an district, Xiamen. This attempt aims to dissolve technological and policy concerns over those who are in need of small loans but have to open accounts online with their ID card. Derivatives of Ant Financial, including Alipay, Yu'e Bao, Zhaocai Bao, MicroCredit, Zhima Credit, credit investigation, insurance, financial cloud computing and other sectors are all designed to help farmers with their financial problems.

Against this backdrop, Rural Taobao needs to step up its efforts of localization. Therefore, in June 2016, it proposed a Three Center strategy: service center, entrepreneurship center and cultural center. Sun Lijun, as the responsible person of Rural Taobao, said that "the eco-service center will link external ecosystems to rural ones. In the near future, on-site maintenance, home-based medical care and other services will be available, so that conveniences enjoyed by city folks are also shared rural dwellers. In a word, we hope to better service the countryside with Alibaba's whole ecosystem. And to make the entrepreneurship center invigorate rural economy, it is important to attract more people to the rural areas".[24]

As a platform to incubate and start businesses, the Rural Taobao strategy was launched at counties simultaneously, making Rural Taobao a channel for people to sign up and learn. From then on, every county can invite owners of large chicken farms and experts in raising chickens through the networks of Rural Taobao to borrow their experiences. An entrepreneurship and incubation platform is built up to provide training, channels and financial support to rural residents who start their own businesses. "As for the cultural center, we believe that improving living conditions and material conditions alone is not enough to change the rural areas thoroughly. Spiritual progress is more important" (Fig. 5.6).

Rural Taobao hopes that the whole society could care about the lives and health of women, old people and children living in rural areas. To help those left-behind children, Alibaba launched the Super Curriculum Initiative in its Cultural Festival, and granted the Best Teacher Award and the Internet-based Education Award. As for women, the Cultural Center opened dance and music classes and encouraged them to pay attention to their fitness, mental conditions, health and beauty, not only providing them with facilities for a better life, but also caring about their psychological status. In terms of the old people living in rural areas, Ali Health will provide nationwide remote medical treatment and hospital appointment services in the next step. At the current 500 pilot villages in Hunan and Hubei province, all villagers can receive medical treatment through a tiered-medical system based on the Internet.

The localization work quickly progresses through the three centers. Alibaba's rural business unit, consisting of a dozen business units, is calling upon local merchants from different places, including P&G, Unilever, Midea, Xiaomi, AFS JEEP and Diyifei, to meet their local demands, shift their focus to local products and build a localized ecosystem. To meet the grand project of covering 200 million villagers in 100,000 villages of 1000 counties, it requires a large number of local businesses to provide quality products. According to Alibaba's database, villagers have strong purchasing power and great demands for affordable and new products. It even proposed new advertising slogans that read "New Customer: rural-inhabited housewives and post-95s become driving forces of online shopping; New Setting: the first Spring Festival Shopping Spree received orders worth 200 thousand yuan". Rural Taobao launched a Local Life channel, initially consisting of six categories: home appliances, digital and mobile phone maintenance; car repair, maintenance and car washing; wedding ceremonies and beauty salons; house renovation, furniture and home decoration; tutoring, interest-oriented classes and vocational training; labor intermediary. Leading merchants in those trades could sign up with the help of responsible persons and partners of Rural Taobao and promote their products through the mobile app of Rural Taobao and its website.

---

[24] Wan Yu,万禺."从2.0升级到3.0,农村淘宝又在谋划什么新布局?_电商在线"[Upgrading From 2.0 to 3.0, What Is Rural Taobao Planning Again?]. 2016. Imaijia.Com. http://www.imaijia.com/xyct/8a04289956c12b880156d5d1eb7e02f5.shtml.

Fig. 5.6 Rural Taobao invites a famous preschool English teacher to give online English classes. *Source* China Daily ("阿里巴巴助力农村幼儿英语教育 - 中国日报网" [Alibaba helps rural children's English education]. 2016. Cn.Chinadaily.Com.Cn. http://cn.chinadaily.com.cn/2016-05/17/content_25326696.htm)

You are wanted in Alibaba's Rural Business Unit[25]

The unexplored market of nearly 10 thousand villages is awaiting you!

It has already reached out to 17,000+ villages in nearly 300 counties of 28 provinces across the country, covering 35+ million rural residents;

It is planning to cover 100,000 villages of 1000 counties, or 200+ million rural residents;

P&G, Unilever, Midea, Xiaomi, AFS JEEP and Diyifei are already here. Well-known brands are taking the lead, covering 6 industries including fast-moving consumer goods (FMCG), home appliances, home decorations, clothing, agricultural products and automobile and motor fittings;

New Customer: rural-inhabited housewives and post-95s become driving forces of online shopping;

New Setting: the first Spring Festival Shopping Spree received orders worth 200 thousand yuan within 12 h;

New Founding: sales volumes of a car washer brand and a body care brand overtake that of the urban online market during the same term;

If you don't want to miss out this opportunity to make your remarkable business;

If you are willing to contribute to the improvement of rural areas;

---

[25]"重磅丨你知道吗?农村淘宝招募本地生活商家啦!"[Big Bang丨 Do you know? Rural Taobao recruitment]. 2016. Mp.Weixin.Qq.Com. http://mp.weixin.qq.com/s/AMMi66G74u1HYV4p-ixLTg.

Then join us today! Our destination is the vast rural land, with enormous unknown beauties!
Click "Read the original text" at the page end to sign up.
Introduction to the Ali Rural business unit:
As one of the three strategies (big data, globalization and rural e-commerce) of Alibaba Group, Ali Rural aims to give full play to the e-commerce to break through bottlenecks in logistics and information flows by conducting in-depth cooperation with local governments and building a two-tiered service network at county- and village-levels, so as to build a two-way circulation system to bring online goods to the rural areas and agricultural products to cities, further integrate rural and urban areas, attract more talents to start their own businesses in their hometowns and in lay solid foundations to achieve modernization and build a smart countryside.
A single location, product and merchant
Three centers
Two-stage logistics
To join Ali Rural, you need to meet the following requirements:

(1) You must be an owner or designated and authorized distributor of a branding business.
(2) You must be registered in Alipay with a new business account and finish real name authentication.
(3) You must turn in 100 thousand cash deposits.
(4) You must having related certifications.
(5) You must agree and comply with service commitments of your corresponding items.

Procedures of joining Ali Rural:
Send applications—Submit documents—Reviewing—Sign the cash deposit and withholding agreement—Release your products.

To Alibaba case study, we can see the quick response made by a locally organized network to the changes of flowing powers. These localization attempts are the reactions made by the county to look after the benefits of stakeholders in the online service.

All these require the presence of a new networking system and urban-rural structure.

References

1. “陆兆禧现身直播间 6亿农村人将创造另一个阿里”. [Interview with Lu Zhaoxi, 600 million rural users may bring out another Taobao and another Alibaba] 2014. Zjnews.Zjol.Com.Cn. http://zjnews.zjol.com.cn/system/2014/11/11/020351463.shtml
2. “周其仁:让互联网惠及更多人” [Zhou Qiren; Let Internet benefit more people]. 2014. News.Ifeng.Com. http://news.ifeng.com/a/20141022/42264895_0.shtml
3. “马云:未来的生意将是C2B模式 - 财经 - 中国日报网” [Jack Ma: the future of business is the model of C2B]. 2015. Caijing.Chinadaily.Com.Cn. http://caijing.chinadaily.com.cn/2015-03/16/content_19824786.htm
4. “阿里巴巴总裁金建杭:美丽乡村 + 农村电商,再造中国农村 -资讯-阿里研究” [Alibaba president Jin Jianhang: beautiful rural + rural electricity business, rebuilding China’s rural areas]. 2015. Aliresearch.Com. http://www.aliresearch.com/blog/article/detail/id/20537.html
5. “农业发展需要有胆有识的年轻人 _寿光评论_新闻中心_中国寿光网” [Agricultural development requires a young man with knowledge]. 2015. Sgnet.Cc. http://www.sgnet.cc/news/201509/11/639279.shtml
6. “阿里巴巴CEO张勇:把农村的机会留给创业者-资讯-阿里研究院” [leaving opportunities in rural to entrepreneurs]. 2015. Aliresearch.Com. http://www.aliresearch.com/blog/article/detail/id/20536.html
7. “宿迁日报:贺沈新创业有“三坚”” [Suqian Daily: the key to the pioneer of He Shenxin]. 2016. Sihong.Gov.Cn. http://www.sihong.gov.cn/art/2016/12/26/art_30_319384.html
8. “拆解网商银行:最不像银行的银行” [Network bank: the most-unlike-bank bank]. 2015. Antfin.Com. https://www.antfin.com/newsDetail.html?id=57b2cb44e059e41b67e00a06
9. Wan Yu, 万禺.“从2.0升级到3.0,农村淘宝又在谋划什么新布局?_电商在线” [Upgrading From 2.0 to 3.0, What Is Rural Taobao Planning Again?]. 2016. Imaijia.Com. http://www.imaijia.com/xyct/8a04289956c12b880156d5d1eb7e02f5.shtml
10. “阿里巴巴助力农村幼儿英语教育 - 中国日报网” [Alibaba helps rural children’s English education]. 2016. Cn.Chinadaily.Com.Cn. http://cn.chinadaily.com.cn/2016-05/17/content_25326696.htm
11. “重磅丨你知道吗?农村淘宝招募本地生活商家啦!” [Big Bang丨Do you know? Rural Taobao recruitment]. 2016. Mp.Weixin.Qq.Com. http://mp.weixin.qq.com/s/AMMi66G74u1HYV4p-ixLTg
12. “农村电子商务“常山标准”出台-中国国际电子商务网” [Rural e-commerce with “Changshan standard”—China International Electronic Commerce Network]. 2015. Ec.Com.Cn. http://www.ec.com.cn/article/ncds/201509/5358_1.html
13. “习近平:加快推进网络信息技术自主创新 朝着建设网络强国目标不懈努力-新华网” [Xi Jinping: Accelerate independent innovation of network information technology Make unremitting efforts towards the goal of making China an Internet power]. 2016. News.Xinhuanet.Com. http://news.xinhuanet.com/politics/2016-10/09/c_1119682204.htm

Chapter 6
Spatial Regeneration of Regional Restructuring

With an increasing number of counties and rural areas gaining access to the network via online service sector, these changes have created a new space model conducive to urbanization. These are supportive of Castell's concept of "grass-rooted flow of space," which underscores the fact that insufficient rural infrastructure (especially public facilities and services) has propelled the development of Network Society[1] below county level. For example, the "metropolis malady" is largely the result of ignoring the development of surrounding rural areas. The sustainable development of a city can, in fact, be measured based on the development and affluence of its neighboring counties. Rural residents are forced to urban slums due to poverty and environmental pollution. Developed cities and the widening gap between urban and rural areas will lure more poverty-stricken rural dwellers into urban areas, creating more slums, as is the case in South America and India where excessive urbanization led to more slums and put social order and security in jeopardy. Therefore, the real victory of a city comes after the coordinated development of its neighboring villages and even those in farther areas that share social and industrial ties with the city. These in turn are all built upon indigenous features of a locality, or the functional shift of a space driven by regeneration that serves the online service system. As closely related to the increasingly globalized Chinese rural and urban communities, this shift has been there for a long time and has begun to gain momentum recently. By focusing on different aspects of the county and rural areas, we will explore and analyze how the online service sector shapes each area.

[1]The Network Society is mentioned by Manual Castells in *The Rise of the Network Society* [1], the first part of his trilogy *The Information Age*.

L. Zi, *Online Urbanization*, Advances in 21st Century Human Settlements,
https://doi.org/10.1007/978-981-13-3603-4_6

6.1 The Broad Picture: New Landscapes in Rural and Urban China

AliResearch released the development indices of e-commerce in different cities and counties, as well as the distribution data of Taobao villages. Though the original data is unavailable, we can draw a rough comparison of e-commerce development between difference regions based on their rankings (Fig. 6.1).

When analyzing the development of digital economy in urban areas, we put equal stress on the development of online service sector, especially e-commerce in counties. These are some findings after reviewing the development indices of e-commerce at county-level, which were released by AliResearch in 2014 (Table 6.1).

What Are the Top 100 Best-Performing Counties in E-Commerce in 2014

Based on the AEDI (Alibaba's E-Commerce Development Index) released by AliResearch, the list of top 100 best-performing counties in e-commerce in 2014 was created. Yiwu topped the list, followed by Shishi, Yongkang, Tongxiang, Haining, Tiantai, Dehua, Kunshan, Qinghe and Changshu.

From the provincial level, the listed counties are widely distributed in 17 provinces and cities, among which 71% are located in Zhejiang, Fujian and Jiangsu provinces. Out of the list of counties, 41 are in Zhejiang. 16 counties are in Fujian, 14 in Jiangsu, and 6 in Hebei. None of the other 13 provinces have more than 5 counties that enter the final list.

Table Distribution of Top 100 Best-Performing Counties in E-Commerce in 2014[2]

From the city level, the listed counties are distributed in 47 prefecture-level cities). Among these cities, Quanzhou is home to 7 listed counties. Jinhua, Taizhou and Wenzhou are home to 6 counties respectively and Jiaxing, Lishui and Ningbo to 5 respectively. E-commerce development in these cities is closely related to their economic prosperity (Tables 6.2 and 6.3).

To break this down, AliResearch has another finding. Whether e-commerce of a certain region would prosper depends on the willingness of local small businesses, entrepreneurs and consumers to put it into practice. As we mentioned, Yiwu ranks first in the list. In 2014, business transactions on e-commerce platforms amounted to 115.3 billion yuan. Local online traders opened a total of more than 240 thousand accounts on major e-commerce platforms, far more than the number of brick-and-mortar stores.

[2]"2014年中国"电商百佳县"榜单揭晓-资讯-阿里研究院" [Top 100 Best-Performing Counties in E-Commerce in 2014]. 2014. Aliresearch.Com. http://www.aliresearch.com/blog/article/detail/id/20431.html.

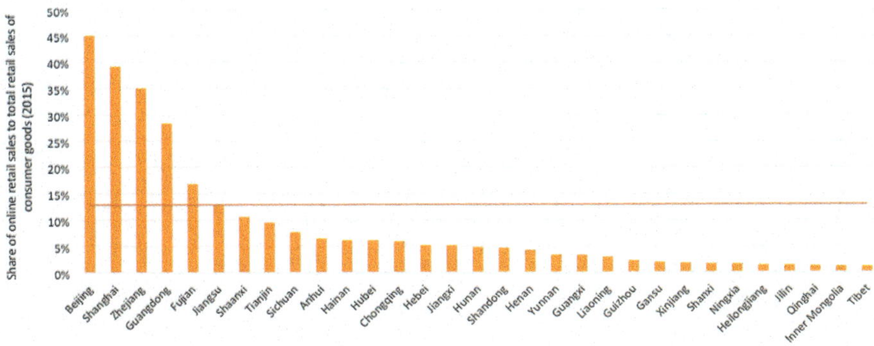

Fig. 6.1 Share of online retail scales of consumer goods (2015). *Source* AliResearch

Besides, in certain counties where e-commerce thrives, rural e-commerce has risen to prominence in recent years. Lots of villagers have started their own businesses on e-commerce platforms, as manifested by a number of "Taobao Villages". Qinghe of Hebei is home to 8 Taobao villages, Boxing of Shandong 6 Taobao villages, Wenling of Zhejiang has 7 and Anxi of Fujian 5, to name just a few.

Edited by the author, source: website of AliResearch.

http://www.aliresearch.com/blog/article/detail/id/20431.html

Alibaba also consolidated and analyzed the statistics of urban e-commerce development in 2014 (Fig. 6.2 and Tables 6.4, 6.5).

6.1.1 The Impact of E-commerce on County Development

The top 100 best-performing counties in e-commerce are clustered in the Yangtze River Delta. Shanghai, Hangzhou and Nanjing underwent swift e-commerce development. Consumptions in the counties of Jinhua, Taizhou, Wenzhou, Jiaxing, Lishui and Ningbo were therefore greatly boosted. Zhejiang province is home to the largest number of e-commerce counties accounting for 41 counties on the top 100 list (Table 6.3) Jiangsu province has 14 listed counties. Jinhua, Taizhou and Wenzhou have 6 listed counties respectively, Jiaxing, Lishui and Ningbo have 5 respectively. 4 counties of Suzhou entered the list of Top 100 E-Commerce Counties. Those counties witnessed rapid development of online shopping, and online businesses have also been thriving. Taking a proactive stance, urban and county clusters in the Yangtze River Delta are building on their technological advantages to grow their service sector based on e-commerce platforms.

Table 6.1 Top 100 best-performing counties in E-commerce

Ranking	County	City	Province	E-commerce index	E-shopping index	E-commerce development index
1	Yiwu	Jinhua	Zhejiang	43.825	25.207	34.516
3	Yongkang	Jinhua	Zhejiang	21.543	15.424	18.483
4	Tongxiang	Jiaxing	Zhejiang	13.71	20.389	17.049
5	Haining	Jiaxing	Zhejiang	15.482	16.358	15.92
6	Tiantai	Taizhou	Zhejiang	14.988	15.883	15.436
11	Pinghu	Jiaxing	Zhejiang	11.735	16.693	14.214
12	Cangnan	Wenzhou	Zhejiang	14.434	12.102	13.268
14	Yuyao	Ningbo	Zhejiang	11.358	13.217	12.287
15	Cixi	Ningbo	Zhejiang	10.574	13.801	12.187
19	Leqing	Wenzhou	Zhejiang	9.849	13.068	11.459
20	Dongyang	Jinhua	Zhejiang	9.878	12.485	11.182
21	Pingyang	Wenzhou	Zhejiang	9.068	12.989	11.029
22	Wuyi	Jinhua	Zhejiang	10.181	11.518	10.849
23	Anji	Huzhou	Zhejiang	9.901	11.357	10.629
24	Yongjia	Wenzhou	Zhejiang	9.387	11.392	10.39
25	Pujiang	Jinhua	Zhejiang	10.87	9.874	10.372
29	Rui'an	Wenzhou	Zhejiang	8.668	11.364	10.016
32	Haiyan	Jiaxing	Zhejiang	8.233	11.084	9.658
34	Wenling	Taizhou	Zhejiang	8.339	10.696	9.518
37	Yunhe	Lishui	Zhejiang	8.382	10.207	9.294
39	Jiashan	Jiaxing	Zhejiang	6.362	11.861	9.111
41	Tonglu	Hangzhou	Zhejiang	7.345	10.644	8.994
43	Yuhuan	Taizhou	Zhejiang	6.465	11.39	8.928
44	Zhuji	Shaoxing	Zhejiang	7.202	10.62	8.911

(continued)

Table 6.1 (continued)

Ranking	County	City	Province	E-commerce index	E-shopping index	E-commerce development index
45	Fenghua	Ningbo	Zhejiang	6.7	11.002	8.851
46	Lin'an	Hangzhou	Zhejiang	6.094	11.479	8.786
47	Ninghai	Ningbo	Zhejiang	6.804	10.626	8.715
52	Shengzhou	Shaoxing	Zhejiang	7.813	8.944	8.379
53	Deqing	Huzhou	Zhejiang	6.129	10.446	8.288
54	Jinyun	Lishui	Zhejiang	6.673	9.826	8.249
55	Qingyuan	Lishui	Zhejiang	7.227	9.263	8.245
56	Xianju	Taizhou	Zhejiang	6.537	9.942	8.24
57	Sanmen	Taizhou	Zhejiang	6.566	9.882	8.224
62	Dongtou	Wenzhou	Zhejiang	4.133	11.844	7.988
65	Xinhang	Shaoxing	Zhejiang	6.058	9.608	7.833
67	Linhai	Taizhou	Zhejiang	5.752	9.591	7.672
69	Songyang	Lishui	Zhejiang	5.495	9.509	7.502
71	Xiangshan	Ningbo	Zhejiang	3.873	11.109	7.491
72	Pan'an	Jinhua	Zhejiang	7.175	7.754	7.465
73	Jiande	Hangzhou	Zhejiang	5.855	9.044	7.45
78	Longquan	Lishui	Zhejiang	5.436	8.971	7.204
51	Ruili	Dehong	Yunnan	6.489	10.303	8.396
84	Wujiaqu	Wujiaqu	Xinjiang	0.856	13.216	7.036
59	Linzhi	Linzhi	Tibet	4.157	12.009	8.083
80	Jinghai	Tianjin	Tianjin	4.996	9.279	7.138
18	Pixian	Chengdu	Sichuan	3.078	21.222	11.65
28	Shuangliu	Chengdu	Sichuan	4.861	15.172	10.016
97	Houma	Linfen	Shanxi	2.112	11.095	6.603

(continued)

Table 6.1 (continued)

Ranking	County	City	Province	E-commerce index	E-shopping index	E-commerce development index
88	Jimo	Qingdao	Shandong	6.578	7.221	6.9
91	Longkou	Yantai	Shandong	3.555	10.049	6.802
93	Jiaozhou	Qingdao	Shandong	5.556	7.989	6.773
96	Boxing	Binzhou	Shandong	5.985	7.27	6.627
8	Kunshan	Suzhou	Jiangsu	8.062	21.789	14.925
10	Changshu	Suzhou	Jiangsu	13.419	15.419	14.419
13	Haimen	Nantong	Jiangsu	11.8	14.576	13.188
16	Taicang	Suzhou	Jiangsu	7.214	17.092	12.153
35	Lianyungang	Suzhou	Jiangsu	5.554	13.207	9.38
38	Jiangyin	Wuxi	Jiangsu	5.408	12.939	9.174
58	Yixing	Wuxi	Jiangsu	5.635	10.645	8.14
61	Danyang	Zhenjiang	Jiangsu	6.297	9.683	7.99
74	Jingjiang	Taizhou	Jiangsu	5.061	9.653	7.357
85	Jianhu	Yancheng	Jiangsu	5.058	9.003	7.03
87	Donghai	Lianyungang	Jiangsu	5.883	7.981	6.932
89	Yangzhong	Zhenjiang	Jiangsu	3.881	9.879	6.88
90	Xinghua	Taizhou	Jiangsu	5.065	8.597	6.831
92	Suining	Xuzhou	Jiangsu	6.743	6.835	6.789
68	Yanji	Yanbian	Jilin	4.893	10.236	7.565
64	Changsha	Changsha	Hunan	3.843	11.85	7.847
82	Lengshuijiang	Loudi	Hunan	3.466	10.727	7.096
98	Jishou	Xiangxi	Hunan	2.186	10.984	6.585
60	Suifenhe	Wudanjiang	Heilongjiang	3.662	12.35	8.006
40	Xinzheng	Zhengzhou	Henan	3.206	14.865	9.035

(continued)

Table 6.1 (continued)

Ranking	County	City	Province	E-commerce index	E-shopping index	E-commerce development index
9	Qinghe	Xingtai	Hebei	13.901	15.374	14.638
31	Gaobeidian	Baoding	Hebei	11.747	8.017	9.882
42	Anping	Hengshui	Hebei	12.014	5.897	8.955
50	Nangong	Xingtai	Hebei	8.349	8.335	8.442
66	Xianghe	Langfang	Hebei	6.501	9.068	7.784
86	Bazhou	Langfang	Hebei	5.97	7.998	6.984
27	Dongxing	Fangchenggang	Guangxi	7.763	12.392	10.078
77	Pinxiang	Chongzuo	Guangxi	3.71	10.705	7.207
36	Enping	Jiangmen	Guangdong	7.254	11.38	9.317
49	Huidong	Huizhou	Guangdong	6.558	10.525	8.41
81	Sihui	Zhaoqing	Guangdong	5.146	9.09	7.118
95	Heshan	Jiangmen	Guangdong	4.809	8.518	6.664
2	Shishi	Quanzhou	Fujian	15.309	22.195	18.752
7	Dehua	Quanzhou	Fujian	12.727	17.6	15.164
17	Minhou	Fuzhou	Fujian	6.239	17.429	11.834
26	Xianyou	Putian	Fujian	6.689	13.504	10.096
30	Jinjiang	Quanzhou	Fujian	7.506	12.373	9.939
33	Wuyishan	Nanping	Fujian	5.062	14.034	9.548
48	Fu'an	Ningde	Fujian	6.29	10.796	8.543
63	Zhenghe	Nanping	Fujian	5.347	10.538	7.942
70	Nan'an	Quanzhou	Fujian	4.785	10.218	7.502
75	Anxi	Quanzhou	Fujian	6.691	7.988	7.34
76	Fuqing	Fuzhou	Fujian	4.268	10.217	7.242
79	Changle	Fuzhou	Fujian	4.043	10.319	7.181

(continued)

Table 6.1 (continued)

Ranking	County	City	Province	E-commerce index	E-shopping index	E-commerce development index
83	Tuorong	Ningde	Fujian	4.41	9.744	7.077
94	Hui'an	Quanzhou	Fujian	4.506	9.035	6.771
99	Yongchun	Quanzhou	Fujian	3.152	10.006	6.579
100	Shaxian	Sanming	Fujian	3.216	9.939	6.577

Source Report of China development index of E-commerce model cities, 2014 ("2014年中国"电商百佳城市"榜单揭晓-资讯-阿里研究院" [Report on the Development Indices of E-Commerce in Model Cities]. 2014. Aliresearch.Com. http://www.aliresearch.com/blog/article/detail/id/20472.html), AliResearch

Table 6.2 Top 10 province with largest number of listed counties 2014

Province	Number	Province	Number
Zhejiang	41	Henan	1
Fujian	16	Heilongjiang	1
Jiangsu	14	Jilin	1
Hebei	6	Shanxi	1
Guangdong	4	Tianjin	1
Shandong	4	Tibet	1
Hunan	3	Xinjiang	1
Guangxi	2	Yunnan	1
Sichuan	2		

Source AliResearch ("2014年中国"电商百佳县"榜单揭晓-资讯-阿里研究院" [Top 100 Best-Performing Counties in E-Commerce in 2014]. 2014. Aliresearch.Com. http://www.aliresearch.com/blog/article/detail/id/20431.html)

Table 6.3 Top 10 cities with largest number of listed counties 2014

City	Number	City	Number
Quangzhou	7	Ningbo	5
Jinhua	6	Suzhou	4
Taizhou	6	Fuzhou	3
Wenzhou	6	Hangzhou	3
Jiaxing	5	Shaoxing	3
Lishui	5		

Source AliResearch ("2014年中国"电商百佳县"榜单揭晓-资讯-阿里研究院" [Top 100 Best-Performing Counties in E-Commerce in 2014]. 2014. Aliresearch.Com. http://www.aliresearch.com/blog/article/detail/id/20431.html)

In the meantime, e-commerce is also penetrating village-based industries and productions. Township enterprises and rural workshops are plugged into the local grid. Taobao villages [2] first appeared in 2006, with 24 located in Jiangsu. The most prominent one was Dongfeng village, Suining county, Xuzhou city north Jiangsu province. It becomes the first Taobao village in China through its furniture production and processing industry. The whole industry chain of has been expanded to cover villages within a 15 min drive, including Xiawei village, Xingguo village, Dingchen village, Zhumiao village and Dazhong village in Sucheng district of Suqian. These areas are increasingly urbanized. Zhejiang is home to 62 Taobao villages, including Bainiu village (which sells nuts and roasted seeds) in Lin'an of Hangzhou and Beishan village (which sells outdoor goods) in Jinyun county of Lishui. Suichang county is another example. It develops a unique model of agricultural products rural- urban upstreaming and industrial products urban-rural downstreaming.

Zhejiang Takes the Lead in Rural E-Commerce with Its 62 Taobao Villages

By the end of 2014, 62 Taobao villages had been founded in Zhejiang, accounting for 29.2% in its total number. As of last year, there were 212 Taobao villages across the country altogether. Zhejiang is therefore home to the largest number of Taobao villages, followed by Guangdong (54), Fujian (28), Hebei (25) and Jiangsu (25).

In terms of geographical distribution, the 62 Taobao villages in Zhejiang are located in nine prefecture-level cities, namely Hangzhou, Huzhou, Jiaxing, Jinhua, Lishui, Ningbo, Shaoxing, Taizhou, Wenzhou. Except for Quzhou and Zhoushan, each prefecture-level city in Zhejiang has its own Taobao village, with Taizhou and Jiaxing ranking first in the list, 13 villages each.

Zhejiang is also a top runner in terms of Taobao town. Based on the current distribution data, the existing 19 Taobao villages were located in Zhejiang (6), Guangdong (5), Fujian (2), Jiangsu (2), Shandong (2) and Hebei (2).

It is reported that the 62 Taobao villages in Zhejiang represents 15 thousand Taobao stores. If each store in a Taobao village creates 4 jobs, the Taobao villages in Zhejiang has offered jobs for 60 thousand people.

Three major factors that contributed to the rising of Taobao village in Zhejiang

Zhejiang boasts time-honored commercial and cultural traditions, which have significantly underpinned the formation and growth of Taobao villages. Barter trade, as an example, finds deep roots in Yiwu, Zhejiang, where people traded chicken feather for sugar since long time ago. It is this catalytic tradition that facilitated the rising of Taobao villages in the Internet era. As a result, one of the first Taobao villages, Qingyanliu village, was born. Other villages were also coming to the fore in neighboring regions. By the end of 2014, 5 Taobao villages were found in Yiwu.

The massive economic basis further bolsters the growth of Taobao village. If we take a closer look at the distribution of Taobao villages, we may find that many of them are founded on the basis of the original economic blocks. In the meantime, Taobao villages have transformed and restructured traditional industries, hence becoming a model of "Internet + industry cluster" pattern.

Well-positioned governance is a more important factor than relaxed policies in bringing Taobao villages in Zhejiang to the forefront position. In Zhejiang, local governments attach great significance to rural e-commerce, or Taobao villages to be more specific. A good relationship with government can mean better financial support, the ability to attract higher talent, and cooperation on key issues (such as land and logistics) for entrepreneurs. Taobao villages are then able to enjoy conducive policies and strong government support.

Based on *The 2015 Report on Taobao Villages in Zhejiang* Released by AliResearch (Tables 6.6 and 6.7).

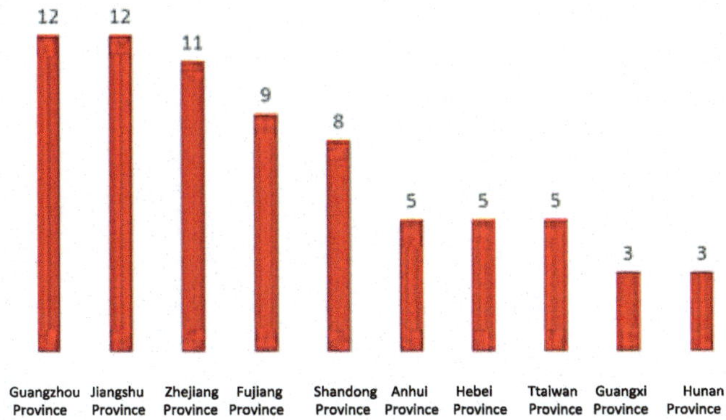

Fig. 6.2 Top five provinces with the largest number of listed counties. *Source* AliResearch ("2014年中国"电商百佳县"榜单揭晓-资讯-阿里研究院" [Top 100 Best-Performing Counties in E-Commerce in 2014]. 2014. Aliresearch.Com. http://www.aliresearch.com/blog/article/detail/id/20431.html)

The ecommerce index of cities and counties was addressed to explain the general situation of national scale in China with comparison of different regions' ecommerce condition through Alibaba's data. It's just one aspect to understand the impact on the urban-rural relationship from ecommerce.

In top 100 counties or cities with the Development Indices of E-Commerce, the Suichang county is not included. In fact, Suichang is a small or middle scale county out of around 2800 counties in China with 260 thousand residents. The meaning of this case study in Suichang is its innovation in providing an ecommerce service system in cooperation with the local ecommerce association. From this aspect, we can watch closely its structure and processes. The following development is therefore not about the quantity of ecommerce in Suichang and this is why I chose it as a case study in Chap. 4 (Fig. 6.3).

In those index, we can also notice the unbalance distribution of ecommerce development among counties and cities from different regions, which constitutes the first challenge faced by ecommerce actors. Therefore, it may be relevant to focus on this unevenness by comparing the counties' GDP and the distribution of ecommerce services across China. For instance, the maps showing the distribution of GDP per capita on a province scale, the Online Shopping Index and the Online Business Index geographic distribution from 2013 to 2015 highlight this asymmetry. However, it seems that ecommerce would not be a sufficient answer to solve this issue (Figs. 6.4, 6.5, 6.6 and 6.7).

> While China's economic development as always been uneven—richest counties being located on the east part of the Heihe–Tengchong Line[3] (the line separating China from Heihe to Tengchong), ecommerce seems to be following the same trend. Therefore, even

[3]Wang and Pan [3].

Table 6.4 The 2014 e-commerce index in some demonstration cities (based on the data of 52 sample cities)

National ranking	City	E-commerce development index	National ranking	City	E-commerce development index	National ranking	City	E-commerce development index
1	Shenzhen	26.926	27	Fuzhou	10.689	66	Yinchuan	7.011
2	Guangzhou	24.102	28	Changsha	10.548	67	Xuzhou	6.985
4	Hangzhou	19.694	29	Hefei	10.353	76	Yantai	6.594
6	Xiamen	15.854	30	Chengdu	10.116	78	Lanzhou	6.537
8	Dongguan	15.217	31	Jinan	9.873	84	Zhuzhou	6.175
9	Beijing	15.062	32	Xi'an	9.691	86	Changchun	6.04
10	Suzhou	14.922	34	Nanchang	9.493	89	Jieyang	5.973
13	Putian	14.661	35	Qingdao	9.297	92	Weifang	5.763
14	Shanghai	14.221	36	Taiyuan	9.183	97	Chongqing	5.451
15	Ningbo	14.041	42	Shantou	8.367	100	Ha'erbin	5.415
16	Wenzhou	13.517	45	Tianjin	8.251	110	Luoyang	5.159
17	Nanjing	12.743	48	Wuhu	7.993	123	Guilin	4.904
18	Quanzhou	12.42	52	Kunming	7.752	127	Yichang	4.835
19	Wuhan	11.964	57	Guiyang	7.554	133	Ganzhou	4.681
20	Taizhou	11.747	58	Shenyang	7.542	147	Jilin	4.327
22	Wuxi	11.24	60	Nanning	7.232	171	Xiangyang	3.97
24	Changzhou	11.042	62	Shijiazhuang	7.076			
25	Zhengzhou	11.01	64	Huhehaote	7.038			

Source Report of China development index of E-commerce model cities, 2014 ("2014年中国"电商百佳城市"榜单揭晓-资讯-阿里研究院" [Report on the Development Indices of E-Commerce in Model Cities]. 2014. Aliresearch.Com. http://www.aliresearch.com/blog/article/detail/id/20472.html), AliResearch

Table 6.5 The 2014 e-commerce service index in some demonstration cities (based on the data of 36 sample cities)

Ranking	City	E-commerce service index	Ranking	City	E-commerce service index
1	Hangzhou	29.92	19	Wuhan	0.662
2	Shanghai	8.592	20	Shijiazhuang	0.61
3	Guangzhou	5.442	21	Zhengzhou	0.607
4	Beijing	5.156	22	Chongqing	0.56
5	Shenzhen	5.059	23	Fuzhou	0.53
6	Wenzhou	1.637	24	Shantou	0.501
7	Suzhou	1.429	25	Qingdao	0.492
8	Dongguan	1.378	26	Changsha	0.48
9	Nanjing	1.259	27	Xi'an	0.462
10	Taizhou	1.169	28	Nanchang	0.42
11	Quanzhou	1.15	29	Putian	0.367
12	Ningbo	1.036	30	Changzhou	0.338
13	Chengdu	0.983	31	Shenyang	0.307
14	Hefei	0.728	32	Xuzhou	0.268
15	Xiamen	0.711	33	Kunming	0.19
16	Wuxi	0.71	34	Taiyuan	0.182
17	Jinan	0.694	35	Harbin	0.175
18	Tianjin	0.671	36	Nanning	0.111

Source Report of China development index of E-commerce model cities, 2014 ("2014年中国"电商百佳城市"榜单揭晓-资讯-阿里研究院" [Report on the Development Indices of E-Commerce in Model Cities]. 2014. Aliresearch.Com.http://www.aliresearch.com/blog/article/detail/id/20472.html), AliResearch

> though it may have been suggested that ecommerce could absorb such development inequalities, it has been actually confirming this pattern according to the study of the evolution of ecommerce from 2013 to 2015. The maps presented above (Fig. 6.3) clearly show that the geographical distribution of both ecommerce practices and counties' economic performances are overlapping. Therefore, counties where indexes such as the GDP per capita, the share of the GDP in secondary and tertiary sectors are higher have a much higher OSI (Online Shopping index) and OBI (Online Business index).

Alibaba and other platforms started urban ecommerce at the end of the 90s, much earlier than the development of rural ecommerce (the concept of the Taobao village was firstly defined in 2006, and the first phenomenon of ecommerce association in county level emerged around 2010). The urban ecommerce, especially in first to third class cities, is developing better than in counties and villages nearby. Moreover, nowadays, based on low levels of ecommerce service, rural ecommerce develops faster than the urban ecommerce by the data in national scale. Ever since, main ecommerce stakeholders have been dedicating themselves to fill the development gap between rural and urban areas, which is the second challenge they will have been tackling for the past few years and that they will keep facing in the future.

Table 6.6 Provincial distribution of "Taobao villages" 2014

Ranking	Province	Number of Taobao villages	Ranking	Province	Number of Taobao villages
1	Zhejiang	62	6	Shangdong	13
2	Guangdong	54	7	Sichuan	2
3	Fujian	28	8	Henan	1
4	Hebei	25	9	Tianjin	1
5	Jiangsu	25	10	Hubei	1

Source Research Report on China's Taobao Villages (2014) (http://i.aliresearch.com/img/20141223/20141223163126.pdf)

Table 6.7 Number of Taobao towns of district/county as of 2014

Index	Province	City	District/county	Town/township/village	No. of Taobao villages
1	Guangdong	Guangzhou	Zengcheng City	Xintang Town	9
2	Guangdong	Guangzhou	Baiyun District	Taihe Town	7
3	Shandong	Heze	Cao County	Daji Township	6
4	Hebei	Xingtai	Qinghe County	Gexianzhuang Town	6
5	Hebei	Baoding	Gaobeidian city	Baigou NewCity	5
6	Shandong	Binzhou	Boxing County	Jinqiu Street	5
7	Zhejiang	Wenzhou	Yongjia County	Qiaoxia Town	5
8	Jiangsu	Xuzhou	Juning County	Shaji Town	5
9	Fujian	Quanzhou	Anxi County	Shangqing Township	5
10	Zhejiang	Jinhua	Yiwu City	Jiangdong Street	4
11	Zhejiang	Taizhou	Tiantai County	Tantou Town	4
12	Zhejiang	Taizhou	Wenling City	Zeguo Town	4
13	Guangdong	Jieyang	Puning City	Zhanglong Town	4
14	Fujian	Putian	Xianyou County	Bangtou Town	3
15	Jiangsu	Nantong	Tongzhou County	Chuanjiang Town	3
16	Guangdong	Guangzhou	Panyu District	Nancun Town	3
17	Zhejiang	Hangzhou	Lin'an District	Qingliangfeng Town	3
18	Guangdong	Guangzhou	Huadu District	Shiling Town	3
19	Zhejiang	Huzhou	Wuxing District	Zhili Town	3

Source Research Report on China's Taobao Villages (2014) (http://i.aliresearch.com/img/20141223/20141223163126.pdf)

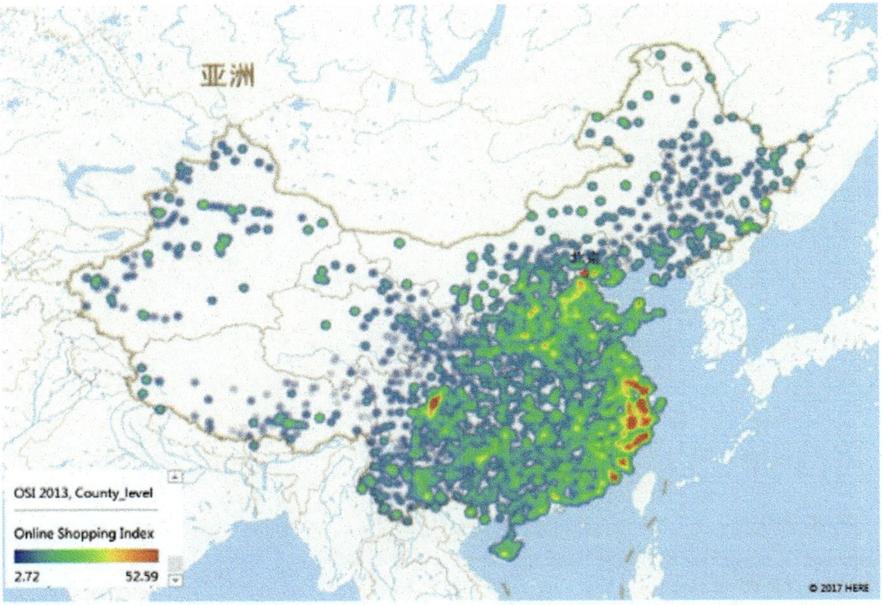

Fig. 6.3 Online shopping index geographical distribution 2013 (county-level). *Source* AliResearch

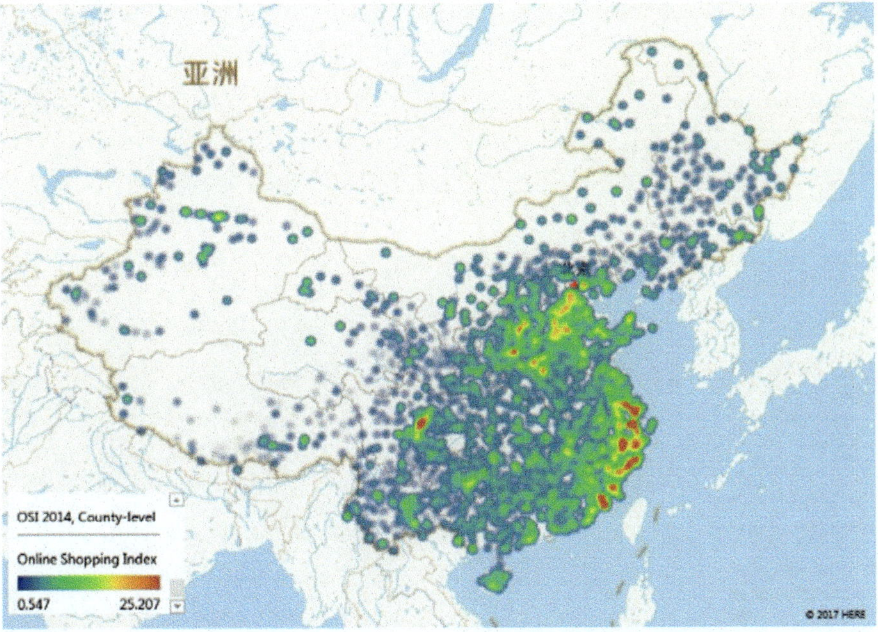

Fig. 6.4 Online shopping index geographical distribution 2014 (county-level). *Source* AliResearch

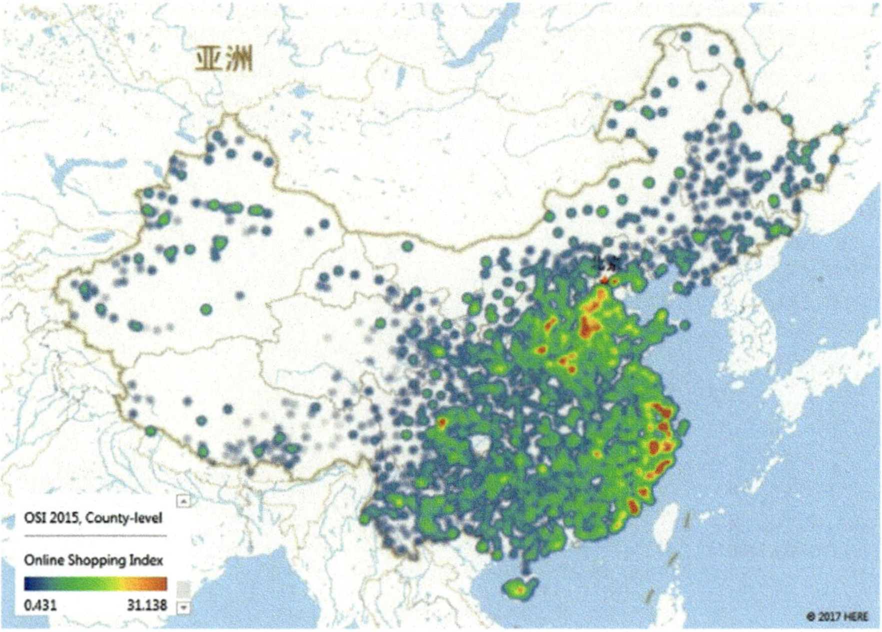

Fig. 6.5 Online shopping index geographical distribution 2015 (county-level). *Source* AliResearch

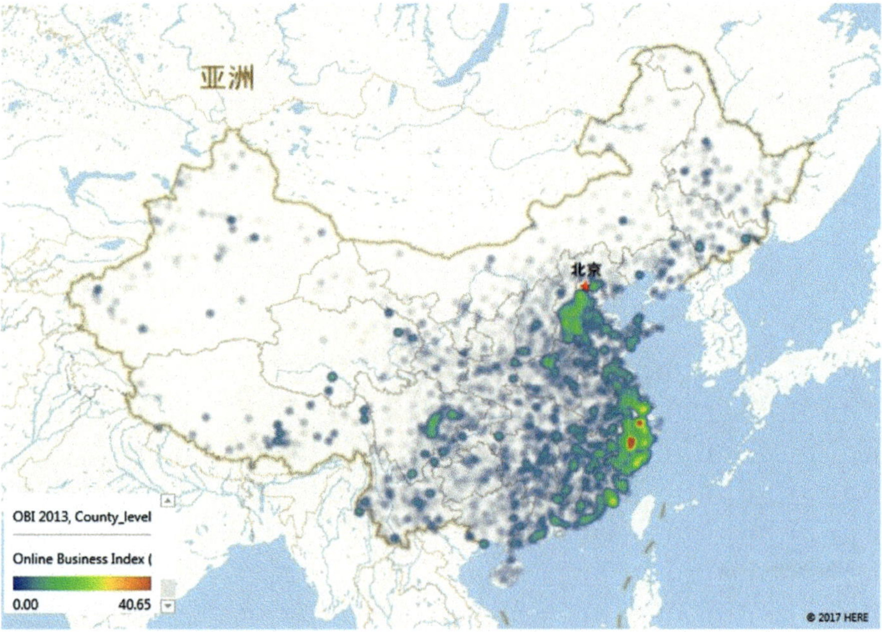

Fig. 6.6 Online business index geographical distribution 2013 (county-level). *Source* AliResearch

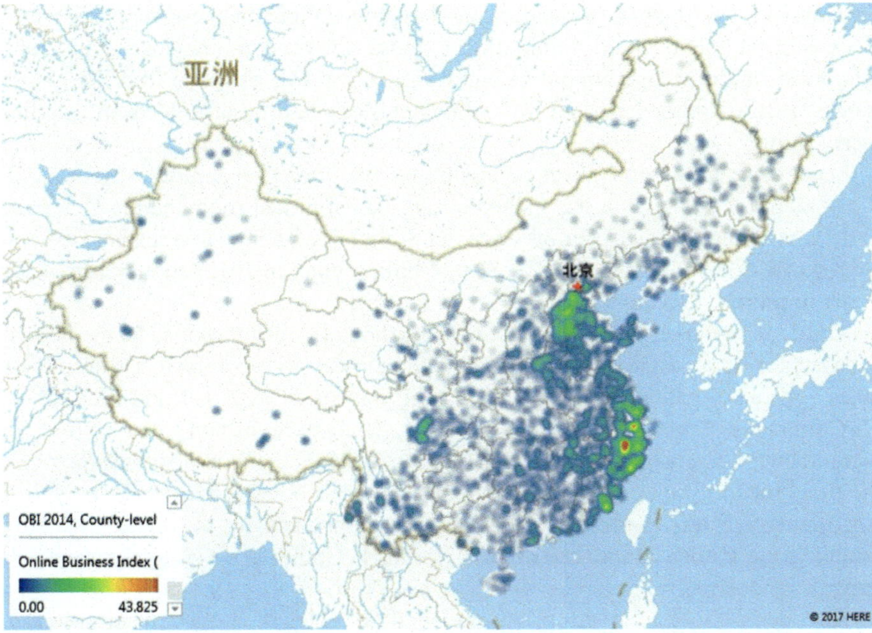

Fig. 6.7 Online business index geographical distribution 2014 (county-level). *Source* AliResearch

While ecommerce will enable counties and villages to become nodes of information and flows, crucial to their development, their connection to the cities' cluster could be an opportunity when facing this second challenge.

6.2 Nodes that Construct Different Levels of Urbanization

Now let's illustrate the flowing nodes from the perspective of city, county, village and rural household.

(1) City level

Hangzhou is a very typical case, as it is leading the national e-commerce service industry. Hangzhou is a pillar of growth in the online service sector, integrating the service sector of the whole Delta.

According to the 2014 Report on the Development Indices of E-Commerce in Model Cities released by AliResearch in 2014, Hangzhou's leading position in e-commerce is embodied in the following aspects:

First, it has the most comprehensive service portfolio in e-commerce. According to one rough estimation, Hangzhou is home to over one third of the nation's e-commerce websites. At the same time, many professional e-commerce service providers choose their headquarters in Hangzhou, their business scopes covering electronic payment, cloud computing, express delivery, online marketing, information technology, operational services and so on. We can also find the world's biggest B2B e-commerce platform, online retailing platform and electronic platform in Hangzhou.

Second, e-commerce revenue continues to increase rapidly. Since 2002, e-commerce in Hangzhou has gained strong development momentum. This sector underwent a rapid growth period since 2008, with its e-commerce revenue growing from 4.002 billion yuan in 2008 to 74.024 billion yuan in 2014, an increase of 17.5 times in merely 7 years.

Third, innovative ideas abound in Hangzhou. In recent years, Hangzhou has been exploring a sustainable and systematic pathway to e-commerce, where it also takes the lead nationally. In 2008, Hangzhou was awarded the title of the "E-Commerce Capital in China". In 2011, Hangzhou became one of the first e-commerce demonstration cities in China. In 2014, Hangzhou also became one of the first cities to pilot cross-border e-commerce, and opened the first Cross-Border E-Commerce Park. In 2015, Hangzhou was authorized by the State Council to establish the China (Hangzhou) Cross-Border E-Commerce Comprehensive Pilot Area.

Anyone who once lived in or travelled to Hangzhou has experienced the sophistication and convenience of its e-commerce services. A smart phone can almost take care of every aspect in people's daily lives. And these services are extending towards the whole Yangtze River Delta.

(2) County level

Tonglu is a good example here. In Tonglu, export-oriented township enterprises were once the mainstay. Now, inter-market enterprises have developed the e-commerce industry to transform not only itself but the development model of its counties and villages.

As previously mentioned, by 2014, the industrial structure in Tonglu has matured. It has become a model in the development of traditional economy. Tonglu becomes a typical case in that it supports its export-oriented processing industry with local rent, cheap cost of manpower and other resources. However, the economic landscape continues to change, RMB depreciates, the international market shrinks, and OEMs are moving to Southeast Asia and other places. All these factors have reduced market shares of SMEs in towns and townships, brought about fiercer competition and eaten away profits. Industrial structure in counties is in urgent need of transformation. All these challenges have put its SMEs in a positive position.

As Hangzhou develop is rural and cross-border e-commerce, Tonglu has been seizeing this opportunity to engage in regional integration. It has basically finished building an ecosystem for county e-commerce. 57 e-commerce companies have been admitted into the existing three county-level e-commerce industrial park. Besides, the 6 county incubation parks have incubated 165 e-commerce companies. The 8 local supporting platforms have provided services to over 4600 e-commerce business entities and individuals. 9 e-commerce warehousing and logistics platforms are already in service. 6 e-commerce public education bases have provided training for over 10 thousand people. Rural Taobao and rural service stations in Tonglu have come into service and achieved full coverage, which is unprecedented in China. In Taobao and Tmall alone, we can find 5100 local businesses. There are 52 key enterprises in Tonglu whose annual sales volume reaches 5 million yuan or more. Online sales in Tonglu exceed 1.454 billion yuan. Based on these achievements, Tonglu becomes the E-Commerce Demonstration County in Zhejiang. Its marketing and business zones become expansion areas for National E-Commerce Demonstration Cities. In 2013, online sales in Tonglu County quadrupled, registering an increase of 201% over the previous year. Sales volume in 2014 increased by 142% over 2013. It is estimated that 2015 will witness another increase of 150%.

Tonglu has adopted two strategies to develop rural e-commerce. On the one hand, it deploys rural e-commerce service stations to the whole county to ensure that rural logistics is available all over the county. On the other hand, it creates more marketing channels and expands its online market by building platforms such as e-commerce industrial parks for agricultural products. On top of these two strategies, it leverages the microcredit services of Ant Financial to address the shortage of funds. To be more specific, it acquires funding from credit loans from Rural Taobao and startup-targeted microcredit, in a bid to attract people to start business here. With the innovations made by grassroot efforts, Tonglu is able to smooth the relations between the government, business and the market. The online service sector, especially e-commerce, has made its way into other sectors to extend the industrial chain both upward and downward.

(3) County and Village

We will illustrate this aspect with Dongfeng village, Shaji. By observing the development of this Taobao village, we may find clues as for how the online urbanization links villages into the global and regional space of flows.

Dongfeng village, Shaji is a very representative Taobao village. We can learn a lot from its growth, especially from the interrelations between Dongfeng village, Shaji town and the Gengche town. Gengche town locates right in front of Dongfeng village. It is a very typical township enterprise in the 80s and the prototype of Gengche Model.[4]

Genche town stands next to Shaji town in Suqian city, north of Jiangsu. It was originally an impoverished village until 1987 when it was turned into a town. From 1984 to the early 90s, it developed the garbage and waste processing industry, a new and omnichannel service system. It reached multiple levels including towns, villages, household unions and individual households, and spanned across multiple industries including manufacturing, commerce, construction, transportation and service sectors. Genche town developed its collective and family-based economy in

[4]Zhou Erliu, Zhang Yulin. (1994). *Research on the Development in Urban and Rural China*. Hong Kong, China: Oxford University Press.

a balanced and coordinated way, while engaging and cooperating with urban businesses, universities and research institutes in various forms. Therefore, Genche became a successful model of urban-rural integration in north Jiangsu, and was spoken of highly by Mr. Fei Xiaotong by referring to this model as "Genche" model.

In the early 1980s, there were 19 villages in Genche town, with only 8200 households or a population of 43,000. Much of the 7018 acres of arable land were salinized with low yield. Some villages were so poor that many of their residents were reduced to beggars. In Huating village, the Master of Junk Dealers Zhou Shuocai and his son Zhou Deji led their fellow villagers to recycle and reprocess ragged cloths and worn-out cottons. It worked so well that later on, workshops and plants managed by individual households or household unions sprang up like mushrooms in the town. As of 1989, there were altogether 5863 township enterprises reprocessing recycled goods. These enterprises recycled over 10,000 tons of discarded items annually from other places and sold reprocessed products to over 10 provinces and cities. In this way, a niche market for recycled and repurposed goods was created. What's more, the various trades that each village once depended on to make a living were gradually industrialized. For example, by building on its wooden toy industry, Sanyi village gradually expanded its line of business to produce other sought-after wooden products including high heels, handles of wooden spoons, table and bed legs, cloth racks, etc. Over 100 kinds of products were sold to other provinces. Dongfeng village, which locates at 10 min drive away from Sanyi village, Genche town, also followed its example by developing recycling industry.

In 2006, Dongfeng village, Shaji town began to set foot in the e-commerce industry when the graduate of Nanjing Forestry University, Sun Han opened the first Taobao shop to sell assembled furniture. By 2010, Taobao villages had undergone tremendous development across the whole Shaji town. "Shaji Model"[5] was then created.

As of 2010, there have been over 600 farmers turned online merchants, more than 2000 online stores, 16 delivery companies, 6 panel processors, 2 furniture and accessory markets and 1 e-commerce service provider. In 2010, the online sales reached over 300 million yuan, a real industrial cluster therefore came into being. Here is Wang Xiangdong's remarks at the updated Shaji Model: it is the second stage of a bottom-up rural e-commerce development model. To break this down, it refers to a preliminary industrial ecosystem that consists of online merchants and multiple components. Those online merchants are mostly farming households who turned to rural e-commerce to make a living. With a third-party e-commerce platform, they can spring up spontaneously, multiply and expand rapidly, and organize themselves voluntarily.

[5]Wang Xiangdong's, "Shaji Model 2.0". Followed-up Research on a Rural E-Commerce Model, second issue of Ali Business Review "Small Towns, Profound Impact".

Fig. 6.8 Busy logistic during the night at Dongfen village. *Source* Sun Han

Industrial aggregation will naturally create more jobs, require better commercial and public service facilities and boost urbanization process. Online-aggregated industries in Shaji generates a sales volume of 3 billion yuan. Its industries and population are on the threshold of urbanization, but the unaddressed public service issues (medical care, education, etc.) still put those family-owned or collectively-run businesses under considerable stress.

Shaji town is at the jurisdiction of Xuzhou city and is very close to Suqian city, the latter two are prefecture-level cities. Due to the geographical advantages, Shaji town is able to establish close relations with Genche town. In the same way, in 2014, Genche town also joined in the furniture industry, a more environmental-friendly one. Both of the towns attract job hunters from a dozen miles away. An e-commerce-driven industrial cluster was hence created. And if this cluster continues to expand, we wonder whether it will share the public service facilities in Suqian, and be linked to the industrial cluster and regional space of flows with Genche town and Shaji town at its core. Besides, if the cluster is to be expanded to form a wider ecosystem, let's say 20 or 30 miles, it is imperative to explore a new business model and industrial chain (supply-demand relations) to underpin it. In this case, we need to focus on more aspects in practicing and studying rural e-commerce, such as public service, supplementary service, jurisdiction, cultural identification, capital flow, human resource allocation, land distribution, information flow, logistics, to name just a few (Fig. 6.8).

6.3 City Cluster Online

Furthermore, E-commerce at county-level and Taobao villages share similar development trajectory with city cluster:

6.3.1 The Yangtze River Delta

Since the year 2000, the city cluster in Yangtze River Delta has taken shape and therefore grabbed much public attention. A city cluster centered around Shanghai was formed, surrounded by major cities,[6] as well as neighboring towns and villages. By 2015, the population in the city cluster of Yangtze River Delta was 800 million [4] based on a rough estimation and the urbanization rate in core areas exceeded 60%. Not only did Shanghai become an international financial center and the Asian headquarters of many conglomerates, the peripheral villages and towns also experience rapid development for being linked to the global production chain. We find it similar to the development approach of the Pearl River Delta. In *Towards Competition and Cooperation: Comparing the Economic Growth between the Pearl River Delta and Yangtze River Delta*, author Zhu Wenhui notes that rural private enterprises benefited most from the industrialized villages in Jiangsu.[7] In 2001, township enterprises in Jiangsu invested 70 billion yuan in fixed assets, an increase of 10 billion yuan over last year. The region spanning from South Jiangsu to Nanjing is rapidly overtaking Pearl River Delta to become the most popular destination for foreign investment. In 2002, Jiangsu used more foreign investment than Guangdong, ranking first in the country. Besides, it is important to mention that 24 counties (cities) in Zhejiang were shortlisted in the Top 100 Counties (Cities) in China, which was unparalleled nationwide. Those developed counties started by selling specialized products in their peripheral market and improving quality of their offerings. Their leading industries are getting stronger day by day. We may find three features that are distinctive to this region: first, they are selling petty commodities in a grand market and yielding high returns; second, trivial capitals are accumulating extensively; third, exportation has become the mainstream.

In 2008, however, China's export-oriented economy confronted many obstacles, bringing forth an urgent need for county economy to transform itself. In this regard, Tonglu county and Changshan county in Zhejiang have explored their unique ways to transform.

Tonglu county is the first place to pilot Rural Taobao, therefore, it can reap the first mover advantages on rural e-commerce. If Suichang develops rural e-commerce merely to shake off extreme poverty, Tonglu, an affluent county in Zhejiang or even China, on the other hand, makes this choice only to transform itself. As noted by county magistrate Mr. Fang Yi, it does so because it has no choice.

---

[6]Including Nanjing, Suzhou, Wuxi, Hangzhou, Ningbo, and Changzhou, Zhenjiang, Yangzhou, Taizhou, Nantong, Huzhou, Jiaxing, Shaoxing, Zhoushan, Taizhou, Lianyungang, Xuzhou, Yancheng, Huai'an, Suqian, Wenzhou, Jinhua, Quzhou and Lishui

[7]Zhu [5].

The economic landscape continues to change, RMB depreciates, the international market shrinks, and OEMs[8] are moving to Southeast Asia and other places. All these factors have reduced market shares of SMEs[9] in towns and townships, have brought about fiercer competition and have eaten away at profits. Industrial structure in counties is in urgent need of transformation. As the export-oriented economy in coastal areas of eastern China losing its market share and profit margins, the jeopardized SMEs in those areas may end up in the dock. As the result, the government and enterprises have to reflect on how to survive by expanding the domestic market, since export-oriented economy can hardly be sustained in those counties. However, in making such changes, they may find it hard to handle insufficient independent brands, design capabilities, teams and marketing networks. Previously, their orders came directly from foreign trade companies rather than consumers, which meant that they themselves had no market. In terms of brand, enterprises in Tonglu does not own any independent brands as OEMs do. In terms of design, OEMs make products by following samples, instead of designing on their own. These are the hurdles standing in the way of county enterprises. If they expand domestic market under a traditional business model, they would be short of both funding and time, and they also have to confront with fierce competition.

From August 2012 to the end of 2013, Tonglu launched a Head Start program to foster a strong sense of crisis and opportunity. It reminded government departments and enterprises of the fact that the exiting market of e-commerce is not only enormous, but highly potential. To this end, Tonglu freed up minds, integrated resources, including human, product and platform resources, and leveraged the expertise of Alibaba, so that government officials and entrepreneurs could embrace new ideas in a short time.

Later on, Tonglu county adopted a "1234 Initiative" to transform the development approach of counties and villages. The Initiative includes:

One comprehensive plan to define short-term and long-term objectives, organize development phases, choose what and how to support chosen programs.

Two centers, which refer to the e-commerce public service center and warehousing and logistics center.

Three parks and four platforms consisting of two e-commerce industrial parks, one agro-product e-commerce industrial parks and their respective industrial platforms.

Logistics and express delivery industry in Tonglu also underwent swift development.

As we can see, e-commerce is an enabling tool for various counties to explore their own path to urbanization.

---

[8]An original equipment manufacturer (OEM) is a company that makes a part or subsystem that is used in another company's end product.

[9]Small Medium Enterprises.

6.3.1.1 The Fujian Province

Fujian has four major cities: Fuzhou, Quanzhou, Zhangzhou and Xiamen. It bridges Yangtze River Delta and Pearl River Delta. 16 counties in Fujian entered the list of Top 100 E-Commerce Counties, and 6 were in Quanzhou and 3 in Fuzhou. Quanzhou therefore becomes home to the largest number of e-commerce counties in Fujian, and the credit should be given to its strong industrial clusters. According to the 2015 Report on the Work of the Quanzhou Government, Quanzhou focused on industrial agglomeration to provide a platform for the vigorous private sector to leap forward. The advanced industrial clusters in Quanzhou are built upon the existing niche markets. This is why Quanzhou leads other townships to form a textile and garment cluster (urban areas, Jinjiang, Shishi and Nan'an), a footwear cluster (Jinjiang), a building ceramic and stone cluster (mainly distributed in Jinjiang, Nan'an and Hui'an), as well as a handiwork cluster (Fengze, Jinjiang, shishi, Hui'an, Anxi, Dehua and so on) [5]. These clusters continue to upgrade with e-commerce. And Quanzhou, the city where the Maritime Silk Road begins, will become a pioneer in e-commerce in Fujian.

Fujian is home to 28 Taobao villages. The most representative two are villages that produce bamboo mats, one is Peixie village, Xinluo District, Longyan City, and the other is Qianbu village Shishi City, Quanzhou City (Fig. 6.9).

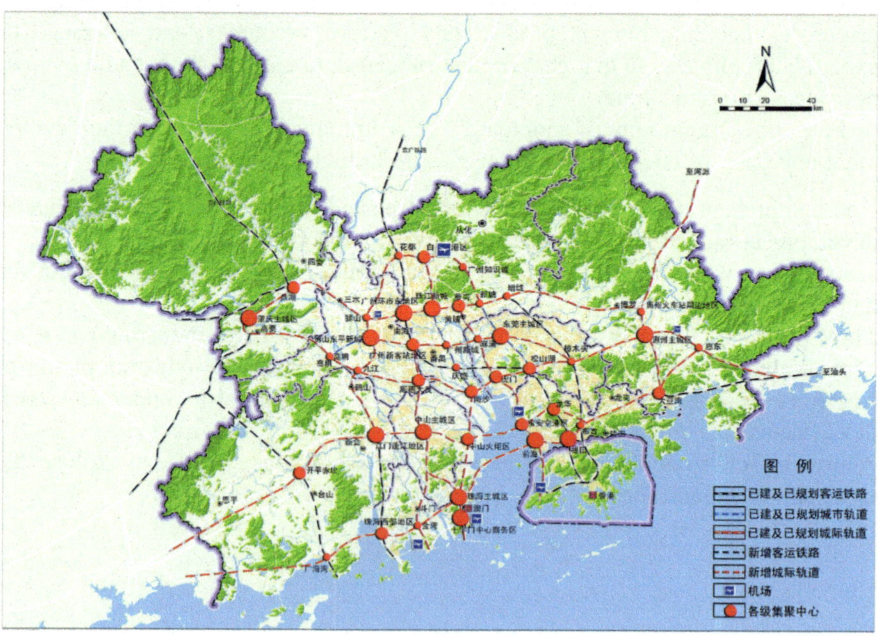

Fig. 6.9 City cluster in the Pearl River Delta. *Source* Planning on the urban-rural integration program in The Pearl River Delta (2009–2020) ("珠江三角洲城乡规划一体化规划 (2009–2020年)" [Planning on the Urban-Rural Integration Program in The Pearl River Delta (2009 to 2020)]. 2013. Zwgk.Gd.Gov.Cn. http://zwgk.gd.gov.cn/006939756/201506/t20150626_587371.html?keywords

6.3.2 Pearl River Delta

The city cluster in the Pearl River Delta began to take shape in late 1990s. It covers Hong Kong, Shenzhen, Guangzhou, Zhuhai, Macau, Huizhou, Dongguan, Zhaoqing, Foshan, Zhongshan, Jiangmen and the small towns and villages in this region. This cluster not only includes cities, but also links rural areas to its grid. We can find some traces in the shifting of Hong Kong's manufacturing industry towards rural areas in the Pearl River Delta, as described by Manuel Castells. To be more specific, Castells noted that from mid-1980s to mid-1990s, investors and entrepreneurs in Hong Kong have taken notice of the great potential of rural families and villages in the Pearl River Delta. Later on, large-scale industrialization took place. These investors and entrepreneurs funded over 10 thousand investments and invested in more than 20 thousand processing plants. The Pearl River Delta therefore attracted nearly 10 million laborers across the country. Rural areas in the Pearl River Delta were rapidly urbanized. Excluding urbanization data of Hong Kong, by the end of 2008, urbanization rate in the Pearl River Delta reached an 80.5%, average density population at 863/km^2 and lands reserved for construction reached a total area of 8790 km^2, 16% of the total land area in the Pearl River Delta.

The Pearl River Delta is now guided by Shenzhen, Guangzhou and Hong Kong. Its online service sector and e-commerce are showing great momentum. Measuring against the development index, Shenzhen and Guangzhou (Hong Kong excluded) are the two top performing cities in e-commerce, even the counties therein are becoming increasingly prominent in e-commerce development. Let's put it in this way, four of the top 100 e-commerce counties are in Guangdong, namely Enping, Huidong, Sihui and Heshan. By following the development pattern of township enterprises in the Pearl River Delta, as we mentioned earlier, Guangdong gains further edges in regional competition. Another 54 Taobao villages are linked into the regional network. The neighboring area within 30 min drive covers 10 villages from 3 districts.[10] The effect of aggregation provides favorable conditions to this region, where the mobile phone industry thrives.

Obviously, when the county-level e-commerce develops in a rapid and sustainable manner, the credit should be given to the involvement and support of local enterprises and partners upstream and downstream, as well as the in-depth integration of e-commerce into county economy.

We can conclude from the distribution pattern that transactions in Taobao happen most frequently in coastal areas of eastern China.

The integrated development of city cluster and counties takes place at different levels on e-commerce platforms.

If we look beyond the new pattern of urban-rural relation, we may find remarkable changes in how people organize their daily lives and production, no

[10]Shiqiaotou village, Jieyang city, Puning city, Xilou village, Xia village, Xinliao village and Dachanglong village, and reaches out to Dongbei village and Zhilan village in Chaonan district, Shantou city, as well as Donglong village and Xincuo village in Chaoyang district.

matter where they live. It is Internet technology and global capital that begets these changes. Suichang is a telling example to testify this judgment. By launching the Suichang Net Union, a localized public service platform for agricultural products is created under an "association + enterprise" model. The Union plays the role of an e-commerce server for agricultural product suppliers, so that it can probe into the rural market (farmers, cooperatives and rural enterprises). In the meantime, Ganjie.com and rural e-commerce service stations find their ways into each village to ensure that villager's needs are met. They also perform other jobs such as purchasing agents, traders of life necessities and agricultural products, and quality supervisors at the grass-root level. In the case of Suichang, a fairer, more transparent and extensive marketing platform is created by leveraging the Internet and mobile telecommunications. This platform grants rural market entities lower trading cost and more affordable land rent. In the future, a diversified urbanization model will be created. Besides, rural e-commerce practitioners receive training and proper financial and professional support so that they are better prepared to confront challenges in conducting businesses. Furthermore, Ganjie.com deploys offline sites and reaches out conventional village stores. In this way, it is possible for the real economy to transform and improve production, operation, resource utilization, community organization and spatial layout. Backed by Suichang Net Union and Ganjie.com, villages build supply platforms to match demands, foster more talents and improve public services. These undertakings aim at bolstering weak spots in government-provided public services in rural areas. The task of providing public service is delegated to the market and NGOs, not only improving government performance, but also narrowing urban-rural gaps.

References

1. Castells M (1996) The information age: economy, society, and culture. Volume I: the rise of the network society
2. Guixin W, Zehan P (2016) The robustness of China's migration and Heihe-Tengchong line. Chin Popul Today 4:8
3. "2014年中国"电商百佳城市"榜单揭晓-资讯-阿里研究院" [Report on the Development Indices of E-Commerce in Model Cities]. 2014. Aliresearch.Com. http://www.aliresearch.com/blog/article/detail/id/20472.html
4. "2014年中国"电商百佳县"榜单揭晓-资讯-阿里研究院" [Top 100 Best-Performing Counties in E-Commerce in 2014]. 2014. Aliresearch.Com. http://www.aliresearch.com/blog/article/detail/id/20431.html
5. Zhu W 朱文晖 (2003) *Zouxiangjinghe: zhusanjiao yu changsanjiao jingji fazhan bijiao 走向竞合: 珠三角与长三角经济发展比较 [Towards Competition and Cooperation: Comparing the Economic Growth between the Pearl River Delta and Yangtze River Delta]*. Tsinghua University Press: 清华大学出版社有限公司
6. "珠江三角洲城乡规划一体化规划 (2009—2020年)" [Planning on the Urban-Rural Integration Program in The Pearl River Delta (2009 to 2020)]. 2013. Zwgk.Gd.Gov.Cn. http://zwgk.gd.gov.cn/006939756/201506/t20150626_587371.html?keywords

Chapter 7
Conclusion: Urban Rural Flows with Online Urbanization

The urban and rural structural patterns are related to their social relations. The combination of technology and local communities has rendered the space of flows more grass-rooted, and has expanded the space of flows paradigm to much larger scale. The Internet of everything is coming upon us. The Space of flows is so pervasive, that maybe there is practically no non space of flows. As discussed previously, the phenomena in rural China are references of this trend.

7.1 Answer to the Research Questions

1. What is rural ecommerce in China?

Nowadays, rural ecommerce in China includes lot of styles, and in this book, I introduced two typical styles, Suichang Ecommerce Association model and Alibaba Rural Strategy (including Taobao village). I will then define rural ecommerce from the consideration of these two case studies.

Rural ecommerce is the phenomenon in which a large number of residents in towns and townships begin to use the Internet (including mobile commerce and other businesses and public services opportunities provided by the Internet) to enter the market and join the urban and rural production chain and local lives, build socializing networks, promote products online, and organize offline production, acquisition, transportation and community building, achieve local development, create jobs and improve business and public services. Rural ecommerce actors include farmers, small commodity producers, couriers who deliver packages and ecommerce practitioners who engage in online trading but also services such as healthcare. They are networkers in the information economy, as well as netizens in the cyber society. Carrying on the traditions upheld by cities and towns in the south of Yangtze River and heritages of countryside markets network during Song, Ming and Qing dynasty, rural ecommerce including local rural ecommerce platforms

L. Zi, *Online Urbanization*, Advances in 21st Century Human Settlements,
https://doi.org/10.1007/978-981-13-3603-4_7

(ex. Suichang ecommerce association) and national rural ecommerce platforms, or even international rural ecommerce platform (ex. Alibaba Rural Taobao villages and virtual communities came into being.

2. **What is the urban-rural spatial relationship under the influence of rural ecommerce in China?**

At the local level, the process of space renewal brought by rural ecommerce and other new media is actually a reconstruction of rural life, the upgrading of rural industry and the improvement of rural environments. The internet, and new media bring everyone online, and in doing so provide new opportunities for rural entrepreneurs, instigate private and public services, and make possible the creation of a deeply connected organization among rural societies, families and ethnic groups. The organization is based on social relationship and identities, including common cultural recognition and a shared value system, which continues to link to cities via the virtual space of Internet, connecting the local communities and outside network as a whole. The Internet breaks the barriers of traditional top-down administrative systems, as well as business system with many intermediaries, regaining the faded extraordinariness and glory in virtuality and reality. The space renewal becomes an extension of local lifestyle, social relationship and business eco-system.

At the regional scale, ecommerce is rising swiftly, giving momentum to the development of city clusters, and improving private and public services as new paradigm in China. It is manifested in five aspects: fostering and flowing of urban and rural human resources, the improvement of urban and rural logistics supply chain, the narrowing of urban and rural information and Technology gap, the effective resource allocation and urban-rural cultural progress. The urban and rural areas are unified as one network. A larger-scale city cluster is taking shape—the cluster that bridges Yangtze River Delta and Pearl River Delta, connects central and northern Zhejiang province and extends all the way to Shenzhen of Guangdong province. The rising of this cluster is perhaps the most significant event of urban development in the 21st century. Core areas of Yangtze River Delta (Shanghai, Suzhou, Hangzhou, Nanjing and so on) and Pearl River Delta (Hong Kong, Shenzhen, Guangzhou and so on) have all witnessed the emergence of vigorous towns, counties and villages. Empowered by the Internet and information technology, villages of these regions have gained access to the space of flows and therefore been turned into different nodes. Employment, business and public services therein are now on a par with their urban counterparts. These regions have become hubs of production and consumption activities as well as bases for innovative technologies and business models.

I thus define this phenomenon as "online urbanization "to analyze the updated urban-rural relations brought by online services (private and public services), creating jobs. The spatial transformation from city cluster (including county scale) and regeneration local township and village to the conservation of public or private space is what characterize online urbanization

7.2 Contribution About Online Urbanization

In order to discuss the impact of the Internet in the urban rural spatial relationship, I addressed some key authors on urbanization and spatial distribution, such as Saskia Sassen, Henri Lefebvre, and Manuel Castells. The definition of space of flows can be simplified as the global network and urban spaces formed by the Information Network and Financial Capital. However, space of flows and the grassrooting of space of flows in Euro-America and other more developed regions are aggressive, and does not adequately account for urban-rural relationships such as one in China. In China, the integration of space of flows is clearly reflected in the urban-rural unity and social practices, epitomized in the emergence of rural ecommerce. One of the main contributions of this research is to attempt to use China as a reference to gauge the accuracy of these theories.

As I mentioned before, Karl Polanyi put the technical reformation/innovation, economic globalization into the corresponding social transformation/reformation[1] From his mind, the First World War and the Second World War are part of the results of industrial revolution, due to the conflict between technical innovation, economic globalization and existing social structure. He discussed about the transformation of rural life with urbanization from Britain to all the Europe through industrialization and globalization. Nowadays, the informalization and digitalization expand from urban area to rural area all over the world, especially in China. In this term, Henri Lefebvre's in-depth analysis of globalization in *The Urban Revolutio*n[2] is helpful to understand the urban space is the kind of production of global capitalism. He asserted that with the expansion of the financial, commercial, and industrial networks, the traditional social structure and morphology of the city would suffer from disintegration. From the cases study about rural ecommerce in China, I may assert that the rural space can also become a part of the results of global capitalism. Maybe this is why the architect Rem Koolhaas recently talked about Generic Village[3] after Generic City when he said: "Husbandry of the land is now a digital practice, and the countryside in terms of how we work is becoming very similar to the city. The farmer is like us—a flex worker, operating on a laptop from any possible location"[4]. In this statement, he may have already felt that the digitalization and globalization make a new kind of rural space. Because his observation is based on his experience in European rural area, he cannot think about the phenomena of China's rural ecommerce and social media. Because of the Chinese civilization continuity and its unique urban rural relationship in history, I may still wonder how "generic" the villages in China will become. However, digitalization can both maintain local community's social and family's relationship,

[1]Polyani, Karl. The great transformation: *The political and economic origins of our time*. Beacon Press, 2007.

[2]Lefebvre, Henri. *The urban revolution*. U of Minnesota Press, 2003.

[3]https://www.gooood.cn/generic-village-study-of-village-by-rem-koolhaas.htm.

[4]https://www.iconeye.com/architecture/features/item/11031-rem-koolhaas-in-the-country

as well as introducing an innovative business model with the use of local social capital. This hypothesis is based on the observation made in Suichang Ecommerce Association and Alibaba Rural Strategy and from their practices such as building local logistic, creating local ecommerce services station, structuring online financial system. Therefore, we can assert with great certainty that the digitalization of rural China will become one of most important issues of globalization.

How to measure this rural transformation through digital services and globalization? Scholars who do research on urbanization and globalization have been bringing inspiring of methods to me. For example, Saskia Sassen analyzed global cities[5] when it comes to five topics including major stock exchanges and indexes on flows of Capital (1), international political affairs and cultural institutions on Cultural identity (2), media hub on Flow of information (3), transit networks and airport and impact on transport and logistic (4) and skyline on spatial distribution (5). Therefore, with online service and especially ecommerce as a part of globalization and a new technical reformation, I observed and analyzed the rural ecommerce in China's urban rural context through this economic, social reformation and spatial relationship. It includes 5 aspects: human resource, flow of capital (etc. investment), logistic, informational tech and cultural interaction.

Manuel Castells analyzed the space of flow[6] with at least three layers: material supports by a circuit of electronic exchanges (virtual space) (1); its nodes and hubs (place) (2) and the spatial organization of the dominant, managerial elites that exercise the directional functions around (elites) (3). The rural commerce system can also be thought as a system of virtual space and nodes. When it comes to the analysis of online services and their impact, online urbanization became a new paradigm to grasp the urban rural spatial relationship in China.

Therefore, Online urbanization can be defined as a Chinese paradigm of urbanization:

"Online urbanization" is a new urbanization phenomenon based on the integration of online services[7] system, offline urban and rural infrastructure (high-speed rail, subway, aviation, roads, waterways and other infrastructure) and public and commercial service facilities. The integration of online services and offline urban and rural infrastructure and facilities promotes convection of urban and rural production and living factors. It bridges the gap between urban and rural public services, business services and employment, and achieves urban and rural services and employment fair. Towns and villages in the Yangtze River Delta, Pearl River Delta, Beijing-Tianjin-Hebei region, etc., are integrated into the global virtual economy and social activities through digital technology, offline infrastructure and service facilities. The production supply chain and the life service chain have been

[5]Sassen, Saskia. *The global city: New York, London, Tokyo*. Princeton University Press, 2001.

[6]Castells, Manuel. *The rise of the network society: The information age: Economy, society, and culture*. Vol. 1. John Wiley & Sons, 2011.

[7]Online services are accurate, economical and convenient services provided through Internet business (including ecommerce, long distance education, long distance health care, logistics, financial technologies and so on.

regenerated through the digital interaction. “Online urbanization” includes the urban and rural flows which are manifested in five aspects: fostering the flow of urban and rural human resources; the urban and rural logistics supply chain; information flow; effective resource allocation; and ecological and cultural progress. This can be summarized as the flow of people, goods, information, capital, ecology and culture:

> Fostering the flow of urban and rural human resources (the flow of people): train ecommerce operators, provide relevant expertise and financial support to create high-caliber human resources and mobilize them.
>
> Logistics supply chain (the flow of goods): take advantage of the thriving online shopping and services based on the Internet and mobile phone, build a set of Internet infrastructures by cloud computing and big data, combine with traditional enterprises and logistics, and develop the supply chain system for urban and rural logistics.
>
> Circulation of information (information flow): through the use of information technology, the Internet and mobile communications technology establish a fairer and more transparent market access to a wider range of goods and services, so that an Infobahn is established through of a variety of Internet platforms in urban and rural areas.
>
> Effective resource allocation (the flow of capital): increase the investment of rural areas over global capital allocation; provide support for agriculture-related small and micro businesses in rural areas and financial services for rural residents to narrow the urban-rural gap in terms of financial services.
>
> Urban-rural ecological and cultural progress (the flow of ecology and culture): ecommerce and social media are essentially a new media, they raise the value of agricultural product, increase concern about the ecological environment and culture, establish correct values for urban and rural residents, and prompt people to realize that a simple, earnest and dutiful model of production is also able to create profits and values. Therefore, the outstanding traditional Chinese culture heritage, such as the “heaven-human harmonious” outlook on the environment, can be passed on in the Internet era.

The online urbanization is an alternative phenomenon of urbanization to land urbanization, which I critiqued before. During China’s urbanization in past decades, the land was found more urbanized than the people who lived there. I mentioned this point when I discussed the urbanization crisis in China in Chapter 2. In 2015, 260 million migrant workers had yet to be granted urban residency by the cities they were working in, so they were not entitled to the benefits shared by other citizens (Fig. 7.1).

By switching concentration of online services and online urbanization, China can rebalance the urban and rural areas in a dynamic way, forge new economic relations, social patterns and distribute resources more evenly. In this way, China can find pathways to resolve the dilemma faced by its villages and towns, such as uneven industrial distribution, brain drain, an aging population and environmental degradation.

To go into a deep discussion, I have to explain why online services and online urbanization are based on the context of local and central government political system.

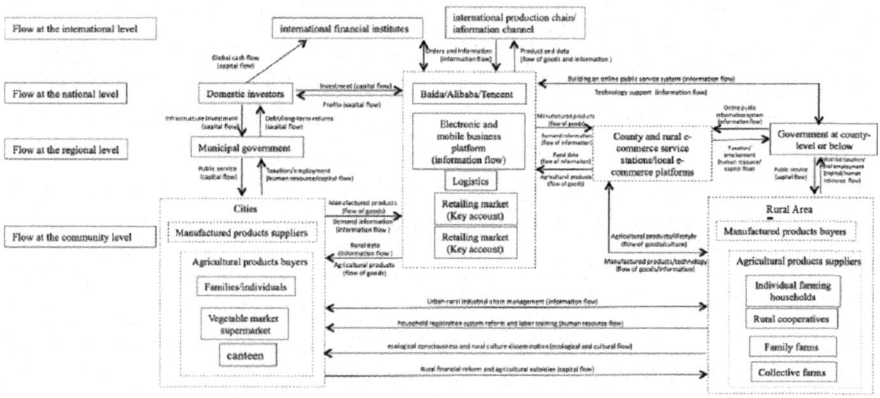

Public services: social security / education / medical care/ other public services
Industrial chain management: product adjustment / supply and demand evaluation / quality control / branding
Agricultural policies in 2015: grain direct subsidy policy/agriculture loan subsidy policy /seed subsidy policy / Agricultural machinery purchase subsidy policy/ pilot subsidy policy for scrapped or upgraded agricultural machinery/ policy for raising the minimum purchasing price for wheat and rice/rewarding policy for major food/edible oil producing counties/ rice/rewarding policy for major farm pig raising counties

Human resource flow: human resource training and flowing
Flow of goods (Logistics): improving the supply chain of logistics
Information flow: urban and rural information exchanges
Capital flow: effective allocation of urban and rural capital
Ecological and Cultural Flow: urban and rural ecological culture publicity

Fig. 7.1 Analysis of the flowing pattern of five factors during the process of Online Urbanization. *Source* Author

7.3 Partnering with Local and Central Governments

When we consider the thriving ecommerce in rural China, it is first important to highlight the existing hardwares that contribute to it. However, we may also mention some other key processes to explain its success, such as the age-long competition between the central and local governments as well as the external and internal cooperation and competition among provinces, cities and counties. These two factors encourage the interactions between Internet technologies and the society as well as participate in the convection of urban/rural capital, human resources, goods, information, eco-culture and other factors. From this perspective, we may wonder how the online services, including rural ecommerce, has affected the urban and rural areas and the flow of factors therein. It may turn out that the regional restructuring brought by online services industry relies, to a great extent, on the local governments; online services industry and ecommerce platforms of all sorts. In other words, the partnering of commercial organizations and local governments would provide an organizational basis and political guarantee to technology publicity and innovation in local communities and the flow of factors between urban and rural areas.

7.3.1 *Regional organizations and structures*

In "*Local and Global–The Management of Cities in the Information Age*"[8], Manuel Castells notes that the local and regional governments, in partnership with more flexible market players, are beginning to emerge and gain importance on the international scale. These authorities remain closely related to their identity foundation, as well as have the potential to transform themselves to gain access to informational trends in various forms.

In "*Regional Advantage: Culture and Competition in Silicon Valley and Route 128*", by drawing a comparison between Silicon Valley and Route 128, Anna Lee Saxenian upholds the same idea that, despite the increasingly globalized production and market, regions remain a major source for competitive edges. Solely relying on spatial clustering is not sufficient to create a mutual dependence that delivers win-win outcomes. It is the organizational structure, rather than the technology or the size of an enterprise that defines the adaptability of a system.

The unprecedented prospects of China's online services in urban and rural places, especially its soaring popularity in the countryside have presented something different: that those arguments are applicable not only in cities, the developed countries, Europe and America, but also in the countryside, the developing countries and the oriental nations. In the meantime, the situation is somewhat different in China.

In this country, the central authorities have been vying with local ones for several thousand years. It boasts a long tradition of political-merchant reciprocity and regional autonomy by local prominent families and gentries (detailed in Chapter 3). As a result, the information technology is bound to interact and integrate with local communities in unique and diverse forms. However, the uniqueness and diversity shares something similar: well-established associations (Suichang Model) and the interaction between commercial organizations and local governments provide an organizational basis and political guarantee for the flow of various factors in urban and rural areas.

7.4 No Non Space of Flows

Information technology, globalization and networking have become closely integrated. These three elements are reflected in the streamlined processing and use of information for more efficient production. They allocate worldwide living factors: capital, labor, raw materials, management, information, technology and markets; they interact on the web with their global configuration, whereby information technology constructs new infrastructures to support the new economic system.

[8]Borja, Jordi, Mireia Belil, Manuel Castells, and Chris Benner. Local and global: the management of cities in the information age. Earthscan, 1997.

It has gradually expanded from an initially unipolar system towards a multi-polar network through globalization. It operates within the context of different cultures as regional systems interact with one another.

After reaching the Information Era, the Network Society emerges[9]. Space of flows and grassrooting space of flows have turned into a phenomenon within the globalized urban development. The definition of space of flows can be simplified to be the global network and urban spaces formed by the Information Network and Financial Capital. These networks and spaces are separated from the daily life of local communities, but are still linked to the 24-h global production and capital industrial chain. This is the globalization in the Internet Era noticed by Castells, in which global information and capital flows are led by international political and economic elites, spatial distribution in configuration and living being brought by them.

Social and cultural differences influence how information is disseminated and received, and how social differentiation arose. As communities filter information, they are strengthened in real and virtual worlds so they are increasingly dependent on information technologies. The Self in the Informational Society[10] is a tricky issue. There is a certain degree of space isolation, embodied in information technology and globalization. This kind of isolation promotes competition and cultivates rebellion.

Thus, the space of flows and the space of places mutually penetrate each other through the popularity of Internet technology. The gap in technology between global elites and local leaders is being progressively obscured.

Therefore, enclave as nodes of global finance and information is gradually being integrated into the traditional local communities. Grassrooting of the space of flows has become a challenge to history, culture and technology. The rule has become simpler: those who make good use of technology have the right to lead.

Moreover, the grassrooting of space of flows in Euro-America and other more developed regions and cities are in contrast with the ones in China as they are more aggressive and less harmonious considering the rivalries within the urban-rural binary structure.

In China, the situation through the lens of globalization in Information Technology and finances, and the configuration of local organizations, and to analyze through the developmental history of cases. There exist both external factors and internal factors. The external factors are the power of national and international financial capital, represented by the Internet giants like Alibaba Group, Tencent and JingDong, from whom they borrowed the platforms and global financing to improve on the infrastructure for rural Internet business. The internal factors are related to local organizations, local governments, and rural ecommerce

---

[9]Castells, Manuel. *The rise of the network society: The information age: Economy, society, and culture*. Vol. 1. John Wiley & Sons, 2011.

[10]Castells, Manuel. *The rise of the network society: The information age: Economy, society, and culture*. Vol. 1. John Wiley & Sons, 2011.

enterprises to provide comprehensive services. As locals who were born and brought up there, they are able to penetrate deeply into every step of production and consumption of villagers. The local government also helps by providing industrial funds and subsidies through supportive policies and appropriate supervision.

The rural internal consumer demands led by the international Internet network and mobile Internet reshape the industrial structure. In the rural, especially in the counties, the Internet and the local communities interact and integrate to untie the knot of China's urban-rural binary opposition, and to bring about reconfiguration. This is the connective point in the development of mega-cities (regional rural clusters) enabled by globalization and informatization, and it is the transition of China's industry within global economic context. The rural communities are empowered within the network, and turn into nodes in the cyber world.

Furthermore, compared with the simplified network of advanced city services to the flow of information and knowledge production of flows from Manuel Castells, another way of definition of flows between rural urban areas have been discussed to fit the realities of urban and rural China. Flow of urban and rural human resources, the urban and rural logistics supply chain, information flow, effective resource allocation and ecological cultural progress are five aspects of flows between rural urban china with services.

The flows and traditional local spaces interact. Decentralization of the Internet combines creatively with rural family-oriented production methods and lifestyle. This is reflected in the spatial-temporal distribution of consumption (demands) and production (supplies), and the emergence of new business models and industrial chains (demand-supply relationship).

Disillusioned by the urban experience as migrant workers, the rural population went back to villages and counties, turning themselves into entrepreneurs to revive their hometowns. This is an expression of their love for homelands. As a result, the virtual community and the real community integrate in Suichang and other places. The spirit and technology of decentralization of the Internet combine with the nepotist society in China's rural area. The Internet brings transparency of information, and the highly efficient market regulations reduce the costs of business, which in turn provide opportunities for local communities.

The congruence of Virtual Communities and Real Communities enables the extension and innovation of ways of community integration. Agricultural products increase whereas the industrial products decrease; the public and commercial service infrastructure and amenities are being improved and the nature and eco-system are protected. Through these pioneers in rural entrepreneurship empowered by mobile and PC Internet, the Internet brings ecommerce and mobile commerce. This has the power to reactivate completely industrial chains, realize the re-construction of hometowns, regional development and high employment rate.

As we have been discussing above, one of this book's main contribution is its extension of Manuel Castells' concept of space of flows. We have indeed stated that the 'non space of flows' described by Castells is no longer relevant to the two case studies presented in this book, considering the predominance of ecommerce. This is why we have been drafting the concept of 'no non space of flows' which means that the notion of space have been completely reinvented by the rise of the Internet, blurring the distinction between the virtual and the real world.

We must now remind that the analysis we have been conducting is however limited for two main reasons. First of all, this research about online urbanization is based on empirical data that apply within Chinese borders and to the specific context of China's rural and urban relationship. However, we believe that the concept of online urbanization is a phenomenon that can be witnessed in other parts of the world, which needs to be further explored. I made this cross sectional research based on a data collection from 2014 to 2017. From the two case studies about Alibaba Rural Strategy (including Taobao village) and Suichang Rural Ecommerce Association Model) in China, we can acknowledge that there is still a small sample size of interviews and observation. As this research was mainly conducted from the angle of urbanism, it has been focusing on the phenomenon of online urbanization by analyzing online services' impact, and especially ecommerce. It is then inevitable to remind the multiple possibilities when it comes to interpret the results gathered. Furthermore, the methodology of this research is based on the ethnographic method and the analysis was inspired by the concepts of Space of Flows and Grassrooting Space of Flows. I tried to create a new method system to adapt this research to Internet business activities, virtual communities, government's policy and spatial transformation in order to analyze the current urban rural relationship. This method still needs to be adapted and extended to other contexts.

References

1. Sassen S (2001) The global city: New york, London, Tokyo. Princeton University Press
2. Castells M (2011)The rise of the network society: the information age: Economy, society, and culture, vol. 1. Wiley
3. Polyani K (2007) The great transformation: the political and economic origins of our time. Beacon Press
4. Lefebvre H (2003) The urban revolution. U of Minnesota Press
5. Borja J, Mireia B, Castells M, Benner C (1997) Local and global: the management of cities in the information age. Earthscan
6. Generic village—study of village by Rem Koolhaas, https://www.gooood.cn/generic-village-study-of-village-by-rem-koolhaas.htm7 Sep 2018
7. Koolhaas R (2014) Countryside architecture, FEATUREShttps://www.iconeye.com/architecture/features/item/11031-rem-koolhaas-in-the-country23 Sep 2014

Postscript: Online Urbanization to Online Community

When people have more opportunities and more time to build their virtual communities, a social movement that takes place online will soon storm the world. When it comes to community, it is more than those that share a sense of place situated on a given geographical area. Virtual communities that go beyond geographical, national, cultural and religious barriers spring up like mushrooms after rain, some of these religions and cultures are out of fashion or even extinct. "Residents" in these online communities break down physical barriers and begin to embrace an online lifestyle. In turn, online communities will also redefine and reconstruct physical communities, so that people can migrate all over the world, or between the physical and virtual world to find their identities.

Online urbanization is the first step of virtualization of society, and this trend have emerged and go deeply and widely.

In recent years I have been following up on the Luohong clan of Li nationality in Dayangpin, Lijiang city, Yunnan province. The history of their clan can be traced back to a thousand years ago. Now they are utilizing Wechat to rally clan members who have been scattered around the world. By now the Luohong clan has found millions of clansmen living around Liangshan mountain. Their success has great cultural, political, economic and social significance. In addition to online communities, their offline counterparts (communities like Dayangpin village) are also agglomerating family forces. Online communities are major players in the networked Chinese society. When thousands more online communities rewrite cultural, social and political structures with the help of new technology, state authorities, if not collapsed, will be delegated to lower levels. The online movement will soon sweep over Western nation-states, or the modern version of European monarchies.

The world will soon be reshaped. With more and more online communities built on similar identities, the state power pattern will make due adjustments. The new governance system and power pattern need to be efficient, inclusive and inspiring enough to soothe the complexities among online communities, both in the virtual

L. Zi, *Online Urbanization*, Advances in 21st Century Human Settlements,
https://doi.org/10.1007/978-981-13-3603-4

and real world. The new governance system will be built on rules that are commonly accepted by online communities. It will respond swiftly, make real-time decisions and execute the decisions. Better enough, people will be entitled to design trouble-shooting mechanisms by themselves. Therefore, it is reasonable to predict that autonomy and decentralization will be the new trends. What is equally important in the future is data collection and processing. Applied properly, data can improve online communities in a comprehensive, precise and proper manner. In real life, a governance system for online payment, e-commerce and social media platforms has taken shape. In other words, Internet and technology tycoons like Google, Facebook and Twitter are competent enough to bring order to online communities. What's more, they are data oligarchs, opinion manipulators, virtual world creators and community governors. They exert greater influence on the economy and society than state authorities. In addition, they can rally the most vigorous communities, no matter their sizes and locations.

To conclude, as an alternative to manpower, technology will link up productive forces, production and consumption to form a closed cycle. It will bring us a new society with rights and interests will be redefined. Online communities that transcend border, cultural and ethnical barriers will emerge. Online communities may create a more powerful system and more solid ideological walls. This dynamic power system will soon penetrate into all aspects of politics, commerce and other areas, providing new solutions to governance.

Those topics will be discussed in my next book about emerging social medias with sharping youths' identities and new spatial transformation in urban and rural China.

Chinese Index

L. Zi, *Online Urbanization*, Advances in 21st Century Human Settlements,
https://doi.org/10.1007/978-981-13-3603-4

Printed by Printforce, the Netherlands